CONTENTS: 1 book
1 CD-ROM

D0887192

The Mid... ...the Future

A Focus on Exploration

Edwin T. Merritt
James A. Beaudin
Patricia A. Myler
Daniel M. Davis
Richard S. Oja

Published in partnership with Fletcher-Thompson, Inc., and
the Association of School Business Officials International

ScarecrowEducation
Lanham, Maryland • Toronto • Oxford

Published in partnership with Fletcher-Thompson, Inc., and
the Association of School Business Officials International

Published in the United States of America
by ScarecrowEducation
An imprint of The Rowman & Littlefield Publishing Group, Inc.
4501 Forbes Boulevard, Suite 200, Lanham, Maryland 20706
www.scarecroweducation.com

PO Box 317
Oxford
OX2 9RU, UK

British Library Cataloguing in Publication Information Available

Library of Congress Cataloging-in-Publication Data

The middle school of the future : a focus on exploration / Edwin T. Merritt ... [et al.].—
    1st ScarecrowEducation ed.
        p. cm.
    "Published in partnership with Fletcher-Thompson, Inc., and the Association of School
    Business Officials International."
    Includes bibliographical references.
    ISBN 1-57886-101-2 (pbk. : alk. paper)
        1. School facilities—United States—Planning. 2. Middle schools—United States—
    Planning. 3. Middle school education—United States—History. 4. Education—Effect of
    technological innovations on—United States. I. Merritt, Edwin T., 1936–

LB3209.M47 2004
373.16—dc22

                                        2003063288

The Middle School of the Future
A Focus on Exploration

by
Edwin T. Merritt, Ed.D., Director of Educational Planning and Research
James A. Beaudin, AIA, Principal, Education Practice Group
Patricia A. Myler, AIA, Director of Pre-K through Grade 12 Facilities
Daniel M. Davis, AIA, Senior Design Architect
and Richard S. Oja, AIA, Senior Project Manager

Fletcher-Thompson, Inc.
Shelton and Hartford, Connecticut, and Edison, New Jersey

with
Barry Blades, ASLA
Blades & Goven Landscape Architects, Shelton, Connecticut

and additional contributions by
Katherine C. Clark, Ed.D.
Timothy P. Cohen
Joseph G. Costa, AIA
East Lyme Middle School Vision Committee
Julie A. Kim, AIA
John C. Oliveto, P.E.
Marcia T. Palluzzi, LA
Robert J. Poletto, P.E.
Jeffrey A. Sells, AIA

Acknowledgments

Many people contributed their talents, skills, wisdom, and experience to this book. First, we would like to express our deep thanks to the principals of Fletcher-Thompson, Inc., for their willingness to support the book's production and their recognition of its importance.

We are especially grateful for the valuable contribution made by Barry Blades, principal of Blades & Goven Landscape Architects, Shelton, Connecticut. This book would be much poorer without his insightful work.

Several educators were of extraordinary assistance in preparing this book. Thanks are due to Jerome R. Belair, principal of the East Lyme Middle School, Niantic, Connecticut; Richard Wenner, principal of the Mount Olive Middle School, Budd Lake, New Jersey; and Katherine C. Clark, Ed.D., principal of the Ocoee Middle School, Ocoee, Florida. Educational consultant Christine Casey, Ed.D., was always ready to contribute her insights.

The many members of the Fletcher Thompson staff who participated directly in this book's creation by contributing ideas or written text to various sections of the book have our great thanks. Over time, the entire Fletcher Thompson Education Practice Group has become involved in this series, and all have exhibited patience and enthusiasm on the many occasions when the books have gotten in the way of revenue-producing work.

Fletcher Thompson administrative assistants Marie Fennessy and Joyce A. Saltes provided invaluable help and always found time to help move the project along. Valuable research assistance was provided by Katie Voelker, a college student who has worked at Fletcher Thompson during the past several summers. Matthew Holst helped prepare the conceptual drawings that appear in chapter 6.

Fletcher Thompson graphic designers Andy Krochko and Brian Russo, with the assistance of Marketing Coordinator Jan Pasqua, deserve our thanks and compliments for their great design and hard work in formatting the book. Marketing Coordinator Diane Kozel was always ready to help with the many details that go into a book's production.

We are grateful, too, for the enthusiasm shown for this project by Managing Editor Cindy Tursman and the staff of ScarecrowEducation, as well as the Association of School Business Officials, and we look forward to continuing our superb working relationship as we bring the other volumes in this series to publication.

And, most important, a large thank-you to James Waller, of Thumb Print New York, Inc., who demonstrated his good humor and editorial skill in scoping the contents of this book, organizing the material, and putting the text into readable shape.

Preface

When a community decides to build a new public middle school, it is taking on a task that is sure to be lengthy, complicated, and expensive. And the job of bringing a new school facility into being is, today, made even more daunting by the fact the nature of education is changing so rapidly. The expanding role that technology plays in schooling our children is, of course, a major force behind these changes. But technology is not the only driver of change. As policymakers and the American people debate the future course of public education in this country, a very wide gamut of issues is influencing—or should be influencing—the ways in which new middle schools are conceived, planned, funded, designed, built, and used.

These issues, to choose just a few, range from large questions concerning the general approach we should take in educating students; to specific questions of curriculum; to concerns about safety and security; to the pressure exerted on finances and facilities by rising enrollments; to the need to conform to burgeoning federal, state, and local laws and regulations enacted to meet the needs of disabled students; to the desire to define the role that middle school buildings play in addressing the facility needs of the wider community.

We at Fletcher-Thompson, Inc.—architects, engineers, interior designers, and educators—plan and design educational facilities. Although the firm is not directly involved in educating students, our long and varied experience in the design of school buildings leads us to understand that each of the issues contributing to the current debate over the future of American public education has—or should have—a substantial impact on how schools are designed and engineered. We say "should be" and "should have," above, because it is our belief that, all too often, this complex of issues is given to little attention in the process by which schools are planned, funded, designed, and built today.

To plan the middle school of the future—one that will truly accommodate the educational needs of five, ten, or even twenty years from now—requires a comprehensive vision. In compiling this book—which we hope will reach state officials, superintendents and other school-district administrators, local boards of education, principals, teachers, parents, and taxpayers—we at Fletcher-Thompson are attempting to begin articulating such a vision. Our point of view is that of designers who have had the privilege of helping to create school buildings across New England and beyond. But we hope that, by gathering together information on the major issues likely to affect elementary school design in the years to come—and by outlining a new collaborative process for the creation of genuinely forward-looking middle school facilities—we will be providing real, practical help to communities across America that are now engaged in setting their future educational agendas.

——Edwin T. Merritt, James A. Beaudin, Patricia A. Myler, Daniel M. Davis,
and Richard S. Oja
Shelton and Hartford, Connecticut, July 2003

Foreword

Think About It *Today*:
The Need for a
Pragmatic Futurist Approach
To School Planning and Design
By Edwin T. Merritt, Ed.D.

We can't stop the future from happening. We're moving into it, every moment of our lives. The future belongs to us, but, more than that, it belongs to *our children*.

These are simple, inarguable truths. So why is it that the future is so often ignored—or given very short shrift—in school planning and design? I can think of several, related reasons.

First of all, it can be *difficult* to think about the future. Not only is the future unpredictable (we all know that), but getting even a limited grasp on the kinds of developments the future might bring requires us to know something about the many trends and forces that are shaping human life right now. That's quite a large field—and so it's no wonder that people feel intimidated before they even begin. Understanding and solving *today's* problems seems challenging enough. Who has the time or energy to think about the future?

Second, thinking about the future can be . . . well, it can be a little *scary*. We Americans are in love with technology; we're thrilled by scientific and technical advances, and we're very quick to welcome the latest innovations—whether they're new features on our cell phones or new gizmos in the doctor's office. But that pleasure is just one facet of what we feel toward technology. Technical advances also frustrate, concern, and—yes—frighten us. The complexity of this emotion is perfectly reasonable. "Technology" doesn't just mean cell phones and MRIs; it means cloning and genetically modified food and sophisticated weapons systems and corporate Big Brothers reading your mind every time you make a credit-card purchase. No wonder our feelings are so mixed—and no wonder that, when asked to think about the future, we so often take refuge in the Scarlett O'Hara syndrome: "I'll think about it *tomorrow*."

Third, planning for the future can seem *expensive*, or financially risky. We sometimes feel that people who want to talk to us about the future are trying to sell us a bill of goods, trying to get us to shell out for costly things that we may never really need—or that will become obsolete before we ever get around to learning how to use them. It goes without saying that this kind of fear—that by thinking about the future, we're opening ourselves up to being taken for a ride—grows more intense during a time of economic instability, when every financial outlay has to be carefully justified.

Finally, thinking about the future can seem *impractical*. For hundreds—perhaps thousands—of years, people have been making predictions about the future that simply haven't come true, or that have come true in ways so very different from what the prophets imagined that it more or less amounts to the same thing. The actual year 1984 didn't look at all like the world predicted in George Orwell's 1949 novel. Y2K was a well-publicized bust, and the year 2001—the setting for Stanley Kubrick's 1968 *Space Odyssey*—passed without any earthling actually engaging in interplanetary travel.

And even when the predictions have been accurate, they've only been partly so. If you'd gone to the "Futurama" exhibit at the 1939 New York World's Fair, you'd have seen the world of 1960 as envisioned by the automakers at General Motors; their vision got some things right—the freeways, the highway cloverleafs—but it also got a lot wrong (the GM folks neglected to mention the rush-hour traffic jams, or the fact that the flight to the suburbs permitted by the automobile would wreak havoc on our cities). Because so little of what I or anyone has to say about the future may come true, anyway—or may "come true" in a way so different from what we envision—why bother to listen?

So, since thinking about the future is so hard, so scary, and so difficult to justify economically, let's not rush right into it. Instead, let's approach the matter "through the backdoor," so to speak, spending a little time thinking about the past and the present—particularly as they relate to the ways we've educated (and continue to educate) our children and to the school buildings we send them to, expecting them to learn.

Backward-Looking Education?

As someone once said, "The past is prologue," and there's no better way to get a handle on the importance of thinking about the future when planning new schools than to examine how well the school facilities built over the past half-century have accommodated the "future." (The future, that is, that's already passed or passing.)

Let's be clear: I'm *not* talking about school buildings that are in bad shape, physically (though there are lots of those, obviously, and there's a crying need for a program of national scope to repair, upgrade, and in many cases replace deteriorating school facilities). I'm talking about *well-maintained schools* in *affluent* school districts. How well have such facilities responded to the great changes that have occurred—technologically and otherwise—in American education over, say, the past 20 years? How well have they adapted to social, economic, and other changes impacting education?

The short answer is: *not* very well.

Let's begin with the very simplest sort of example. The *New York Times* recently reported on a number of Connecticut public high schools that have been forced to restrict the privilege of driving to school to seniors, leaving junior-year drivers grumbling about the indignity—the "uncoolness"—of having to return to taking the bus to and from school each day (Gross 2003). The reason for this harsh new restriction: there's no room for all the cars. This, obviously, is more a social than an educational problem per se, and it's obviously a problem that could only afflict an extremely wealthy society, but it points up something noteworthy. All over the country, high school parking lots are groaning, bursting at the seams from an onslaught of private vehicles—a crisis (of sorts) that these schools' planners and designers never imagined. Snarled traffic has become the norm even at many suburban elementary and middle schools, as parents have increasingly taken to dropping their children off and picking them up rather than relying on the school bus. *Could* yesterday's school planners have anticipated this situation, and taken steps to alleviate it? Perhaps not, but it's certainly an interesting question.

So let's turn our attention to another current space-related issue, one that bears more directly on the educational experience itself. This issue has to do with books. Printed books are physical objects—they take up space. Today, school media centers (which in the days before the "information revolution" used to be known as *libraries*) are, with rare exceptions, designed to store many, many books. They have lots of bookshelves, lots of what librarians call "stack space." So what's wrong with that? We want our schoolchildren to have access to lots of information, right? And doesn't that mean lots of books (and lots of space to store them)?

Well, not quite. Few people seriously doubt that books—printed books—have great value, or that the technology of the printed book, which has been with us ever since Gutenberg, will remain a useful technology for years and years to come. The issue is that, over the past few decades, books—and, for that matter, other printed information sources, like magazines and newspapers—have been supplemented by a wide range of other technologies for conveying and accessing text-based information. *Electronic* technologies.

We all know this. We use these technologies every day. And we know, too, that for many purposes electronic technologies are superior to books as repositories of information. Which is better? A multivolume printed encyclopedia or an online encyclopedia? The "real" encyclopedia takes up several feet of shelf space and gathers dust when it's not being used. It can be physically damaged, and each of its volumes can be used by only one reader at a time. What's more, the pace of advance in scientific and technical fields is so rapid that a printed reference work like this is almost guaranteed to be out of date in certain important respects even before the ink is dry. And obsolescence doesn't just apply to the scientific and technical information such a work contains. Geographical information becomes quickly obsolete (an encyclopedia published in 1991 would have had a long article on the "Soviet Union"). History in all its dimensions—artistic, biographical, cultural, political—continues to unfold, which means that information on the arts, people, governments, and so on all needs to be constantly updated.

A virtual encyclopedia, unlike its tangible, physical cousin, has none of these drawbacks. It takes up no storage space—or not, at least, at the point of access. Its "pages" can't get dog-eared (or cut out); it has no spine to break. It can be used by multiple researchers simultaneously. It can be rapidly and continuously updated. What's more, it can be searched—"mined" might be the better word—for information in a much more thorough, much more creative way than a printed reference work. It can be interactive. And, as if all that weren't enough to convince us of its superiority, subscribing to such an online reference is likely to be vastly cheaper than having to replace that heavy, hardbound printed set every couple of years.

As I say, we all know this. Students today are very much in the habit of taking advantage of electronic resources like the online encyclopedia I've just described (and many, many other such resources besides). *Why* is it, then, that we're still designing media centers to accommodate lots and lots and lots of printed materials? Why are we still dedicating all that valuable, expensive square footage to storage space that, as the years go on, will be less and less necessary?

We all recognize that schools designed even a decade or two ago have in many cases adapted only very uncomfortably to the technological revolution that has so recently transformed virtually every aspect of education. We're all familiar with learning spaces—including media centers—into which computers and other electronic technologies have been "squeezed" in ways that are not very ergonomic and not very aesthetically satisfying, and, most important, in ways that inhibit rather than enhance flexibility. So why do we still design and build new school facilities in ways that probably won't serve future purposes very well?

One reason, certainly, is that we are creatures of habit. We often have trouble seeing the changes that *are* taking place—that *have already* taken place—much less those that lie ahead. We often can't see that solutions to our problems are right at our fingertips.

Let's stay on the subject of printed books for a moment. In December 2002, the *New York Times* carried a story about parents in California and elsewhere around the country who are raising Cain about the weight of all the textbooks that their children are being forced to carry to and from school each day (Dillon 2002). Textbooks have gotten bigger and bigger, heavier and heavier: the story tells of one mother who weighed her daughter's textbook-stuffed backpack, which came in at 28 pounds. Another mother reported that her son's daily textbook burden amounted to 42 pounds. In districts that have eliminated lockers because of concerns about weapons and drugs, the burden on schoolchildren's backs is even greater, since they must lug the books around with them all day long. Backpacks, it seems, are *literally* bursting at the seams; the parents interviewed were of course concerned about the effect of carrying all this weight on their children's long-term health, but they were also angry about the cost of having to replace torn backpacks every few months.

The story mentioned several proposed solutions to the problem: make textbooks lighter-weight; divide them up into multiple (and smaller) volumes; issue students two sets of books—one for use in school, the other for use at home; allow students to bring wheeled packs to school; bring back school lockers in those districts that have eliminated them. What's so interesting here is that the *best* possible solution appears never to have crossed the minds of those parents, educators, and legislators who were interviewed for the story: *Why not just eliminate printed textbooks entirely and replace them with electronic books or other, Web-based products?* The technology for solving the problem already exists, *has* existed for a long time. Why not use it?

Now, granted, there are economic interests at stake here. The publishing companies that produce printed textbooks would have to come up with alternative electronic products. Textbook printers and distributors would no doubt suffer a sharp decline in business. School districts would have to take steps to ensure that each schoolchild could access electronic resources at home. And so on. But changing our basic ways of doing things always has some economic consequences, and in this case it's hard to see how those consequences, as a whole, would be worse than the consequences of what we're now doing—which is virtually guaranteeing that a whole generation of children grows up with musculoskeletal problems resulting from lugging all that weight around.

Now, let's turn our attention away from that old-fashioned technology—paper-and-ink—back to "current" technology (i.e., the computer). Why have I put those quotation marks around "current"? Why, simply because—as we're all aware—computer and computer-related technologies change so quickly that it's very dangerous to describe something as "current." The almost brand-new iMac on which this is being written has a storage capacity of 80 gigabytes—a capacity that would've been unimaginable in a home computer just a few short years ago. What's more, it's networked, wirelessly, to another home computer, a remote printer, and so on. It's perpetually connected to the Internet via cable-TV cable, and access to the Web is virtually instantaneous. Wow, huh?

Well, as you and I both know, such a home setup is hardly unusual these days. And, if you're reading this five or even two years hence, you're probably not thinking, "Wow!" You're probably thinking, "Gee, what a puny little machine. And what a primitive little network!"

I'm hardly trying to brag about how "wired" (or "wirelessly wired"?) I am. The point I'm working toward is that—knowing all we do about the rapidity of change in the arena of computer technology—we continue to design schools for *today's* technology (or even yesterday's), not tomorrow's. There are, of course, some new schools that have been designed in technologically savvy, future-oriented ways, but there are plenty of others whose design is based on the "state of the art" of five or even ten years ago. Face it: Hard-wired computer stations and dedicated computer labs—no matter how well integrated into an overall design—begin to look positively antique in an era when students are carrying cell phones and PDAs that enable them to connect wirelessly, effortlessly, and oh-so portably to the Internet.

In fact, we're not even fully exploiting the *wired* technologies that we have. In many cases, high school science-lab suites are still being designed in ways that don't realize the space- and cost-saving possibilities conferred by virtual laboratory environments—which are now quite sophisticated, highly interactive, and every bit as good for teaching the experimental method, especially in the lower high school grades, as their "real life" equivalents. And we're certainly not utilizing distance-learning and teleconferencing technologies (which already exist) to the fullest extent possible, which would allow schools, districts, regions, and even statewide school systems to share resources more effectively, cutting costs and (probably) enabling space reductions in individual schools.

I should go a step further, here, and say that it isn't at all difficult to imagine the space-related implications of a situation in which all of a school's students (and faculty, and staff) have immediate, personal, wireless, fully portable access to a full range of electronic information resources. This kind of situation—and we're not very far from getting there—would, very simply, eliminate the need for the various sorts of dedicated computer spaces that are still being designed and built into new schools today.

Parking lots. Printed books. Information technology. So far, I haven't even touched on the core aspects of the educational experience—the curriculum itself, the instructional methods used, socialization dynamics, the ways schools are organized (and the ways they make decisions)—or on how these central aspects of education, as they exist today, do or do not relate to today's and tomorrow's realities.

I've just been reading an intriguing little book (you see, I do appreciate the value of paper-and-ink technology!) called *Tomorrow Now: Envisioning the Next Fifty Years,* by futurist Bruce Sterling. Let's listen to Sterling's trenchant take on contemporary American education and its relevance to the world outside the schoolhouse. "My older daughter," Sterling writes

> is a student in high school. . . . [S]he lives in harsh paramilitary constraint. She has a dress code. She fills out permission forms and tardy slips, stands in lines, eats in a vast barracks mess room. She comes and goes at the jangle of a bell, surrounded by hall monitors. . . . My child leads a narrow, tough, archaic working life. Though she isn't paid for her efforts, she'd do pretty well as a gung-ho forties-era Rosie the Riveter. . . .
>
> Today's schoolchildren are held to grueling nineteenth-century standards. Today's successful adults learn constantly, endlessly developing skills and moving from temporary phase to phase, much like preschoolers. Children are in training for stable roles in large, paternalistic bureaucracies. These enterprises no longer exist for their parents. . . .
>
> Today's young students are being civilized for an older civilization than their own. . . .
>
> It's no coincidence that my daughter is appalled by her schoolwork but thrilled by the Internet. Loathing her official school assignments, she spends hours tracking down arcana on the Net, in patient orgies of pop-culture research. (Sterling 2002, pp. 42–44)

Now, certainly Sterling is exaggerating for effect, and he's generalizing from his own child's experience—or his impression of it—to make claims about the experience of all schoolchildren in America today. I'm an educator, and so I know that there's lots that's right about American education, and that conditions in many schools aren't nearly so harsh or so "archaic" as Sterling would have us believe. But, even so, the overall point he's making has some real validity. The enforced routines his daughter is made to follow in school are backward-looking; they have precious little to do with the world outside school—or with the workworld she'll ultimately enter. That workworld's values include an extremely high degree of flexibility, intensive teamwork, the ability to think and act effectively "on your feet" and in "nonlinear" modes. The contemporary and future workworld is (and I'll use a big word here) *protean*—as is the valued employee in that world of work. "Protean" means constantly changing, constantly shifting, constantly *adapting*—and nothing could be further from the inflexible, regimented routines that Sterling's daughter has to endure.

It's clear that that backward-looking approach to education *has* to change.

A Critical Juncture

American public education has reached a critical juncture in its history. The trouble is, the situation is confusing, and no one really knows which of several directions we'll eventually end up moving in. It's likely, in fact, that we'll continue moving in several different directions simultaneously. Let me give some examples.

On the one hand, a concern for diminishing performance in reading, math, and science skills is leading us, as a nation, toward greater standardization in curriculum, with an emphasis on evaluating every schoolchild's performance—and that of every school and school district—through standardized testing. This approach, epitomized in the No Child Left Behind Act passed by Congress and championed by the Bush administration, has its virtues—it demonstrates real concern for academic excellence—and it has many advocates.

At the same time that there's this push toward standardized curricula and standardized testing, however, there's a movement in what seems to be the opposite direction: toward highly exploratory, individualized (and individually directed) learning. There are, for example, teachers, parents, and students across the country who are railing against the practice of "teaching to the test," which, in their view, sucks the life (and a great deal of the value) out of the educational experience. There's the gathering strength of the middle school movement which has always emphasized a highly exploratory, highly interactive educational experience for young adolescents. There's the fact that advances in learning and information technologies make it possible, as never before, to individualize curricula *while* making sure that individual students' performance matches or exceeds standards. (I'm talking, here, about sophisticated "data warehousing"/"data mining" systems that enable an individual student's performance to be plotted against school-wide, district-wide, statewide, and national standards as well as against that student's own past record. Such systems foster the development of individualized curricula that closely attend to students' academic strengths and weaknesses.)

Then there's the growing importance in American education of what's called "multiple intelligences" theory, which emphasizes that children have different gifts, different inherent abilities, and which stresses the need to recognize these differences when designing curricula and instructional methods. And the multiple-intelligences movement, with its emphasis on adapting educational technique to the ways in which children actually learn, dovetails with another trend—that of applying the lessons of neurological science to instructional methods and even to curriculum itself. MIT professor and popular science writer Steven Pinker, whose books describing how the brain works have been bestsellers, is, like futurist Bruce Sterling, very concerned about our schools' failure to adequately prepare children for life outside the classroom. In a recent *New York Times* op-ed piece, he takes American schools to task not only for teaching the "wrong" subjects (he thinks all students should receive basic instruction in economics and statistics, for example), but for teaching *in the wrong way*—that is, by neglecting to apply what science has learned about human cognition to what goes on in the classroom (Pinker 2003). The connection between neurology and education is one to which I'll return, below.

Finally—and perhaps most important—there's the unstoppable movement toward greater *choice* in American public education: the growing number of magnet schools, charter schools, and other "alternative" (theme-based and specialized) schools that are offering parents real alternatives in how their children will be educated.

What's so interesting about this current, conflicted situation—in which "standardization" vies with "experimentation"—is that there *are* ways of making these competing, seemingly divergent, approaches come together. One of the ironies of this critical juncture is that some "alternative" schools—magnets, charters, and others—whose instructional methods, curricular approaches, and modes of organization are *anything but* "standard" may offer the greatest hope of improving students' performance according to standard measures. Magnets, charters, and other specialized schools—highly attentive to the needs of individual schoolchildren and specific populations—stand, in many ways, at the cutting edge of American public education. Alternative schools' potential to transform American education for the better is being increasingly recognized: in February 2003, for example, the Bill and Melinda Gates Foundation—which is turning into one of the most important "movers and shakers" on the American educational scene—gave a grant totaling $31 million to fund the startup of 1,000 new alternative schools across the country (Winter 2003).

Not all such schools are successful, of course, and the jury is still out regarding whether, for example, the charter school movement will live up to its proponents' promise to revolutionize learning, but it is clear that the best magnet, charter, and other specialized schools are doing something that too many "traditional" schools are failing to achieve: they're actually preparing their students for the world—including the workworld—outside the school doors while at the same time ensuring that they "measure up" academically.

Future Schooling—*And* the Future School

At this point, you may be asking yourself what any of this has to do with the school buildings—the physical places—in which we educate our children? The short answer is: *plenty.*

I've described a present-day situation that is, at best, confusing, and I've begun outlining a future in which, it seems, the only certain thing is *change.* Given these realities, it's pretty clear that the most important, overriding principle in school design should be *flexibility.* If a learning space is likely to be used *both* for the traditional, "stand and deliver"–type instruction best suited for preparing students for standardized tests *and* for more exploratory forms of learning combining large- and small-group interaction and individual research, then that learning space *must* be flexible in order to succeed in both its purposes. If, as seems certain, new learning, information, and other technologies are going to continue coming "on line"—and if, as also seems certain, these technologies will quickly be adopted by public schools—then it is *absolutely essential* that schools' learning spaces and infrastructure be designed to flexibly accommodate them.

When you look at the future this way—focusing on the inevitability of change and, therefore, on the need to flexibly accommodate it—"futurism" turns out not to be a flight of imaginative fancy but rather a very pragmatic approach, indeed.

Keeping that in mind, let's take a look at some of the other changes that the future is likely to bring to American education. Some changes, of course, are likely to be expansions or extrapolations of current trends: Because educators increasingly recognize that the performing arts are great tools for building leadership capabilities and fostering the kinds of interpersonal dynamics that enhance teamwork and democratic decision-making, schools of the future are likely to contain a greater variety of (technologically sophisticated) performance spaces, or spaces that can easily be adapted for performing-arts purposes. As everyone grows increasingly conscious of the impact of the physical environment on learning, the indoor-air and acoustical environments of school buildings are likely to be of higher and higher quality. As the manifold benefits of environmental/sustainable, or "green," design become clearer, multiple aspects of a school's interior and exterior environments are likely to be shaped with green-design principles (which cover everything from energy efficiency, to recyclable building materials, to indoor environmental quality) in mind. And as concern grows over increasing rates of childhood obesity, the wholesale retooling of school food programs, with an eye toward balanced nutrition, becomes inevitable. When compared with upcoming technology-based changes, however, these sorts of developments appear tame and relatively uncontroversial. We don't have any trouble envisioning them, and, in fact, we welcome them optimistically and with open arms.

We need to keep that openness and optimism handy when looking at some of the technological advances that lie ahead. Some of the developments discussed below, if and when they are proposed and/or implemented, are likely to be highly controversial and are sure to set off heated debates. But because technology continues to develop so rapidly, I think it's high time that those debates begin, so that the technology-based changes that are introduced into public education result from truly democratic decision-making involving American society at large.

If we don't think about these things now, we're *not* being pragmatic; in fact, we run the risk of letting the future determine us, rather than vice versa.

Human/Computer Interactivity

Even as we prepare this book, the media tell us of successful human-brain chip implants that help disabled people by restoring or simulating sensory abilities, enabling them to function better and more completely by supplementing the brain's power with computer power. It's easy to imagine this kind of technology being more widely applied—for instance, in the form of "remedial reading [or math] chips" implanted in the brains of students with certain kinds of learning disabilities. Such an application would, I think, represent a marriage of education and neurological science like that that Steven Pinker proposes. (And—who knows?—such chips might even eventually enable ordinary human beings to communicate "telepathically," merely by thinking and directing their thoughts at others.)

In a similar vein, voice-activated technologies—in which spoken commands generate computer responses—are a reality today, assisting people with disabilities, those who suffer from repetitive stress injuries, and people who must keep their hands free for non-keyboard tasks. (The 2003 Honda Accord automobile features just such a voice-activated, interactive navigation system.) It strikes me that such technologies naturally lend themselves to educational uses, and that, far from merely "responding" to spoken commands, computers—with whom students will communicate wirelessly—may actually play a role in directing the educational process.

For instance, when the full range of personal data on each student is "warehoused" on school and family servers, the computer will "know" enough about the student to respond to questions such as, "What question *should* I have asked?" The answer will, in effect, control the direction the student takes. As this kind of artificial intelligence advances, it's interesting to speculate about the kinds of answers computers might give to philosophical or spiritual questions. Will the home system give the same kinds of answers as those provided by the school computer? How will school systems deal with church-state questions, and how will parental rights be protected? We don't know the answers to these questions. In fact, we don't even know whether they're the *right* questions—but we can predict with some certainty that this kind of high-level human-computer interactivity will set off some heated debates.

Biotechnical and Genetic Technologies

Interactive technologies like those just described may be supplemented by biotechnical and genetic technologies that enhance mental and physical performance. I can certainly envision the day—perhaps not too distant— when genetic blueprints of each student are available to educators (and their computer "assistants") to help them determine students' inherent strengths and weaknesses and to design individualized educational programs on that basis. I can even foresee educational prescriptions—for both mental and physical activity—being regularly updated (perhaps even daily) through ongoing analyses, conducted in school-based labs, of students' blood chemistry. A changing regimen of dietary supplements and drug therapies would be prescribed to modify and control the changes in students' biochemistry and to prepare students for optimum educational experiences. (If nutritional programs were individualized, you can just imagine how the cafeteria environment might be altered!)

In such a scenario, computers would be involved not only in prescribing dietary/pharmaceutical regimens but in monitoring each student's well-being and measuring and assessing the progress he or she makes. As information was collected, the computer would make the necessary adjustments to the prescription, and teacher/facilitators would monitor the computer-student interaction and intervene when appropriate. "Guidance counseling" would come to include mental capacity mapping, sense acuity diagnostics, and the monitoring of brain and overall physical development informed by an intimately detailed understanding of the student's genetic makeup.

The facility-related impacts of these trends are likely to be extensive— involving, for example, the expansion of today's nurse's suites into small-scale, comprehensive diagnostic and treatment centers, and the transformation of physical education spaces into banks of individual workstations equipped with smart machines that use genetic and biochemical data to help individual students maximize physical performance.

Let's not underestimate the importance or scope of the changes that will be wrought by advances in biotechnical and genetic-engineering technologies. Futurist Bruce Sterling, who devotes a chapter of *Tomorrow Now* to the coming biotech revolution, writes that "Biotech is by no means tomorrow's only major technology[,] . . . [but] if it survives and flourishes, it will become the most powerful" (Sterling 2002, pp. 5–6). So, in thinking about schools of the future, let's try to think about what a school in which educational and biomedical functions are intertwined might look like.

We're making a mistake if we don't at least try to anticipate such changes. Schools designed 30, 20, or even a dozen years ago didn't anticipate the explosion in social, support, and technical services that are, today, common- place features of the educational environment (I'm talking about everything from ESL labs, to planning and placement teams (PPTs), to onsite social workers, to IT support). The result? A situation in which such services are squeezed—uncomfortably—into facilities not designed to accommodate them.

Security, Scheduling, and Environment

Security technology is currently being revolutionized by so-called biometric devices, which "read" and store handprint, fingerprint, and retinal patterns—or even scan and remember human faces—and that permit or disallow access based on whether a person's biometric attributes match those in the security database. Inevitably, biometrics will come to be used in school security systems, providing a much higher level of access control than is possible with the card-access and other, similar systems in widespread use today.

These technologies will reinforce the attitude that the school community is a family, supported by the school's safety and security system. All the members of the community will be connected to one another, and, in effect, the community will protect itself. "Bubbles of caring" will invisibly surround school facilities so that security personnel will be alerted instantly when a problem arises. The technology for this kind networkable system—in which security is based on individual alert buttons worn by all staff and students—already exists and has been implemented at some colleges.

That "bubble of caring" will embrace scheduling, as well. It's more than conceivable that the standard school day will become a thing of the past. As learning programs are increasingly individualized, it will become less and less necessary for all students to arrive at and depart from school grounds at the same times each day. With computerized scheduling and navigational systems in place, there would be no reason why school bus routes couldn't be highly individualized, too, with students being picked up from home, delivered to school, and then taken back home or to after-school activities as their individual schedules require. (In fact, such a system could make sure that the efficiency of a fleet of buses is maximized, potentially leading to reductions in the number of buses needed to serve a school's student population.) Moreover, if students were required to wear or carry chips connecting them to the Global Positioning System, their whereabouts could be constantly tracked and monitored. (Another option would be to surgically implant such chips—making it impossible to lose a student or for a student to elude authority—but this sort of procedure would surely be greeted by outright hostility by some members of the public, making its introduction controversial, to say the least!)

In the school building itself, computers will control the interior environment—not just to modulate comfort conditions as necessary, but also to alter aesthetic characteristics of the environment. We can foresee a day when the colors of walls, floors, and ceilings; images projected on walls; and the amount and quality of light in interior spaces are all controlled by computers, which will change the colors, images, and light as changing educational and recreational activities warrant. On a gloomy day, a ray of artificial (though natural-looking) "sunlight" might stream through the atrium skylight; the mood of a dismal winter afternoon might be enlivened through the projection of a lush lawn onto the floor adjacent to a wall showing a virtual waterfall.

And technology is likely to alter the school environment in another way, as well. Throughout the "Schools of the Future" series, we often speak of the trend—in all public school facilities—toward increased after-hours use of the school building by the larger community. Pursuing that trend further, we can envision a time when educational facilities become even more tightly interwoven with the overall governmental and institutional life of the community. As data resources and support services become ever more intertwined (and instantly, virtually accessible), and as land for municipal construction projects becomes ever more costly (and less readily available), a time may come when it makes a great deal of sense to consolidate many or all municipal functions—governmental, recreational, health, and educational—on a single campus.

The School as "Laboratory"

Whether or not any of the particular changes discussed in the preceding sections is ever implemented, it's clear that technology will continue to radically transform the educational experience. And one of the most sweepingly important aspects of this transformation will be that education—at all levels from preschool on—will become increasingly "experimental" and laboratory-like. Not only will students be in increasingly constant virtual communication with electronic resources, but the seamless interplay between computers and their human users will enable an educational approach that is individualized, problem-solving–oriented, and "experimental" in the best sense of the word. This will be true in all schools—but some magnet, charter, and other alternative schools are even now on the cutting edge of this transformation.

No longer will experimentation be confined to the science lab. Instead, a school building's learning spaces will become all-purpose laboratories in which hands-on and virtual experimentation of many different, interdisciplinary sorts can be carried on. Students—employing personal digital assistants (PDAs) that combine MP3, DVD, cellphone, and laptop computer functions in a single device—will communicate with electronic resources containing vast amounts of information. Wall-mounted "smartboards" will replace blackboards/whiteboards in classrooms and other learning spaces, making even the traditional, lecture-style format a much more interactive experience. Through empirical experiments and heuristic thinking, students will continually be testing the truth and viability of their parents' and teachers' assertions and creatively evaluating the workability and wisdom of schools' organizational structures.

Experimentation, of course, is an ongoing, never-ending process. It involves dialog, the back-and-forth of argument and counterargument, the openness and flexibility required to change one's mind and alter one's direction. It involves interaction—and, of course, interactivity is the foundation of a healthy democratic society. Advances in learning and information technologies don't mean very much—they aren't very valuable—unless they support and extend our ability to work together to find solutions to the challenges besetting us. Education doesn't mean very much—isn't very valuable—unless it prepares our children for the life that awaits them outside the school's doors.

And this, finally, is the earmark of the school building of the future: that it not only enables students to learn interactively, but that it actually nurtures the dynamics of creative, positive, solutions-oriented interaction. It does this in all sorts of ways, from incorporating interactive technological resources into every dimension of learning; to articulating space in ways that enhance human-computer, one-on-one, small-group, and large-group interaction and democratic decision-making; to ensuring that the environment enhances rather than impedes learning.

Does all this sound scary? Well, change always is at least a little scary, and designing facilities to flexibly accommodate change while ensuring that change is for the better is scarily daunting.

But let's not be frightened. To respond effectively to the changes the future may bring, we must ourselves be willing to change our thinking, our strategies, and our priorities. This is a potentially endless task, and one that we—as designers, educators, parents, and citizens—should welcome. Let us, together, begin thinking about the future *now*.

Introduction

Exploring Space: A Vision of the Future Middle School

"The middle school movement is . . . the most successful grassroots movement in American educational history."

——Middle school theorist Paul S. George (quoted in Jackson and Davis 2000, p. 1)

Born of the lived experience of educators who work with early adolescents, the middle school movement has over just a few decades revolutionized the way American public schools educate children between the ages of 10 and 15. From the movement's origins onward, middle school advocates have consistently emphasized the importance of *exploration* in middle-grades education, and the concept of exploration will be a touchstone of this book, as well. As we plan, design, and build spaces for exploration, we ourselves— all the stakeholders in a new school construction project—should be "exploring space," constantly investigating the many ways in which learning activities and learning spaces interact.

For all its success, the middle school movement is still very much a work in progress. The middle school advocates who speak in such recent milestone works as *Turning Points 2000: Educating Adolescents in the 21st Century* (Jackson and Davis 2000) and *This We Believe . . . and Now We Must Act* (National Middle School Association, 2001) are as mindful of the distance yet to travel as they are of the ground that has already been covered, and approaches to middle-grades education are certain to undergo continual refinements as the 21st century progresses. As learning changes, so will— so *must*—the facilities in which learning occurs.

Because this book's major purpose is to help communities plan, design, and build new middle schools, it concerns itself primarily with matters related to architecture, engineering, and construction—and with the collaborative processes that we believe give school construction projects the best chance for success. But decisions about space programming, architectural design, and construction methods and materials are very much dependent on—and closely intertwined with—a community's vision of how it wants to educate its children. That's true of any new school project, but it seems especially so when the school being planned is a middle school, because so much of the innovation that's happening in American education today is taking place at the middle-school level.

Today's middle schools are the result of a broad-based movement, which began in the 1950s and gathered steam during the 1960s and '70s, to reform American school systems' approach to educating early adolescents. For that reason, middle school design—now and in the future—springs from, and proceeds hand in hand with, an *evolving* body of educational theory and practice.

We continue to learn how to build buildings for learning. It's therefore worthwhile to begin our exploration of tomorrow's middle schools by taking a look back to the origins of what came to be known as the middle school movement—to see what this movement for reform was reacting against, to explore at least a few of the important changes it has wrought in the way American schools educate children in the "in-between" years, and to take a look at how those changes have affected school facility design.

The Middle School Movement

As recently as 30 to 40 years ago, the majority of public school districts around the country employed a three-tier organizational model in which pupils attended elementary school from kindergarten through grade 6, then progressed to junior high school (for grades 7–8 or 7–9) before going on to high school proper. The contemporary middle school movement arose in reaction to that model, which its proponents believed ill-served the unique emotional, social, and intellectual needs of early adolescents.

Little High Schools. Physically, most junior highs of the pre–middle school era were closely modeled on high schools, and the educational experiences they provided were very similar to those offered by the typical high school. Many junior highs built through the 1960s—and in some cases even later— were, except for their smaller size, almost indistinguishable from the high schools of the time: Classrooms were situated in long one- or two-story wings. Inside these wings, the classrooms were arrayed along both sides of "double-loaded" corridors, usually lined with lockers. In larger junior highs, the several classroom wings were typically connected by a perpendicular corridor that also provided access to the school's main entrance, administrative offices, and common facilities such as the cafeteria, gymnasium, library, and auditorium.

By the 1950s and 1960s, the organization, schedules, and curriculums of most junior highs also aped those of high schools: The model was that of a "factory," in which authority was centralized and flowed from the top down. The school day was divided up into six or seven class periods of equal length, with perhaps a few "double periods" for special purposes scattered through the school week. In most cases, the curriculum was highly "depart-mentalized." Arriving at school, students would report to homerooms for 15 or 20 minutes, then go on to attend a series of classes, each taught by a different faculty member, each devoted to a distinct subject, and each held in a different classroom. Little effort was made to integrate the curriculum's various components—though English and social studies and/or science and math were sometimes combined in a so-called "core curriculum." Junior highs' increasing resemblance to high schools could also be seen in the fact that students "were promoted or retained on a subject-by-subject basis" and that "[e]lective programs focused on specialization that would lead to quasi-majors at the high school" (George et al. 1992).

Moreover, for junior high pupils, there wasn't much social continuity over the course of the day. Students going from one class to another traveled through those long corridors alone or with shifting groups of friends, and each class brought together a somewhat different mix of students. At the same time that there was little social continuity, however, "grouping patterns based on perceived ability (measured by I.Q.) or prior achievement became characteristic of the junior high school" (George et al. 1992)—that is, through "tracking," a rigid separation was maintained between those students designated as high-achievers and children perceived to be ordinary students or slow learners.

During the 1960s and '70s, a number of educational experts, teachers, and psychologists were coming to the realization that this model's abrupt transition from the homelike atmosphere of the elementary school into the utterly different, high school–like environment of the traditional junior high could be—and often was—psychologically traumatic and educationally counterproductive. Among older Americans who went to public school, there are probably few in their late forties, fifties, and sixties who don't recall the shock of leaving behind the intimate, and intimately scaled, environment of elementary school and entering—without any preparation—the large, disorienting, and relatively anonymous environment of junior high. As middle school advocates William M. Alexander and Paul S. George put it in a 1981 study, "[S]ixth graders in June became high school students in September without adequate readiness or maturity" (Alexander and George 1981, p. 11).

A Vision Lost—And Regained. Interestingly, it's probable that few early middle school advocates realized that the junior high school concept had, at its own beginnings, represented an effort to reform American education that was in some ways very similar to the "new" model that they were proposing. Those educators who in the 1910s and 1920s were founding the nation's first junior high schools were likewise responding to what they believed was an inappropriate degree of influence over middle-grades curriculum exerted by the high schools of their era. As one group of middle school theorists has pointed out,

> Plans for the first junior high schools contained components that would be very familiar to today's middle school educator. The school was to be based on the characteristics of young adolescents and concerned with all aspects of growth and development. It would be a school designed to provide continued work in learning skills while bringing more depth to the curriculum than had been the case in the elementary schools. It would emphasize guidance and exploration, independence and responsibility. . . . None of this should sound strange to contemporary educators; surprising, perhaps, but not strange. (George et al. 1992, p. 3)

Among the curricular innovations introduced by the early 20th-century junior high school movement were practical arts training (industrial shops, home economics), hands-on science experimentation, and citizenship education—this last directed particularly at children of recent immigrants to the United States. As the authors just cited sadly note, however,

"[P]rogrammatically, many a junior high school steadily became more and more a little high school in virtually every way." For the most part, high schools were intended to serve as preparatory schools for the nation's colleges and universities, and the junior high school—which had been established for quite different purposes—gradually became little more than a preparatory school for high school.

There were many reasons for this falling-away from the junior high school's original intention, but one of the major forces driving the trend was the absence from most of the country's teachers colleges of any training specifically geared to serving the educational needs of children in the "in-between" years. Most junior high school faculty—as well as the administrators drawn from their ranks—had been trained to teach high school. Junior high school teachers generally received lower pay than their high school colleagues, and many districts treated their junior highs as less-than-equal components of the overall system, devoting less money and attention to their junior highs than to either their elementary or their high schools. For decades, there was no professional group to advocate for early adolescents or their special educational needs.

The middle school movement filled that void. At first, it represented the efforts of only a few educators. The first genuine middle school was opened in Bay City, Michigan, as early as 1950 (Barton 1976, pp. 168–169), but the movement to reform middle-grades education grew by fits and starts during its first decade and a half. Of course, progress seldom occurs in a strictly linear way. Even though most junior highs had, by the 1950s, reverted to a high school–based model, there was interest, here and there, in changing that pattern.

The 1950s saw a few districts instituting a "democratic curriculum" that encouraged curricular decision-making by the local junior high or even by individual classroom teachers. (Decades later, school-based decision-making was to become one of the rallying points of the full-fledged middle school movement.) Some other districts were ahead of their time in introducing junior high school learning plans that emphasized group process and problem-solving or that "fused" (or "integrated") various aspects of the curriculum, breaking down barriers between traditional subject areas. Still others experimented with block scheduling, with team teaching, and with core curriculums whose purpose was to equip students with basic knowledge of democratic decision-making (Barton 1976).

A few districts scattered around the country even began, in the 1950s, to experiment with the shapes of junior high school buildings and the organization of space within them. Junior high and middle school historian Ronald Rex Barton reports that a school construction boom in the late '50s made possible "opportunities for . . . experimentation," including classrooms of different shapes and sizes: round, semicircular, oval, triangular, quadrangular, pentangular, hexangular, and a few octangular buildings. A number of new buildings contained from six to eight trapezoidal classrooms arranged in a hexagon or octagon with a centrally enclosed room for audio-visual materials and equipment. Some secondary schools [including junior highs] were constructed in the form of several units, e.g., a unit for science, a unit for humanities, a unit for industrial arts, and a unit for administrative offices. . . . (Barton 1976, pp. 156–157)

What's significant, though, is that until at least the mid-1960s all these attempts at reform—of middle-grades curriculum *and* of junior high school facilities—were *definitely* in the minority. It's also true that educational reform and architectural experimentation didn't necessarily proceed hand in hand: undoubtedly, some genuinely progressive educational innovation was happening in traditional-looking buildings, while some new schools that were architectural showpieces were being used in traditional ways that did not exploit these sometimes daring buildings' true potential. Meanwhile, the construction of old-style, high school–like junior highs continued apace: as late as 1971, *Progressive Architecture* magazine was complaining about the number of new—sometimes brand-new—school buildings with "self-contained classroom boxes . . . arranged along a double-loaded corridor, leaving no room for teaching techniques now being used" (*Progressive Architecture* 1971).

"This We Believe." Indeed, by the early 1970s, the "teaching techniques" employed in public schools were undergoing a sea-change in a growing number of districts. The late 1960s and early 1970s—a period of social ferment, generally—marked a high point in public debate about what American public education should be like. Numerous best-selling studies described a "crisis" in the nation's schools, and the theories of a number of educational reformers—some of them quite radical—filtered into the public discourse, which was doubtless intensified by the great number of baby boom children then entering or making their way through the country's public school systems and by the nationwide push for racial desegregation.

In the mind of the general public, the educational and facility-related reforms then being experimented with were probably epitomized by the "open classroom" concept. But the controversy over open-plan classrooms and the relatively unstructured kinds of learning that occurred in them mostly concerned elementary education. In fact, a great deal of the media coverage of educational reform in the late 1960s and early 1970s focused on elementary and early childhood education. Much more quietly, the movement to reform middle-grades education was gathering force. It's perhaps ironic that this movement—not often noticed in media reporting on the educational controversies of the time—was to have a more significant and long-lasting effect on the future course of American public education than the much-discussed open classroom.

The number of middle schools grew steadily throughout the 1960s, with 499 middle schools (in 29 states) in the 1965–1966 school year and 1,946 (in 38 states) in 1968–1969 (Barton 1976, pp. 208–209). By 1973, the movement had gathered enough steam to found its own national professional organization, the National Middle School Association (NMSA), and districts around the country were adopting the sweeping changes in approach to early-adolescent education that middle school advocates were proposing. By 1980, there were at least 5,000 middle schools in operation in the United States (Alexander and George 1981).

From its beginnings, the middle school movement stressed the importance of an integrated (or "integrative"), project-oriented curriculum that would permit young adolescents to explore the world around them, making connections between the different kinds of subject matter that most junior high curriculums had treated as distinct and separate. Just as important, middle school proponents worked for the creation of educational environments that were noncompetitive, that fostered a high level of social cohesion and continuity, and that—by emphasizing guidance and close teacher-student interaction—ensured that no child would fall between the cracks. Over time, the movement's principles were codified in a number of visionary documents, most recently in *This We Believe . . . and Now We Must Act,* issued by the NMSA in 2001 (National Middle School Association, 2001), which lists the following basic characteristics of effective middle school education:

- Curriculum that is challenging, integrative, and exploratory.
- Assessment and evaluation that promote learning.
- Varied teaching and learning approaches.
- Flexible organizational structures.
- An adult advocate for every student.
- Comprehensive guidance and support services.
- A shared vision.
- High expectations for all.
- Positive school climate.
- Educators committed to young adolescents.
- Programs and policies that foster health, wellness, and safety.
- Family and community partnerships.

Besides emphasizing flexibility, curricular integration, and a nurturing, caring school community, middle school educators have over the past several decades articulated and experimented with a number of innovative educational approaches, among the most important and widely implemented of which are these:

- Block, or modular, scheduling and "site-based" scheduling, in which individual school communities collaboratively decide how best to organize the school day and school week to permit a wide range of activities. Schedules are divided up into modules, and different kinds of subjects and different learning experiences are allotted the number of modules they require. This introduces great flexibility in the schedule, which may differ from day to day, week to week. Scheduling decisions are made by—and closely coordinated with the curriculum of—the individual school.

- Teaming, which means more than just "team teaching," in that it involves the participation of the entire learning community—students as well as multidisciplinary faculty—in making the curricular and other decisions that affect the experience of the group.
- "Looping," in which students remain for two years with the same team of teachers. (In a 5–8 middle school that uses the looping model, the same group of students would remain with the same teachers for grades 5 and 6, and then go on to a new team of teachers for grades 7 and 8.)
- Multi-age education, in which students in different "grades" learn together, in the same environment. (The old one-room schoolhouses of rural America were, in fact, employing the multi-age educational model!)

Beyond these innovations, middle school advocates have worked hard to change our basic ideas about children in the "in-between-age" years. While admitting that the years from age 10 to age 14 or 15 are a period of turmoil for most young people, middle school educators have also stressed that early adolescence is "an exciting period—and indeed to observe, work with and enjoy youngsters at this age is exciting" (Alexander and George 1981, p. 9). This perspective has led middle school advocates to transform the very nature of middle-grades education, moving away from a system that focused strictly on the "transitional" aspects of early adolescence to a new vision that puts equal emphasis on the unique educational opportunities that middle-grades education affords.

Architecture + Learning. The new middle school educational program quickly inspired new ways of thinking about school facilities designed for the middle grades. By 1976, middle school historian Barton was reporting that "the design of most new . . . middle schools reflects the educational . . . innovations that have taken place" (Barton 1976, p. 225). It's worth quoting him at length to see just how extensive those facility-related changes had already become:

> Provision [in new middle school buildings] is usually made . . . for learning or resource centers where students may obtain printed materials, engage in study and research, undertake special projects, listen to recordings, and view videotapes, motion pictures, and filmstrips. Separate instructional stations for band, orchestra, and chorus are included . . . as well as space arrangements for block-time teaching and large-group instruction. There are . . . special rooms in which team-teaching members meet to plan their work and discuss their problems. Small and large auditoriums, along with broadcasting studios and committee meeting rooms, are additional features.

Structural flexibility is assured to a certain degree through the construction of demountable walls and the use of movable and operable partitions. Interior spaces can be rearranged quickly and easily for accommodating different kinds of learning activities and experiences. (Barton 1976, pp. 225–226)

Moreover, Barton points out that—in what was certainly a departure from school-building design of the past—much attention was now being paid to "the control of the thermal, acoustical, and visual environment" in new school buildings (Barton 1976, p. 226). (The continuing—indeed, growing—concern for indoor environmental quality in the planning, design, and construction of new school buildings is a major focus of this book; see, for example, chapters 5, 11, and 12.)

Many of the innovations described by Barton in the mid-1970s—or, rather, more sophisticated versions of these innovations—continue to play a role in middle school building design today. (A few do not: For example, Barton reports that school designers in the 1970s were trying to minimize window area. That trend definitely came to an end as awareness grew of the importance of fresh air and natural light to emotional health and academic performance.)

The "House" Concept. As middle-grades educational theory evolved over the next two decades, a set of basic architectural principles regarding middle school design began to crystallize. These are epitomized by the "house" concept (sometimes also referred to as the "pod," or "cluster," or "schools-within-a-school" concept), which was fully developed by the 1990s. Most middle schools being built today—including exemplary projects discussed in this book—utilize some version of the "house" approach to organizing space, which was described in a 1996 article as follows:

"[T]he house concept" . . . literally dissolves the arbitrary boundaries used to divide information into academic subjects. [Houses are] small collections of flexible classrooms and support spaces which can accommodate virtually any type of subject matter and any form of instruction.

. . . [T]he house concept allows students to remain within the house *and have information travel to them.* The key to this, architecturally speaking, is to design instructional spaces within the house to be function-specific rather than subject-specific.

In other words, . . . spaces are designed to accommodate specific functions such as presentation; discussion; individualized learning; technology-based learning; or activities involving the handling and creation of liquid, fumes, dust or other materials that need to be carefully contained. (Sullivan 1996, pp. 3–4; emphasis added)

The author of that article—himself an architect—is also adamant about the need for "participatory" process (we prefer the term "collaborative process") in middle school design. After all, if middle school educational practice emphasizes group process and democratic decision-making by the entire school community, it only stands to reason that facility design should grow from the needs and desires of the community that will actually use the new school building!

No longer are middle-grades students suddenly thrust into the overwhelming, anonymous environment of the old junior high. Among the great advantages of the house concept to middle-grades education is that it breaks the large middle school—which may have a total student population of a thousand or more—into more manageable, self-contained units. In other words, the house concept, especially when combined with the looping and multi-age educational models discussed above, maintains the intimacy and coherence of the elementary school while fostering a diversity of exploratory learning experiences that will prepare students for the departmentalized academic environment of high school. It's instrumental in "making big schools feel small"—the title of one of the most influential recent books of middle school theory (George and Lounsbury 2000).

The fact that middle school design has been somewhat codified doesn't mean, however, that there isn't plenty of room for change and improvement. The "house" model itself has already undergone refinement in the years since its introduction: today, middle school advocates are more likely to speak of "teams" than of houses. Why? Because it began to be felt that, especially in larger middle schools of more than 1,000 students, dividing a school into a few different houses didn't go far enough toward making a big school "feel small." A further limitation on the size of the middle school's basic unit had to be made, and the team concept, in which four or so teachers work with 80 to 100 students, was developed. At some contemporary middle schools, facility design centers on the teams, which may be clustered together in distinct "neighborhoods."

Change is happening elsewhere, as well. For example, the ongoing revolution in educational technology—including the advent and proliferation of wireless technologies—is already rendering the dedicated computer-learning spaces of 1990s school buildings obsolete. The increasing demand for in-school social services continues to amplify the numbers and kinds of support spaces that all new school facilities contain. And middle school educators and designers continue to experiment with variations on the "house" concept mentioned above—exploring new ways of making big schools feel small. As we'll see, those are just a few of the trends that will shape the middle school of the future.

2020 Vision

The Carnegie Council on Adolescent Development's study *Turning Points 2000: Educating Adolescents in the 21st Century* (Jackson and Davis 2000)—itself a follow-up to the groundbreaking *Turning Points* study published by the Carnegie Council in 1989—is one of the recent milestones of middle school theory. It's not necessary to summarize, here, its authors' conclusions about progress in middle-grades educational reform over the previous decade nor their many recommendations for further improving America's middle schools—recommendations that cover areas ranging from academic standards and assessment to instructional methods, middle-school teacher training, the organization of the school community, school governance, environmental health and safety, and community involvement. Those and related topics are touched on frequently throughout this book, and, in any case, people interested in contemporary thinking about middle-grades education will certainly want to read the whole of this very comprehensive study for themselves. As designers, though, we were particularly struck by an insight that appears early on in the book, and we think it is worth reproducing here.

After discussing a number of significant successes, in districts around the country, that have resulted from the implementation of middle-school practices such as grade reconfiguration, teaming, and active and interactive instructional approaches, the *Turning Points 2000* authors go on raise the following caution. They write that

> [w]hen reforms are implemented in a limited or scattershot manner, . . . as when changes in grade configuration and teacher and student grouping are not accompanied by substantial changes in teaching practices, improvement in student outcomes is more limited. (Jackson and Davis 2000, p. 6)

In other words, the middle school approach has the best chance of fostering the intellectual growth and emotional and social development of young adolescents when recommended reforms are instituted in an *integrated, holistic* way. That insight resonates with us, as school-building designers, because we recognize that a new school is likewise given the best chance of meeting a community's needs—for years to come—when planning and design processes are approached in the same integrated and holistic manner.

And we believe that an essential element in that integrated, holistic approach involves constantly turning a searching eye toward what the future might bring. Among the educators we consulted in preparing this book is Jerome R. Belair, principal of the East Lyme Middle School in Niantic, Connecticut, and a regular contributor to the *Middle School Journal*. The brand-new East Lyme Middle School opened its doors in September 2002, and, earlier that summer, Jerry Belair spoke with us at length about the collaborative, visionary process that led to the new school's creation. (That process—and the educational specification it produced—are covered in detail in chapter 4, "A Case Study of Collaboration: East Lyme Middle School.") Sitting in his office at the *old* East Lyme Middle School—which is now being renovated to serve as one of the district's elementary schools—Belair wondered aloud whether any of the people responsible for that facility's design (it was completed in 1953) had ever taken the time to wonder what education would be like 10, 20, 30, or more years hence.

Could school designers of the early 1950s have imagined an educational environment in which passive, "stand and deliver" lecture-style teaching was no longer the norm? Could they have envisioned classrooms in which children were not strictly segregated by grade level or perceived ability? Could they possibly—even in their wildest imaginings—have predicted the advent of the personal computer and other electronic technologies and the manifold ways in which these technologies would so change learning?

Undoubtedly they could not, but did they even *try* to speculate about future teaching and learning? In asking this question, the point is not to castigate the creators of yesterday's school buildings for not having had a crystal ball enabling them to prophesy the future. Rather, the point is to underline *our own* responsibility—using our awareness of the great changes that have occurred in education over the past 50 years as well as our knowledge of current trends—to try as hard as we can to imagine the ways in which education will *continue* to change.

In Belair's telling, the East Lyme Vision Committee took its responsibility to the future utterly seriously. The committee that developed the educational specification for the district's new middle school constantly tried to look at least two decades ahead and to weigh all its programmatic decisions against possible changes the future could bring. They wanted, said Belair, to do everything they could to ensure that their new building would remain as workable a facility in the year 2020 as on the day it admitted its first students.

"2020 vision": we like the idea. We well understand, of course, that the future is highly unpredictable—surely, few people (if any!) in the early 1950s could have foreseen the enormous changes in education that began to be wrought by electronic technologies three and four decades later. (Who could even have predicted the enormous diversity of contemporary American life—and how that diversity would be reflected in our nation's classrooms?) Even so, we are convinced that it is *very* possible to increase a facility's ability to accommodate future changes by looking at, and extrapolating from, current trends. Working from that conviction, let us use the remainder of this introduction to examine a few of the major trends and to speculate about their long-term impact on middle school design. (A much longer and detailed list of specific principles guiding middle school design is developed in chapter 5)

Using Workplace-Design Strategies for Learning Spaces. One trend that's certainly affecting current school design—and that's likely to exert ever-greater influence in years to come—is a growing consensus that public education should prepare students not just for further academic training but *for life in all its many dimensions.* This isn't the abandonment of an earlier academic ideal but rather the expansion of that ideal to include not just preparation for more schooling (though intellectual development remains extremely important, as the authors of the *Turning Points 2000* study are quick to emphasize; Jackson and Davis 2000, pp. 23, 26) but also preparation for participation in family life, in the political and cultural life of a democratic society, and in the world of work.

This transformed perception of the goal of public education is influential across all the grade levels, but it may be having its greatest impact on middle schools, which—since the beginnings of the middle school movement—have emphasized exploratory learning, mentoring, cross-grade learning, the development of problem-solving skills, teaming, and nonhierarchical organization, and whose leaders have recognized the value of accommodating students of varying interests and "multiple intelligences" within the same learning environment, of making school-day schedules fluid enough to permit a wide range of different kinds of projects, and of mixing group and individual activities in ways that enable students to master the many different dimensions of a given subject matter.

Imagine it: a space in which a highly diverse group of people—of differing interests and skill-levels—are concentrating on a number of different projects, in which they work by themselves or in groups (whose size and composition differ according to the nature of the task), in which they mentor and help one another, in which solving problems is a consistent focus, and in which collaborative decision-making affecting the life of the group is constantly going on. What *kind* of space is this? Well, it certainly shares many characteristics with the contemporary workplace. But, in salient ways, it also represents the ideal middle-grades learning environment.

This resemblance—and the concomitant need to base at least some aspects of middle school learning spaces on real-world working environments—was one of the first points raised by East Lyme principal Belair in our discussion with him. Emphasizing that every decision regarding the design of East Lyme's new facility had been "program driven," Belair noted that even the selection of furniture for the school's learning spaces was performed with this imperative in mind. Just as *flexibility*—which includes the ability to easily reconfigure furniture to permit a wide range of individual and group activities—is a key value in contemporary office design, it has also become a critical principle in the design of classrooms and other learning spaces for middle-grades students.

Let us be clear: by focusing on the resemblances between (well-designed) middle-grades learning spaces and contemporary workplace environments, we are in no sense advocating a return to the "vocational education" concept of years past. Granted, there will always remain a need, on both the middle and high school levels, for training in specialized skills, and some of that training requires the provision of specialized spaces. (You can't have a culinary arts program without a kitchen.) But what we're suggesting here is that the *entire* middle school learning environment is being reconceptualized to resemble—in certain key aspects—the environment of the contemporary workplace. We don't, of course, mean the stultifying "Dilbertvilles"—those undifferentiated seas of cubicles that still characterize too many corporate offices—but rather the *best* in modern workplace design, which emphasizes flexible, nonhierarchical organization; which facilitates communication, creative interaction, and teaming; and which permits the simultaneous pursuit of many different kinds of projects—and quick changes of direction—through easy reconfiguration of furniture and the other components of the space.

In this connection, one of the concepts we'll introduce in the course of this book is that of "non-precious, experimental" space. The idea behind this concept is that truly creative, exploratory learning gives children the opportunity to "get their hands dirty" and to engage in work where they can't always be worrying about not causing damage to a space's furniture and finishes. We'll have more to say about this in chapters 5 and 6, where we'll also show ways in which non-precious, experimental spaces—they might also be termed "lab" spaces, if we broaden the meaning of *lab* beyond the traditional science laboratory—can be integrated into middle-school floorplans. But let us say here that this concept requires the design of *extremely* generic spaces (capable of hosting a very wide range of activities) that are also extremely durable. Let's acknowledge the fact that certain kinds of work—exploratory, experimental work—can get pretty messy, and let's build spaces to accommodate these activities. (We know that this might be a tough pill for architects—who are generally so invested in creating beautiful, perfectly groomed spaces—to swallow!)

The best workplace designs don't neglect a central fact about human nature: that every person likes to have a place to call his or her own. This critical aspect of good workplace design should not be neglected in the design of middle school classrooms. That is, the classroom should include places that individual students feel "belong" to them—places to which they can retreat, when appropriate, from group work to pursue individual projects.

Another point needs to be made about the growing correlation between middle-school learning space and workplace environments. One of the factors that's likely to exert a continuing influence on middle-grades education is the increasing adoption, by districts around the country, of the *magnet school concept.* It used to be that the magnet school concept was more or less limited to the high-school level, but today a number districts are refashioning existing middle and even elementary schools as magnets, creating brand-new magnet schools on the elementary and middle-grades levels, or even reconceptualizing their entire educational program along magnet-school lines. It makes sense to mention magnets here, while we're discussing the relation between learning and workplace environments, because, of course, so many magnet schools' programs are organized around career-related themes, which means that some planning and design attention must focus on creating learning spaces that to some degree replicate the real-world workplaces of specific occupations. (We deal with this issue in detail in a forthcoming book in the "Schools of the Future" series: *Magnet and Charter Schools of the Future: A Focus on Specialization and Choice*.)

Reconfiguring Grade Patterns. Classically, middle schools have embraced grades 6 through 8, though there's always been some diversity of opinion about which grades a middle school should include. That diversity has, in fact, been growing—a function of differing views of psychological and social development during late childhood and early adolescence as well as of the changing facility needs of particular districts. Today, it's easy to find school districts that depart from the classical, 6–8 middle school model. Many—including the East Lyme district—are opting for a pattern that includes the fifth grade in the middle school; other districts (though fewer) are having students transition to high school in the eighth grade. (Fewer districts include grade 9 in their middle schools—there seems to be a general consensus that ninth-graders are too physically, psychologically, and sexually mature to interact well with younger children.) Some communities' middle-grades schools include grades 4 through 8, though these are usually termed "intermediate schools" rather than middle schools. And, finally, some districts—especially urban ones—are locating the elementary *and* the middle grades within single, K–8 facilities, in an effort to enhance the continuity of educational experience for disadvantaged youngsters. (Such schools typically use the house, or schools-within-a-school, model to ensure that the size of the school doesn't overwhelm the children who go there, as well as to segregate younger from older children and to enhance the faculty and administration's ability to monitor students.)

We can't say which of these grade configurations is "best," and on this score we're in very good company: the authors of the *Turning Points 2000* study themselves refrain from recommending any particular grade configuration (Jackson and Davis 2000, p. 4). What we can say is that it's very likely that opinions will continue to differ about which grade configuration is most appropriate, that changing demographics and facility needs will continue to alter grade-configuration strategies in particular districts, and even that the nature of adolescence itself will continue to change, which could eventually lead to the reconsideration of the configurations preferred by many educators today. The important point that should be drawn from the actual current diversity—and probable future diversity—of middle school grade configurations is that stakeholders need to take this into account, too, as they plan new middle schools for future flexibility. (Chapter 1 of this book, which focuses on recent—and we believe exemplary—middle-grades educational facilities, features schools employing a number of different grade configurations, including the K–8 model.)

The grade-range of a given middle school can influence planning and design in a number of ways. First, of course, there's the obvious fact that a 5–8 school is likely to serve a larger student population than, say, a 6–8 school, entailing the need for more classrooms and more (and perhaps larger and more complex) shared areas and support facilities. But it's also the case that a wider grade-range might exacerbate the problem of bullying—one of the chief safety and security issues faced by middle schools—requiring specific design strategies to maintain separation between the youngest and the oldest children, or to enhance the ability of teachers and administrators to monitor students. Also, the possible future need to change grade configurations—which might necessitate facility expansions—needs to be considered when selecting a site for a new building and, for example, when deciding whether or not to build-in the additional structure that might be necessary to accommodate a future expansion.

Using Technology to *Save* Space. Fifteen or more years into the "technological revolution" in education, we find ourselves especially intrigued by one effect of technology on school design that has only lately begun to reveal itself. For a long, long time, burgeoning educational technologies *added* to schools' space needs. Classrooms had to be made larger to accommodate dedicated computer stations; schools at all levels had to find ways of physically accommodating computer labs; proliferating electronic devices required additional classroom space (and space for storage!); technology infrastructure took up an ever-greater share of schools' gross square footage; and so on and so on. But, although the space pressure exerted by technology hasn't exactly abated, we are finally seeing signs that technology can also provide some ways of *decreasing* schools' overall space needs.

One of the areas in which this is already happening is the school media center. To put it quite simply: new information technologies—the Internet, electronic books—are reducing the amount of space that must be dedicated to library stacks. At the new East Lyme Middle School, the decision was made to shave square footage off the media center and to use that space instead to enlarge the group learning spaces in all of the team clusters. Granted, the idea of making media centers smaller has met with resistance on the part of some traditional-minded librarians, but it strikes us as a simple, undeniable fact that the need for space to store printed books will continue to decline over the coming decades. Eventually, we believe that as much as 50 percent of library stack space can be cut.

Meeting Children's Individual Needs. A commitment to addressing each individual student's needs—and to ensuring that not a single child "falls between the cracks"—has always been a guiding principle of the middle school movement. This means attending, of course, to individual children's differing interests, talents, and capabilities, and in this respect middle grades educators have been enormously influenced by the "multiple intelligences" theory put forward in the early 1980s by Harvard University education professor Dr. Howard Gardner. Multiple-intelligence theory now pervades the pedagogy being taught in the nation's teachers' colleges and is dramatically changing the ways in which curricula are being designed across all grade levels. Although the theory is complex and has been extended and refined by Dr. Gardner and his many followers in the years since it was first proposed, the basic premises of multiple-intelligence theory can be put rather simply

- Children (and the adults they become) have different ways of grasping and *intelligently* interacting with the world around them.
- These different kinds of intelligence can be identified and categorized. (Dr. Gardner has so far described eight distinct kinds of intelligence. A given individual may, of course, demonstrate strength in several of the categories.)
- Our educational system has traditionally focused on developing only two of these kinds of intelligence: what Gardner calls the "linguistic" and the "logical-mathematical" intelligences. It has rewarded those whom it deems verbally and/or mathematically/scientifically talented, while neglecting, ignoring, or actually (though inadvertently) punishing those whose gifts lie elsewhere.
- To be truly effective—to make sure that no one gets left behind because his or her gifts, strengths, and talents don't correspond to a certain lopsided value system—education must address *all* the intelligences.

Pedagogically, multiple-intelligence theory has been especially influential in the development of new instructional styles in which the teacher functions as a facilitator and new ways of designing lessons that depart from the traditional lecture format and that are highly interactive and/or self-directed. This departure from traditional modes has had an enormous impact on the ways educational space is conceived and designed—in the classroom and throughout the school. To take the simplest example: when a lesson includes a diverse set of activities aimed at developing a diverse set of interests and strengths, classroom space and components (like furniture) must be altered to accommodate that range of activities.

But besides fostering children's differing talents, an individualized approach to education recognizes that different kids have different psychological, emotional, social, and medical needs, as well. In recent years we've seen the growth of a support system—or, rather, a variety of support systems—intended to meet those needs, and this, too, is having a wide-ranging impact on the way that schools at all levels are designed.

The most obvious of the ways in which the recognition of differing needs is changing school design is in the area of special education. "Special education" is an increasingly broad rubric—one whose meaning is continuously being expanded and extended. In chapter 13, "Exceptional Kids Need More Feet," we use the term loosely to embrace the many kinds of assistance that have been developed to equalize educational opportunity for all children—from accessibility requirements for the physically disabled, to programs for the learning disabled, to strategies for dealing with anger and a whole range of emotional and behavioral problems. And, in that chapter, we show how all these interventions intensify space demands in new elementary, middle, and high school buildings.

But there are a host of other ways in which attending to children's differing individual needs is influencing how schools work and how they are designed. For example, the traditional school day, ending at about three o'clock in the afternoon, wasn't designed for children whose parents both work outside the home or children of employed single parents. Responding to the problems of "latchkey kids," some districts have instituted what amount to before- and after-school daycare programs.

Children's differing medical needs are also being focused on much more strictly and comprehensively than in the past. Gone are the days when the school nurse did little more than apply first aid to scratches and scrapes, dispense the occasional aspirin tablet, and take a feverish child's temperature, sending him or her home if warranted. We're now seeing nurse's suites that are equipped to access any student's medical history and that are stocked with a wide range of pharmaceuticals administered, per doctors' instructions, on a regular basis to certain children (e.g., diabetic kids, children with mental-health issues, asthmatic children) or available to be used in case of emergency. As the function of the school nurse becomes more complex, the need for onsite medical space increases.

Finally, a great deal more attention is being paid to the ways in which children differ ethnically and linguistically. Today, it isn't at all unusual for a public school—even in a suburban district—to have a student population that mixes kids from scores of ethnic backgrounds, who speak dozens of different languages at home. Those long-lived controversies over the wisdom and efficacy of bilingual (usually meaning Spanish/English) education begin to seem quaint nowadays, when a typical school might have students whose first languages are Urdu, Fujianese, Portuguese, Tagalog, Kréyol, Bengali, Arabic, etc., etc. Districts have responded to this veritable Babel by inaugurating a range of academic programs (ESL, remedial programs) and social services that help children and, in some cases, their families adapt. These programs and services, too, require space.

Accommodating differences and celebrating diversity are—no surprise—expensive propositions. An ever-larger percentage of the space in the typical middle school is being earmarked for special programmatic and support uses—in some cases, uses that weren't even envisioned as recently as two or three decades ago. The list of such special spaces is a long one, and includes expanded nurse's suites, planning and placement team (PPT) conference suites, family resource rooms, "time out" rooms, after-school daycare facilities, and so on. Not only is this list incomplete, but it doesn't count any of the space that may be added to many areas of a school building to ensure accessibility by physically disabled students.

All these trends toward greater attention to individual children's talents and needs are likely to become more pronounced in the future. We at Fletcher Thompson are proud to belong to a society that takes great pains to accommodate difference and to ensure not only that all children have an equal chance but that every child has the opportunity to explore his or her own interests and develop his or her own particular skills. But we also know that this celebration of diversity costs money and can lead to discomfort and frustration on the part of boards of education and building committees, who, given the always-present reality of limited budgets, must make hard choices among many different programmatic alternatives. Our appreciation of the difficulty of that decision-making process is one important reason behind the creation of this book, since we believe that, to make good decisions, stakeholders must be informed about *all* the factors that impinge on school building design. But we also train our eye on saving money wherever possible—and on cutting costs in a way that doesn't reduce the fullness or richness of public education.

Community Use. Yesterday's schools were worlds unto themselves, in most ways fundamentally disconnected from the communities that sent their children to them. There were, to be sure, occasions on which the larger community (especially parents) was "invited in"—PTA events, Parents' Days, the school play, a yearly or seasonal school festival, and so on—but these occasions were infrequent and highly structured interruptions of the normal routine. The school's participation in the civic life of the wider community was likewise limited: a lobby might be used as a polling place on Election Day; a gym or cafeteria might be called into service as a temporary shelter during a local emergency. But, for the most part, the school building served the school community only, and it sat empty and unused during hours, days, and months when school was not in session.

But a public school is not only a community building in the sense that it belongs to the community in which it stands and which, to a greater or lesser degree, has paid for its construction. A public school can also be *community-building* in the sense of bringing the wider community together. For a relatively long time, communities have realized that high schools can serve this purpose and have insisted that new high schools be designed to accommodate community uses ranging from hosting town meetings, to providing classroom space for continuing education programs, to serving as venues for performance by local theater groups and the athletic events of local sports teams, and so on. It's been much more recently, however, that we've witnessed a widespread recognition that, if properly designed, middle and elementary school buildings can be community-builders, too.

We should also note that, in virtually any new school planning project these days, it's critically important that voters be made aware from the very start that the new facility will accommodate after-hours community use. East Lyme's Jerry Belair told us that he believes that the fact that that new middle school's gym will have two full courts—available for use by community teams—was instrumental in winning approval of the project at referendum.

There are, to be sure, a host of design challenges that accompany this trend toward opening the school building to use by the wider community—challenges that involve everything from onsite parking, to outdoor lighting and electric power needs, to the need to segregate (for security reasons) common, or core, areas used by community groups from off-limits academic areas. As the trend toward inviting the wider community into the middle school continues to gather steam—as we believe it will—solutions that are tailored to communities' specific needs will be found for all of them. (Community-use issues related to site design and security are treated in some detail in chapter 8, "Site Design and Landscape Architecture for the Future Middle School," and chapter 9, "Middle School Security: Closed Yet Open," respectively.)

In emphasizing community use, we do not forget that the primary responsibility of those who participate in the planning and design of the middle school of the future *is to the students who will learn there*. Architectural and engineering elements have a great bearing on students' safety, comfort, and sense of well-being. For example, a decision to maximize the use of low-maintenance, durable building materials will not only save a district money in the long run by reducing maintenance expenses, it will also foster an environment in which students take pride. (And, as chapter 9 details, experience clearly shows that damage begets damage, and that clean, well-maintained school environments tend to stay that way.) Quality lighting systems that don't create glare or interfere with computer screens, ample natural light, facility-wide air conditioning that supports year-round activity—these and other elements all facilitate learning and demonstrate a community's investment in its children's lives and in their future.

But by "commitment to students" we also mean a commitment to *overall design excellence*. We realize, of course, that the real world can be a tough place—one in which genuinely future-oriented visions can be pared down or simply set aside when visionaries come up against the hard realities of budgets, referenda, bureaucratic intransigence and red tape, and simple human inertia and resistance to change. Compromises will always and everywhere be made. But it's our belief—strengthened by Fletcher Thompson's decades of experience of designing schools in the Northeast—that design excellence and futuristic vision can survive the rough-and-tumble processes by which new schools actually come into being. To repeat: There's a much better chance of that happening when stakeholders are well-informed about *all* the factors impinging on school design, when they understand the consequences of their decisions, and when they work collaboratively. Hence this book.

Part I: The Middle School of Today

Chapter 1

The Middle School of Today: Six Exemplary Projects

In an important sense, there is no such thing as "the" middle school of today. True, architects and educators are coming to share a core philosophy of middle-grades education—many of whose central themes are developed elsewhere in this book—and a generalized set of principles guiding middle school design continues to evolve. Still, every school planning and design process must respond to a large number of particularities. These might include—to choose just a few examples—budget limitations, site constraints, the size and demographics of the student population, the degree and kind of community use the building will house, and/or the specific educational vision the school is intended to embody and foster. As we emphasize throughout this book, *every school construction project is unique*—or should be—and there is, therefore, no single model for a successful middle school design.

This chapter presents six school projects that we believe to be exemplary. (Four of the projects emerge from our own studio; two represent the work of other design firms.) In many important respects, these schools are very different from one another. They vary in size. Some are new construction; others are renovations or renovation-and-addition projects. But perhaps the most important characteristic distinguishing them from one another is the particular grade configuration each serves. Though four of the schools have "classical" middle school configurations (grades 5–8 or 6–8), two do not, and their inclusion here is intentional. By including them, we hope to show that districts can creatively respond to challenges (burgeoning enrollments, tight budgets, etc.) without sacrificing quality in their educational facilities. (In this regard, the Wexler-Grant Community School is particularly important; this renovated facility in New Haven, Connecticut's revitalized Elm Haven neighborhood is an outstanding example of a trend, ever more common in big city school districts, toward consolidating elementary and middle grades in the same building in order to enhance the continuity of education for at-risk children.)

These exemplary schools' designers were in each case charged with responding to a distinct set of issues and, hence, were called upon to create distinctive solutions that met each particular community's needs. Despite—or because of—these differing emphases, we believe that all of the school designs featured here are very successful. But we also believe that, with one exception—the Ocoee Middle School, in Ocoee, Florida—all of the projects fall short of implementing the truly future-oriented design principles that this book advocates. This chapter is therefore meant to be *descriptive* rather than prescriptive.

Project # 1
Seymour Middle School
Seymour, Connecticut
Grades 6 through 8
Designer: Fletcher-Thompson, Inc.
Project type: New construction
Completed: 2001

by Julie A. Kim, AIA

Key Issues:
Community use
Value engineering
Siting and landscape design

Rendering of Seymour Middle School's "main street": entrance to media center is visible at rear.

Photo of Seymour Middle School's "main street."

The town of Seymour was eager to relieve overcrowding in its existing middle school classrooms—and to give its early-adolescent schoolchildren a genuine middle school experience. The budget for a new middle school in this formerly industrial, largely blue-collar city in southwestern Connecticut was limited, however, and designers faced the challenge of creating a school flexible enough to accommodate a range of learning experiences but "standard" and efficient enough to adhere to tight budgetary guidelines. The resulting 164,000-square-foot facility (for a design population of 750) accomplished these goals admirably, coming in *under* the $34 million allotted for its design and construction.

Community Use. Community enthusiasm for the project was generated and sustained by the decision, early in the design process, to create a building that would naturally lend itself to after-hours use by community groups. The relatively straightforward floorplan of the Seymour Middle School accomplishes this by placing all shared, core spaces (gym, media center, auditorium, and cafeteria, as well as administrative and guidance offices) at the front of the building, arranged along the longer access of a large, T-shaped main lobby that serves as a "main street" and a gathering place for the school and wider communities. (The gymnasium—larger than most middle school gyms—was "oversized" to accommodate community use as well as some of the physical education and athletics programs of the nearby Seymour High School.) The school's overall configuration—with classrooms segregated in three two-story wings, or "fingers," at the back of the structure—allows for the easy zoning-off of academic areas after school hours.

Seymour Middle School's auditorium incorporates the latest accessibility guidelines, with seating for disabled students distributed throughout.

Computer lab.

Value Engineering. Money savings were realized throughout the project through meticulous value engineering, whose goal was to cut costs without sacrificing aesthetic quality or durability. For instance, the interior walls of the school's auditorium are made of layers of sheetrock rather than masonry block; this decision to choose a less costly and less durable material in that space was justified because of the comparatively low level of abuse and wear-and-tear that the auditorium is likely to endure. Finishes throughout the school are plain (for example, VCT flooring is used throughout, except in the administrative offices, media center, and gym), but this plainness is alleviated through the use of a bold, exciting color palette in classrooms.

Because value engineering measures were implemented so carefully and thoughtfully, the value engineering process was not allowed to rob the facility of amenities: Although some design-team members worried during the design process that the school's relatively "opulent" main lobby would be criticized as extravagant, this capacious, light-filled space—offering convenient access to all the other common spaces—has in fact proved a very popular gathering place for the community at large.

Siting and Landscape Design. Designers took advantage of the Seymour school's site, which slopes down from front to back, by situating the two-story classroom "fingers" at the back of the building; the lower (ground) floors of these wings have grade-level egress, as well as access to the large interior courtyard at the center of the school.

As the site was being prepared for construction, an archaeological dig investigated the remains of a farm and farmhouse that had once occupied the site. Among the discoveries made by archaeologists was a set of large paving stones, which landscape architects Richter & Cegan reused to create handsome flooring and seating for the Seymour school's "outdoor classroom." This use of materials found on site establishes a strong historical link with the community's past. Onsite wetlands were designated a "science exploratorium,"; a walkway to this portion of the site permits easy access by student groups studying natural processes.

Exterior view of Seymour Middle School shows gymnasium at far left, canopied entrance at center, and auditorium at right.

Project # 2
Helen Keller Middle School
Easton, Connecticut
Grades 5 through 8
Designer: Fletcher-Thompson, Inc.
Project type: Renovation of and addition to
existing middle school
Completed: 2001

by Joseph G. Costa, AIA

Key issues:
Thorough redesign
Parking and circulation
Large, flexible classrooms
Cafetorium
Cost savings
Construction-phase teamwork

View of lobby inside main entrance.

The "main street" artery connects all levels of the Helen Keller School.

Undertaken for the purpose of relieving overcrowding at area elementary schools, the renovation of the original Helen Keller Middle School—a 60,000-square-foot building that had housed grades 6 through 8—and the addition of approximately 30,000 square feet of new classrooms and shared spaces accomplished much more than merely alleviating the space crunch. The original facility and its site had been marred by numerous poor design decisions, leading to cramped circulation patterns inside and out, inadequately sized and inflexible classrooms that were noisy and poorly lit, and a building that "turned inward," ignoring the lovely vistas of its rural setting. The new addition, together with the redesign of the old building (including infrastructure, mechanical, fire protection, and lighting/electrical/telecommunications upgrades), completely "made over" the school's image, transforming it into a lively, efficient, flexible, and light-filled learning environment. The revamped and expanded facility now houses more than 600 students in grades 5 through 8.

Parking and Circulation. As originally laid out, Helen Keller's site had a single, common bus-queuing and parent drop-off area; as the site has been reorganized, these areas have been separated and new parking areas for visitors and staff have been added, eliminating the clogged and confusing conditions that had prevailed in the past. Circulation inside the building had been just as bad: while changing classes and at the beginning and end of the school day, Helen Keller's students had all traveled through a single corridor, creating congestion and delays.

View of renovated cafeteria/performance space; windows at rear of photo open onto surrounding rural landscape.

Another view of the renovated cafeteria showing clerestory element along roofline.

The addition, as well as some reconfiguration of interior space in the existing building, permitted the creation of a loop circulation pattern. That loop pattern is especially important at this school, whose organizational pattern is a hybrid between newer, middle school practices and an older junior high–type model in which students change classes throughout the school day (while mostly remaining within their grade-level areas). Interior traffic flow has been further eased by the replacement of several staircases and wheelchair lifts with ramps, which also provide better accessibility for physically disabled students.

Large, Flexible Classrooms. Classrooms in the old Helen Keller school averaged about 770 square feet—very small by today's standards. Although those classrooms have been retained in the renovated portion of the new facility, they have been redefined as special education support spaces, and most learning activities have been moved into the new classrooms in the addition, which average about 950 square feet. Besides being small, the original classrooms were poorly lit and were afflicted by extremely poor acoustics resulting from a steel shed roof and brick-finished interior walls.

The renovation of these rooms entailed redoing all the finishes: interior walls are now covered with gypsum wallboard; VCT flooring has been installed throughout; and a dropped acoustical ceiling with recessed fixtures helps control noise while improving ambient lighting. Equipment and furniture have been upgraded, as well: ventilators at window walls have been replaced, and new casework provides adequate storage and countertop space. The new classrooms in the addition were likewise designed to maximize flexibility and acoustical quality; their large windows provide sweeping views of the surrounding landscape, which includes a pond and nearby pumpkin farm. Each of the new classrooms has six computer drops for student use and one drop for the teacher's workstation.

Cafetorium. The limited construction budget ($11 million) did not allow for a purpose-built auditorium. To provide space for performances and larger-group meetings, designers opted for a radical redesign of the existing cafeteria. Although this room had always served as the venue for assemblies and other large gatherings, it was badly lit, cramped, and noisy, and it accommodated such activities very poorly. Besides almost doubling its size, the new design improved daylighting by adding a clerestory—a curving, "pop-up" element along the roofline that terminates at the stage area—and by opening up a previously solid wall, permitting views of the surrounding countryside. Acoustical treatments make this space suitable for a wide range of performances and other town events.

Cost Savings. The tight budget necessitated strict control over every dollar spent. Designers realized significant cost savings by allowing the additional classroom wings to follow the existing sloping topography of the site, eliminating the need for extensive earthwork and backfilling.

This entry area is used by children being dropped off by parents and by after-hours community users; windows at top left look through cafeteria to the landscape beyond.

Construction-phase Teamwork. Though smaller than many school renovation/addition projects, the Helen Keller project was also more difficult because construction had to occur while the building was occupied. The fact that there was no existing swing space into which students could be transferred during construction also meant that the job had to be completely very quickly so as to minimize disruption.

Construction proceeded in two stages: the new classrooms were built first to create the swing space into which students could be moved while the renovation was performed. Though a project of this magnitude would ordinarily take a year or longer, construction at the Helen Keller school was completed in about seven months. The accelerated schedule was made possible through intensive teamwork among the Town of Easton's Building Committee; Fletcher-Thompson, Inc., which provided architectural and engineering services; and the construction manager, the Gilbane Building Company. The success of this highly collaborative effort was recognized by the Connecticut Building Council, which awarded team members its 2002 Project Team Award.

Project # 3
Sarah Noble Intermediate School
New Milford, Connecticut
Grades 4 through 6
Designer: Fletcher-Thompson, Inc.
Project type: Renovation/addition to former
high school
Completed: 2001

by Timothy P. Cohen

Key issues:
Adaptation of existing building for different
grade configuration
Rearrangement of core functions
Interior circulation
Child-friendly design

View of cafeteria/multipurpose space.

Entrance into new media center off main lobby.

The town of New Milford, Connecticut, had originally planned merely to renovate its existing high school; that proposal, however, failed at referendum. Research conducted after the vote revealed that voters believed the proposal to be a half-measure that would not really solve the district's problems. Based on that study, a new proposal was developed that called for the creation of a brand-new, state-of-the-art high school (featured on the cover of the first book in this series, *The High School of the Future: A Focus on Technology*) and for a "like-new" renovation of the existing high school to serve as an intermediate school for grades 4, 5, and 6 that would relieve overcrowding at the district's elementary schools and at its middle school.

The renovated 189,000-square-foot facility—now renamed the Sarah Noble Intermediate School—houses a student population of 1,350 in grades 4, 5, and 6. Not really a middle school per se, it provides a transitional educational experience between the primary-school years and the middle grades, and the environment incorporates features associated with both elementary and middle schools.

Adaptation for a Different Grade Configuration. The old high school, built in 1967, was large, imposing, and sterile, and did not naturally lend itself to becoming a learning environment for much younger schoolchildren. Budgetary considerations and structural issues, however, forced designers to work within in the existing structural shell, relocating only a few of the major core components to solve problems of circulation and delivery of services. In the building's classroom areas (a series of double-loaded corridors

9

The new, inviting entrance is easily identifiable; the canopy offers convenient, protected access for children entering the building from nearby bus drop-off.

grouped around a central courtyard), designers were similarly constrained, unable to change the basic layout or existing classroom modules.

Minor reconfigurations of space—including the demolition of some demising walls, which added 150 to 200 square feet to some classrooms—greatly augmented flexibility, however, and the look of the interior environment was completely transformed through the use of visually stimulating finishes that are durable and child-friendly. Future flexibility is fostered by the use of gypsum board for all new partitions, and the support and office spaces dispersed throughout the classroom areas were designed to adhere to the classroom module, meaning that they can easily be converted to learning spaces should the need arise.

Rearrangement of Core Functions. The most challenging problems associated with the existing building were associated with its core spaces—media center, cafeteria, auditorium, gymnasium. The media center was undersized; the cafeteria and kitchen were located directly adjacent to the main entrance, causing circulation problems (especially during delivery times); and there was simply too much physical education–related space, including locker rooms and an auxiliary gym that, while necessary for the high school P.E. and athletics programs, were irrelevant to a middle school's needs. Though it was a desirable feature in many ways, the pur-

Sarah Noble features a planetarium—a renovated component of the former high school.

The main lobby is flooded with natural light from clerestory windows; careful design consideration was given to visual access of this area from adjacent administrative offices.

View of cafeteria/multipurpose room looking toward stage.

pose-built auditorium would be sacrificed in the new design, which focused on devising ways for *all* the core functions to work effectively and efficiently. In the renovation, the cafeteria and kitchen were relocated to the former auditorium, which was redesigned as a cafetorium; the former band and choral rooms behind the auditorium became the new kitchen, and a new service entrance for food and materials deliveries and trash pickup was created at the back of the school, greatly lessening vehicular congestion outside the building and reducing circulation conflicts within the facility. The new cafetorium—filled with natural light, finished with vibrant colors, and acoustically treated to control noise—is very effective at doing double-duty as a performance and large-group gathering space.

Meanwhile, the media center was transferred to the space once occupied by the cafeteria. Not only is this space larger than that formerly occupied by the media center—large enough, in fact, to have allowed a new computer lab to be placed at the back of the media center—but the redesign creates a welcoming transparency between the media center and the school's main lobby. Technology is everywhere on display: the computer lab behind the media center is fully visible, and the school's main server room is glass-walled so that students can view the technology that enables interactive learning.

The redesigned school contains two other computer labs, as well—situated in what had been gym locker rooms. On a mezzanine adjacent to the main gymnasium, the no-longer-needed auxiliary gym was converted into a multipurpose room that's especially well-suited to musical productions. Almost like a black box theater, this space has proved popular with community groups as a venue for gatherings and performances; a set of portable risers enable it to be used for band practice. Rooms below this mezzanine space have been converted to music classrooms.

Despite the constraints and challenges, the decision to work within the basic architectural framework created by the existing core elements had one decided advantage over tearing them down and building anew—these components, originally sized for a high school, collectively provide many more square feet for core functions than might have been possible with a brand-new middle school, given current limitations on state reimbursements.

Interior Circulation. The reconfiguration of core spaces, in and of itself, alleviated circulation problems. But interior circulation was also improved by increasing the width of existing corridors and by adding another corridor that provides an additional pathway out of the cafeteria and that, combined with existing corridors, establishes a loop circulation pattern. Outside the building, a second bus drop-off/pickup area was created at the rear of the facility, alleviating morning and evening congestion in the main lobby. The bottlenecks the facility had suffered in the past disappeared.

The art room was the former high school's auto mechanics shop; the bay doors were retained, providing lots of natural light for this high-ceilinged interior space.

Child-Friendly Design. During the second of the referendum processes described above, some members of the community continued to oppose the town of New Milford's revised school construction proposal, voicing the opinion that the old high school should simply be torn down rather than renovated. They felt—not without reason—that the facility was simply too "institutional" ever to work as a learning environment for younger children. Some of the strategies for enlivening the atmosphere—for example, the specification of a vibrant color palette for interior finishes—have already been mentioned. But the changes that were made to the school's front entrance and main lobby were just as important in altering the facility's character. The original entrance was all wrong for a middle school—cold, imposing, and off-putting. Replacing it with a canopied entrance (quickly accessible from the front-door bus drop-off) was a big step toward making the building more child-friendly. Refashioning the lobby—raising the roof, adding a series of clerestory windows that introduce natural light into the space, and increasing the transparency between the lobby and adjacent spaces (media center, administrative offices)—was equally important in creating a welcoming, non-intimidating environment.

Project # 4
Wexler-Grant Community School
New Haven, Connecticut
Grades K through 8
Designer: Fletcher-Thompson, Inc.
Project type: Renovation of and addition to
existing elementary school
Completed: 2002

by Julie A. Kim, AIA

Key issues:
Transformation of school and community
K–8 facility: advantages and disadvantages

Wexler-Grant's interior courtyard is designed for outdoor-classroom instruction.

The lobby inside Wexler-Grant's main entrance features a commissioned sculptural work by artist John Rohlfing.

Until recently, the history of New Haven's Wexler-Grant Community School (formerly the Isadore Wexler School) was a tragic one of urban decline. The school, originally built as an elementary school in 1951, was situated at the center of a public housing complex, and for decades the school and its community suffered from neglect and all the ills that typically afflict inner city neighborhoods. After the urban riots of the 1960s, the school was "renovated" as a fortress, its windows bricked up. When the high-rise projects were torn down in 1989, the neighborhood's population decreased, and Wexler became a special ed school serving students from all over New Haven.

Transformation. The reversal of this trend began with the construction of Elm Haven, a residential-style public housing project adjacent to the school's site. As families began moving back into the neighborhood, an extensive renovation of the school was undertaken to create an educational environment that would serve this revitalized community's schoolchildren. The renovated facility was also designed to meet the recreational needs of the wider community.

The new design effects a sharp break with the building's dismal past. Though the school remains a one-story, primarily brick structure, it boasts a new glass-fronted entrance with an arched roof—an entrance that welcomes the community in rather than declaring "no trespassing"—as well as a new main lobby featuring a dynamic sculptural piece commissioned by the district. The new lobby and the other added spaces wrap around a new central courtyard, outfitted with benches and plantings, that floods the lobby with natural light.

13

The dramatic new main entrance welcomes school children and the community into the Wexler-Grant school.

An interior "portico" leads into the study area of the school's media center.

The palette of yellows and reddish-brown tones makes Wexler-Grant's renovated auditorium a soothing, welcoming space for assemblies and performances.

K–8 Facility: Advantages and Disadvantages. As part of its transformation, the 92,000-square-foot school was reconceived as a K–8 facility. Like some other cities across the country, New Haven is engaged in a push to consolidate elementary and middle school grades in the same buildings. The rationale behind this movement is a simple one: It's believed that, in urban school districts marked by decades of poor academic performance, K–8 schools provide much-needed continuity of educational experience. Early studies of this trend seem to bear out the notion that children in economically deprived urban neighborhoods respond well when they are schooled within their home communities for a longer period of time, and that their motivation is improved by long-term interaction with teachers they know, in an environment that is comfortable and familiar.

That said, when a school building houses such a wide age-range, measures must be taken to separate younger from older children. The Wexler-Grant school accomplishes this separation in two ways. Architecturally, the school's classroom corridors are zoned into distinct K–2, 3–5, and 6–8 areas; during the course of an ordinary school day, there is no reason for a student from one of these zones to cross into either of the others. Children attending Wexler-Grant are also required to wear uniforms, whose color differs according to grade level, enabling administrators and faculty to immediately identify any youngster who's in the wrong place at the wrong time.

The Wexler-Grant school is blessed with what is a very large site (9 acres) for an urban school, and the extensive site also assists in separating children of different ages, in that there is room for multiple playgrounds, with play equipment designed for younger and older children.

The benefits of the K–8 configuration are, of course, balanced by some sacrifices. The traditional configuration of its classroom zones and the school's relatively small overall population (600 students total) limit the school's ability to implement some of the more experimental aspects of middle school educational practice discussed in this book. Nevertheless, working within a very tight budget, Wexler-Grant accomplishes quite a lot: The new science lab, used by students in the upper grades, is on par with similar facilities in affluent suburban middle schools; the middle-grades zone contains two foreign-language classrooms; and the school's two music rooms and large art room are very good by contemporary urban-school standards.

Moreover, the decision to renovate the existing building rather than demolishing it and building anew proved extremely advantageous in terms of the amenities the school offers its students and the surrounding community. The original structure's auditorium and sizable gym were retained in the renovation; if these had been demolished, prevailing reimbursement standards would have necessitated a much smaller gymnasium and would have eliminated the possibility of the school's having a separate, purpose-built auditorium. These facilities are extremely important in the life of the school and that of the neighborhood: the gym, especially, is in almost constant after-hours use by community sports teams.

Project # 5
Mount Olive Middle School
Budd Lake, New Jersey
Grades 6 through 8
Designer: Jordan & Pease, Architects
Project type: New construction
Completed: 2000

Key issues:
"Synergistics" lab and other specialized
learning spaces
Auditorium
Security
Construction management

Students collaborate on a project at a modular computer unit in Mount Olive's Synergistics Lab.

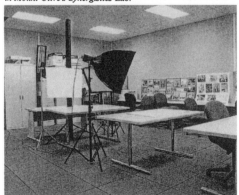

The graphic arts room.

"**I**'ve visited other new middle schools, and thought, 'Well, I'd do this differently, I wouldn't do that,' and so on, but I can truly say that there's nothing about the design of this school that I would have changed," says Principal Richard Wenner, praising the new Mount Olive Middle School in north-central New Jersey town of Budd Lake. The 200,000-plus square foot facility, which opened in December 2000 and serves a student population of 1,150, was the centerpiece of a $50 million county-wide school construction program, undertaken to relieve overcrowding, which also included the retrofitting of the old Mount Olive Middle School (which became an elementary school) and the renovation of three elementary school buildings.

"Synergistics" Lab/Specialized Learning Spaces. At the Mount Olive school, grade levels are organized into teams, and groups of students move from classroom to classroom to study different subjects over the course of the day. Each team, however, stays within its specified team area except when traveling to shared, specialized learning spaces.

These specialized learning spaces are among the features that make the Mount Olive school so noteworthy. The most innovative is the "Synergistics lab," created by Pitsco, Inc.'s Synergistic Systems division, which has installed such labs in more than 2,000 middle schools nationwide. Designed with the specific educational needs of middle-grades students in mind, the Synergistics lab provides a venue for projects that combine computer work with hands-on, experimental learning experiences. The Synergistics lab curriculum is based on age-appropriate modules—

The industrial technology room.

The auditorium.

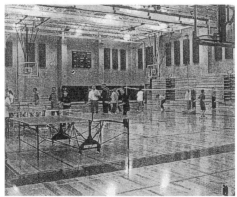

Recreational activities such as Ping-Pong and badminton form part of Mount Olive's physical education curriculum.

ranging from Kite Making (for sixth graders) to Audio Broadcasting and Music & Sound to Robots and Rocketry & Space—and the lab has its own designated faculty person to plan programs and coordinate the lab's use. (The lab was funded by a grant from the BASF Corporation.)

A great deal of attention has also been lavished on the school's other shared learning spaces, including science labs (which are on a par with, or better than, those in many high schools), the interconnected art rooms (which open onto a courtyard and are flooded with natural light), specialized vocal and instrumental music classrooms, and a graphic arts room equipped with more than 20 Macintosh computers. (Technological resources are distributed throughout the facility: the media center, for example, contains several computer technology resource rooms.) The main and auxiliary gymnasiums, which house an innovative physical education program combining fitness training (treadmills, stationery bikes) with traditional recreational activities such as Ping-Pong and badminton, are outfitted with a state-of-the-art sound system and high-grade acoustical treatments to control sound levels.

Auditorium. Mount Olive's resources include a full auditorium that has proved its worth time and again since the school's opening. For the school community, the auditorium (which features a state-of-the-art sound booth) not only provides a venue for assemblies but is frequently used for large-group learning activities. Beyond these uses, however, it also serves as a performance and meeting space for the wider community, and is solidly "booked" throughout the year. Rentals of the auditorium to community groups (dance and theater groups, educational training seminars, etc.) generated approximately $18,000 in additional income for the school during the 2001–2002 school year.

Security. Electronic security at the Mount Olive school is more advanced than that found at many middle schools, incorporating full video surveillance of both the exterior and the interior of the building. About the video surveillance system, Principal Wenner says, "It makes you feel as if you have control of the facility," and he credits the system with aiding in discipline and with preventing damage or misuse by after-hours community users.

Construction Management. In discussing the steps leading up to the Mount Olive school's creation, Principal Wenner reserves special praise for Turner Construction Company, which coordinated the public relations effort leading up to the successful school bond referendum and which managed construction for the Morris County Board of Education. Based on his experience with Turner, Wenner strongly believes that the construction management project-delivery method, by providing strict oversight of contractors, results in many fewer change orders, and he commends Turner's CM team with bringing the project in on time and under budget.

Project # 6
Ocoee Middle School
Ocoee, Florida
Grades 6 through 8
Designer: Fanning/Howey Associates, Inc.
Project type: New construction; reutilization
of existing gymnasium
Completed: 2001

by Katherine C. Clark, Ed.D.

Key issues:
Flexible design
Indoor environmental quality
Audiovisual enhancement
"Smart cards"
Integrated, "break-the-mold" technology-
based learning
Lab-based learning
Fine and performing arts education

Aerial view of Ocoee Middle School site.

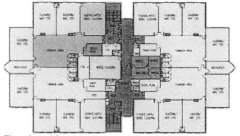

*Floorplan of Ocoee Middle School shows relationship
between classrooms and large common areas.*

*[Editor's note: Of all the exemplary projects discussed in this chapter,
Ocoee Middle School may come closest to realizing the ideals of the
middle school of the future as they are outlined in this book. Its planners'
and designers' dedication to putting the principles of middle-grades educational theory into practice throughout the school and their concern to
integrate advanced technology into every aspect of school life have produced a truly remarkable facility. Principal Kate Clark, who wrote this
section, is justly proud of the new school, and has hosted scores of visitors
from around the country, all of them eager to emulate what Ocoee has done
in their home communities. Ocoee Middle School and the various technologies it incorporates have been featured in numerous magazine stories
(see the "Sources" section at the end of this book). In the fall of 2002, the
school received an Impact on Learning Award from School Planning &
Management magazine for its success in accommodating technology.]*

Through actions of the Florida state legislature and with the help of the
Orange County Public Schools, Ocoee Middle School was selected to become Florida's Demonstration Middle School. This important project was
assigned to the SMART Schools Clearinghouse, whose goal was to develop
a "break-the-mold" technology-based facility. (The acronym "SMART"
stands for Soundly Made, Accountable, Reasonable, and Thrifty.)

At the project's inception, SMART Schools assembled a design team,
which decided how architectural selection would be performed. Others par-
ticipating in the planning/design process included Dr. Katherine C. Clark,

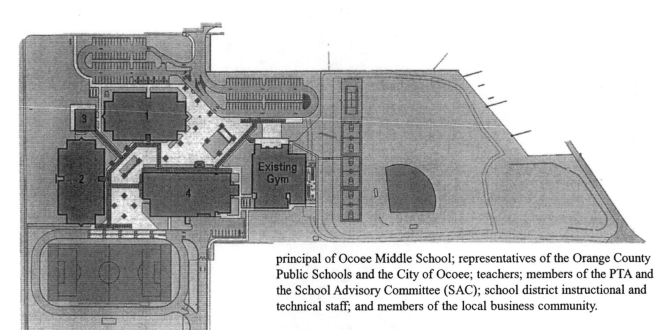

Site plan of Ocoee Middle School.

principal of Ocoee Middle School; representatives of the Orange County Public Schools and the City of Ocoee; teachers; members of the PTA and the School Advisory Committee (SAC); school district instructional and technical staff; and members of the local business community.

In early 1998, architects were asked to present their most innovative design concepts for enhancing the middle school learning process to the architectural/engineering selection committee, which chose Fanning/Howey Associates, Inc., one of the nation's leading educational design firms, as the project architect. The team assembled by Fanning/Howey included educational-design experts, consulting engineers, landscape architects, and food service designers. The project's construction manager, James A, Cummings, Inc., played an essential role in problem-solving during the design process.

The design of the school emerged through a highly collaborative process that included extensive research, exploration, discussion, and planning, all focused on how middle-school-age children learn. In developing the design, the team took into consideration issues ranging from instructional approaches, to use of technology, to community use of the school. Because of the Ocoee school's visibility within the community, the new buildings have been carefully designed to complement surrounding residences, featuring a metal roof and vernacular, "Cracker-style" design elements.

The large common areas outside classrooms are used for individual and group projects; lockers are located in these shared spaces.

Flexible Design. At Ocoee, academic spaces are organized into flexible team areas that support a variety of teaching methods. Classrooms are connected by large common areas rather than by corridors, and students are able to access and work with technology in both the common areas and the classrooms. Beyond providing additional instructional space, this conversion of circulation space into extended learning areas augments supervision. Teachers can easily monitor the activities of students as they use the common areas to visit lockers, travel to restrooms, study individually, or work in small groups. Operable walls between classrooms and common areas further enhance flexibility, allowing a wide variety of spatial configurations. Teachers can easily collaborate, team teach, work in stations, or interact with small or large groups of students.

Teachers at Ocoee wear wireless microphones to enhance speech intelligibility.

Smart cards control access at Ocoee Middle School.

Indoor Environmental Quality: Natural Light and Oxygen Monitoring. During the planning process, the design team explored the impact of natural daylight on students' ability to learn. In the resulting design, all classrooms within the learning areas have walls facing the exterior, meaning that Ocoee Middle School has nearly double the amount of windows required by state standards. To ensure high-quality indoor air, Ocoee's air conditioning system maintains appropriate oxygen flow by monitoring CO_2 levels throughout the day.

Audiovisual Enhancement. Because teachers had ranked audio enhancement as their number one technology priority, the design team put special emphasis on sound control. The school is the first in the nation in which every classroom is equipped with an infrared audio enhancement system—which amplifies teachers' voices to about 10 to 12 decibels above classroom noise levels. Teachers wear wireless microphones and transmitters that send infrared signals to classroom receiver-amplifiers. Speakers, mounted to the acoustical tiles in the ceilings, project the sound within the classroom.

Beyond this sound reinforcement system, the school incorporates other advanced audiovisual technologies and enhancements in all the learning areas. Instead of traditional wall-mounted video monitors (or monitors on movable carts), classrooms are equipped with six-foot-wide video screens and ceiling-mounted LCD projectors. The sound for this system is run through the built-in audio system. Acoustical control within the learning areas is augmented by the movable wall panels, which have sound-blocking capabilities similar to those of fixed walls.

"Smart Cards." Ocoee Middle School is one of four Schools Interoperability Framework (SIF) pilot sites in the nation. Students use "proximity cards" ("smart cards") to access the building and the different grade-level areas, to purchase food in the cafeteria, to use library services, and to access computers. Time restrictions can be placed on building access for students and staff, and the cards can be programmed to limit access to

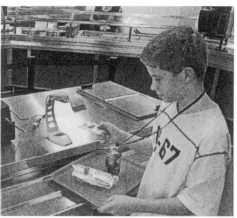

Ocoee students use their smart cards to purchase food in the school's cafeteria.

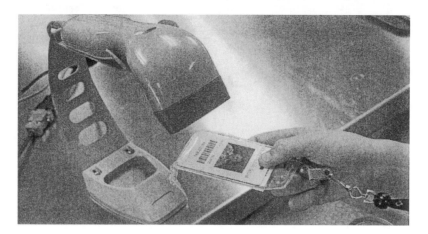

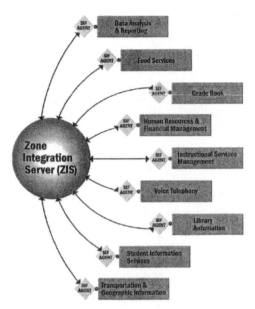

Diagram of Schools Interoperability Framework (SIF) network used at Ocoee Middle School.

Library checkout is one of the many functions that have been computerized at Ocoee.

certain areas. Parents can access information about their children—including grades, attendance, discipline, and homework completion—via the Web, and, ultimately, parents will even be able to check on the status of books checked out of the library, to view cafeteria accounts, and even to see which foods their children are eating for lunch.

"Break-the-Mold" Technology. Technology is fully integrated throughout every area of the Ocoee facility. In addition to audiovisual and SIF technology, Ocoee Middle School has a T1 connection for Internet access, as well as numerous video channels and phone lines. Shared cabling technologies support broadband distribution, media retrieval, and voice/video distribution. Campus buildings are linked electronically via a fiber-optic distribution system. Voice/data, fire alarm, security, video, and other systems all use the common cabling system, and infrastructure design allows the easy addition of new types of cable in the future. While most schools today have 100-megabit backbones, Ocoee features a gigabit backbone with 100 megabits to the desktop.

Lab-based Learning. Ocoee Middle School possesses five different kinds of technology laboratories, all designed to enhance the learning process and provide students a wide diversity of educational experiences:

*   The *Tech Design Lab* offers a modular instruction system in which students learn principles and applications through multimedia-based instruction and develop technical knowledge and skills through hands-on activities.
*   The *Business Communications Lab* features a system enabling students to learn the various features of Microsoft Office.
*   The *Pre-Engineering Robotics Lab* is a hands-on laboratory in which students, using Legos, build and program robots.
*   The *Television Production Lab* introduces students to the world of broadcast communication.
*   The *Tech Science Lab* combines basic earth science skills with technology.

Fine and Performing Arts Education. It has been proven that arts education increases self-confidence and nurtures creativity in middle school students, and Ocoee Middle School offers a full program in fine and performing arts. The school boasts a classic, full-size wooden stage (designed for community as well as school use) and dressing rooms. In addition to band and choral rooms, the music suite also contains a keyboard laboratory, two Wenger practice rooms, and auxiliary storage rooms for uniforms, instruments, and sheet music. The art suite includes facilities for ceramics, sketching, painting, and other art media.

Chapter 2

Cost, Change, and School Construction

Today, the conflicting realities of new-school construction are creating a difficult and many-pronged quandary for educators, government officials, architects, and parents and other taxpayers. On the one hand, school design is changing rapidly. Communities across the country are racing to catch up with advances in learning technology and are coming to grips with the need to build schools that are both larger and more complex than the schools of the past.

On the other hand, however, the design of new public schools is not changing as greatly or as quickly as it should, if we are truly to meet the educational challenges of the future. As it stands, the processes by which new schools are proposed, approved, funded, designed, and built do not easily accommodate the kinds of change that the future demands.

Over the past decade—and in the midst of these contradictory trends—there was a widespread perception that increases in the cost of new schools were greatly outpacing the general rate of inflation. Whether or not that's true, it is certainly the case that costs rose, and these rises in the price a community had to pay for a new school building resulted from a very large number of factors—some only poorly understood by decision-makers. Responding to these increases in a nonsystematic way, communities all too often shortchanged their own children and future generations of students by attempting to control cost by restricting or eliminating genuinely innovative, genuinely necessary change.

As all readers of this book are well aware, the country's general economic picture has been in great flux during 2002, and as of this writing it remains unclear how economic trends will influence the construction market over the next few years. But it is not unreasonable to suppose that school construction costs might continue to rise.

Under these somewhat confusing circumstances, how can decision-makers know which kinds of change are good (and should be promoted and supported) and which are not? Further, what steps can be taken by superintendents, boards of education, building committees, state and local officials, parents, and other community members—in other words, by *all* the stakeholders in a new school construction project—to control costs while directing change in ways that truly serve their interests? We believe that, if they want to create school buildings that are truly future-oriented, stakeholders must first acquaint themselves with the wide range of factors creating the current impasse. And we believe, too, that there are a number of actions decision-makers can take to facilitate the kinds of change that will transform their communities' new schools into *schools of the future.*

John C. Oliveto and Robert J. Poletto contributed to this chapter.

Factors Driving Change: Technology

New public school buildings—elementary, middle, and high schools—are in some ways very different from schools that were constructed even as recently as a decade ago. On an obvious level, new schools are being designed to accommodate a much greater quantity of educational technology—as well a whole gamut of learning technologies that, a mere ten years ago, were either undreamt-of or too expensive for public schools to buy and use.

Paralleling the growth in the amount of technology in schools, we've been witnessing a revolution in the uses to which learning technologies are put. For a long time, computers in classrooms (and elsewhere) in elementary, middle, and high schools mostly served the purposes of *computer training*—that is, acquainting students with hardware and software and developing their proficiency in computer skills. We can gauge just how much that's changed merely by considering how out-of-date a term like "computer literacy" sounds nowadays, when virtually all students (except, perhaps, some in the earliest elementary grades) possess basic computer know-how.

In other words, the use of technology is no longer just an "add-on" or supplement to the curriculum. Rather, technology-related skills have become essential tools in the learning process *in virtually every part of the curriculum*—as crucial to the acquisition of knowledge and to the development of lifelong learning skills as the ability to read and write.

What's more, we believe that we're still just *beginning* to see the changes that technology will cause—both in the way learning happens and in the kinds of skills that will be taught in the public schools. Lately, some educators have begun to say that we've reached a "plateau" in terms of the creation, adoption, and use of new learning technologies. They're wrong. In fact, continuing evolution of learning (and other) technologies and their application will likely *accelerate,* due to pressures of competition in all industries and ongoing globalization of economies. Education in the use of new technologies (and in their operation, maintenance, etc.) will become an ever more essential part of public school curricula, as will instruction in the critical-thinking skills needed to live and work in a world where massive amounts of information, good and bad, are instantaneously available.

Directly related to this explosion in learning technologies are the greater demands placed on the mechanical and electrical systems that serve today's schools. It may be difficult to remember that, just a few decades ago, schools were relatively simple buildings, when looked at from a technical standpoint. Back then, the typical school had one or two electrical outlets in most classrooms; it was heated by steam (there was no air conditioning); ventilation occurred through windows; and makeup air arrived indoors through a simple process of infiltration. By contrast, today's schools require controlled environments for media centers, computer labs, spaces for servers and other information technology equipment, kitchens, science labs, art rooms, music rooms, auditoriums, and gymnasiums. Year-round schools need to be fully air conditioned. Often, a computerized building management system controls the classroom environment by constantly monitoring and adjusting indoor air quality to meet environmental quality standards. Every new school has a built-in telecommunications infrastructure, and—because electrical needs have grown inexorably—is equipped with a power distribution system that's much more generous and sophisticated than those of the past. These aspects of change bear mentioning, in part, because they have had such a significant impact on the first costs of new schools, a subject to which we return at length, below.

Factors Driving Change: The Need for Space

The incorporation of more—and a greater variety of—educational technology is hardly the only way that schools have changed, however. New school buildings are, at every level and in almost every case, *significantly larger* than schools of the past and contain a much greater range of facilities than did their predecessors.

It isn't unusual, for example, for new middle schools to be purposely designed to accommodate a wide variety of after-hours community functions, playing host to events and groups that range from town hall–type meetings, to senior citizens' activities, to plays produced by community theater companies, to continuing education programs. (This trend toward the "synergistic" off-hours use of school facilities by other community interests is frequently powered by the need for community support of a pending school's funding commitment.)

Other factors—just as important—that are driving the demand for larger and larger schools include:

- *The need for custom-designed spaces for specialized programs.* At the middle school level, these include spaces for various kinds of hands-on learning.
- *Demographics.* In many areas of the country, enrollments have been growing and will continue to grow. (In fact, the trend is unlikely to diminish for the next decade or so.) The fact that we have more school-age children means that we need bigger schools (and, of course, more schools) to accommodate them, but demographic changes have another effect on school size. The increasing ethnic/linguistic diversity of our school-age population means, for example, that schools must incorporate space for ESL instruction and for newcomer orientation rooms.
- *Remedial and related programs.* Space demands are also exerted by programs aimed at helping students and their families integrate with the school and wider communities (e.g., "family resources" programs).
- *Accessibility requirements related to the Americans with Disabilities Act (ADA) and other (state and local) legislation and regulations.* Accessibility regulations increase space needs in all sorts of ways. To

take just one example: ramps providing wheelchair accessibility to bleachers in a gymnasium might increase the total seating area by as much as twenty percent. Moreover, the ever more widespread desire to provide education for severely disabled youngsters in their home communities (rather than busing them to regional centers) is also adding to local schools' size and complexity. (This topic is discussed in much greater detail in Chapter 13, "Exceptional Kids Need More Feet.")

- *Special education classroom and support space needs.* Relatedly, as more and more students are categorized as having some special education needs, space dedicated to support spaces (including conference rooms where planning and placement teams can meet) grows.
- *The push—sometimes mandated by law—for reduced class sizes.* The arithmetic here is simple: reduced class size = more classrooms = larger school facilities.
- *Environmental (especially indoor air quality, or IAQ) requirements.* In some cases, greater concern for the quality of schools' indoor air, as well as the push to fully air-condition schools as the typical school year lengthens, means that more room is needed for mechanical equipment.

And, of course, the learning-technology explosion also pushes space needs upward, not only because of the need for specialized instructional spaces for certain kinds of learning technologies (spaces that are often equipment-intensive and therefore cannot be used for other purposes), but also because of the variety of support spaces that high-tech applications require, such as equipment rooms, offices for IT personnel, and so on. (The too-well-kept secret, which we'll get to a bit later, is that technology can also lead to *reductions* in space needs in some programmatic areas.)

One critical aspect of what can validly be called the "space crisis" has to do with the ratio of gross to net square feet. Generally, the ratio of overall square footage (gross) to square footage actually used for programmatic purposes (net) has been growing, in large part because of accessibility requirements and the heightened need for mechanical, electrical, and technological support spaces. Expressed as a fraction, gross-to-net now averages about 1.5 (that is, 3:2). Why is this important? One reason is that state reimbursement levels, which are based on gross square feet per student, have remained static for years. As gross square footage grows in relation to net, a greater proportion of overall construction costs are borne by the local community.

But this growth in the gross-to-net is difficult to control, and efforts to rein it in may not even be to a community's advantage. Many kinds of building enhancements—for example, large atriums that can also serve as gathering spaces for a large portion of the school community—add to gross square footage but also may improve the way a building works. All too often, concern for the bottom line leads building committees to focus on controlling the gross-to-net, eliminating such enhancements. Decision-makers need to proceed cautiously: if architects are handcuffed by the budget, these alternative spaces are not going to happen.

The Construction Cost Upswing

As communities across the country are realizing, *bigger schools are more expensive schools*—a situation made all the more painful by the lack of change in state reimbursement levels. But size—as important as it is—is not alone responsible for the increases in new school design and construction costs that affected the market in the 1990s and that we may very well see again. The point must again be made that *many* factors have driven this trend. Before we turn to those other factors, however, let's take a brief look at some numbers to see just how much costs have risen over the past few decades.

Fletcher-Thompson, Inc. has been designing schools in the New England region for a long time. Our own records indicate that, from 1968 through 1970, new school projects averaged between $26 and $30 per gross square foot. By 1980–1985, typical costs had risen to $60–$65 per square foot. And by 1998–2000 costs were hovering at about $120 per square foot. For projects due to begin construction in 2002–2004, some construction managers are estimating costs at $160 per square foot and higher— meaning that school construction costs will have increased at least 615 percent over the past thirty or so years.

Why have costs risen so greatly? Well, there are several reasons that go beyond the fact that prices in general have gone up. These reasons include:

- *Site development.* Historical data reveal that, thirty years ago we were budgeting as little as $10,000–$12,000 per acre for site development on school construction projects. Today, it isn't unusual for those costs to range from $200,000–$250,000 per acre. The reasons behind this enormous jump? In most communities, there are few if any sites that can be used for schools *without* significant remediation and/or preparation (extensive grading, rock removal, etc.). In most places, there are no more "perfect" sites for the construction of new schools. And, paralleling this decline in the number and quality of suitable sites is the growth of regulatory agencies and regulations—regarding wetlands and other environmental issues, traffic patterns, site accessibility, preservation of trees, and so on—that must be satisfied before construction can proceed.
- *Shortages of skilled labor and building materials.* During the super-hot construction market of the mid-1990s through 2000, costs were driven up by materials and labor shortages. As we say, the situation has recently become much less clear—in part because of the economic aftermath of the attacks of September 11, 2001, and in part because of stock market trends of early to mid-2002. But even if the construction market cools down elsewhere, it strikes us as likely that some labor and materials shortages will continue to be felt, especially in the Northeast, because of the rebuilding effort that will soon be under way in New York City.

Materials and labor fall into what are called the "hard costs" of construction. But the bottom line has also been affected by what are termed "soft costs"—for example, the "escalations" that construction managers (CMs) build into their estimates when trying to predict the ultimate cost of a school that is being planned or designed now but that won't be completed for another three to five years. These escalations are, in effect, hedges against future uncertainty extrapolated from available data. Historically, such estimates have tended to err on the high side, for very good reason. State approval and local referendum processes require that there be an estimated dollar-figure for new school construction; if estimates are too low, a community might have to go back to the state and/or the voters to get more money, which could endanger a project or, at the very least, greatly delay its being built. Even though escalations generally overshoot the mark, it will come as no surprise that communities find ways of spending the difference between the estimated and actual construction cost, which means that these escalations play a real part in pushing up inflation.

This situation of shortages described above worsened during the late 1990s and early 2000s by a general (and understandable) reluctance on the part of CMs and contractors to take on public-sector jobs, including public schools, when there was plenty of high-paying, faster-paying private-sector work available. As we indicate above, this may be changing, but it needs to be mentioned here among the factors that have made new school construction a more problematic enterprise.

Perhaps the best way of characterizing all these factors, grouped together, is *project complexity.* In every conceivable way—from the addition of learning technology, to the imposition of accessibility requirements, to the exigencies of the construction market (and so on and so on)—our public school buildings and the process by which they are planned, designed, and built have become more complex.

Impediments to Change: The Process

Unfortunately, we're stuck with a process for proposing, approving, and funding new schools that does not accommodate this increased complexity very well. We've already indicated that state reimbursement levels have not risen to meet contemporary schools' increased size and complexity. But this is hardly the only way in which the process, as it now functions, impedes change for the better. Here's a brief list of some of the other ways the process raises hurdles to change:

- Onerous deadlines (related to state approvals) that require communities to make decisions too quickly and without sufficient consideration.
- A lack of information, on the part of boards of education and building committees, regarding the real costs/benefits of a wide range of innovative features that are typically rejected because they are seen as too expensive. These kinds of features include (among many others) air conditioning for the entire school; soundproof, easily operable room

dividers to allow flexibility in classroom size; ceiling-mounted, computer-friendly projection screens in each classroom; ergonomic furniture; "zoned" electronic security systems.

- A foreshortened educational specifications process, in which a (perhaps innovative) mission statement is adopted but then forgotten, because there isn't the time or knowledge to work out how that mission can be furthered by truly future-oriented design.
- A referendum process that rewards a traditional, conservative approach.
- A tendency for political concerns to overpower educational needs.

Impediments to Change: Traditional Attitudes

Everyone fondly remembers how things were "back then"—when he or she was in school. In many ways, that nostalgia is a good thing, since it provides a emotional link between adult decision-makers and today's public schools. But it can also foster a conservatism that resists change. On the most obvious level, this traditionalism strongly influences how school buildings look. People rightly feel that a school building "should look like a school building," and architects agree. But there is a world of difference between an attitude that insists that new school buildings rigidly copy past architectural styles and one that allows architects to explore ways of acknowledging tradition while creating designs that are also genuinely new.

That traditionalism on the part of the public at large is paralleled by a conservatism among some educators and other school personnel who, used to doing things in certain ways, are also resistant to change. One sees this, for example, among certain librarians who refuse to acknowledge that media centers are now *in transition* and in the future are likely to need much less shelf space for housing paper-and-ink books. Certainly it's true that printed books aren't going to disappear—or not for a long time to come—but it's equally true that, as more and more resources are available electronically, the need for stack space declines. To serve the future, this transition should move forward more quickly. As it stands, media centers are in many cases being oversized—being built for yesterday's rather than tomorrow's book-storage needs.

Space—in schools as in all other workplaces—isn't emotionally neutral. Space is also "turf," and resistance to change can also originate in the desire on the part of faculty and departments to defend their territory.

It's worth noting here that impediments to using learning technologies as effectively as possible don't always have to do directly with space—though they may indirectly affect the amount of space needed. For example, in the state of Connecticut, there is no coordination of school-day schedules among districts, which makes it hard to employ distance-learning technologies efficiently. (The situation may be exacerbated at the middle school level, because at least some middle schools have instituted site-based modular, or block, scheduling—meaning that schedules may differ even between middle schools within the same district.) If school-day periods were the same statewide, or if middle schools within and across districts could set aside certain blocks of time dedicated to distance learning, it would be much easier to schedule real-time distance-learning classes that students at a number of different schools could participate in simultaneously. This would have the twin effect of cutting down on duplication of effort that already exists while expanding the opportunities for employing distance learning.

There's an emotional component, too, to the widespread resistance we see to combining smaller, local schools into larger district-wide facilities. It's widely felt—among educators and the general public—that a number of smaller schools dispersed across a district are psychologically and practically better than a single, centralized facility that serves all of the district's primary, elementary, middle, or high school students. The resistance to this concept is stronger when applied to the lower grades than to the higher, which makes sense: younger children have a harder time adjusting to large schools than do older children, and there is valid concern about the hardship and inconvenience that busing young students for long distances can cause for them and their families. But the large-school concept has met with resistance on the middle and high school levels, as well.

When we say that part of the reluctance to consolidate schools into larger, regional facilities is "emotional," we do not mean that it is "wrong." As we've just indicated, there are understandable reasons for opposing such plans. The problem is that such opposition generally ignores three strong arguments that can be made in favor of consolidating schools into larger, district-wide facilities:

- *Large, consolidated facilities permit economies of scale that aren't possible if students are dispersed among a number of smaller schools.* That is, a large, consolidated school can provide a wealth of educational resources (a greater variety of books in a media center, a greater variety of enrichment programs and faculty to run them) than is possible if education dollars have to be divvied up and distributed among a number of schools serving students at a given level.
- *Consolidated facilities reduce inequities between richer and poorer areas of a district.* When all students—no matter whether they come from high- or lower-income families or neighborhoods—attend the same school, they all receive the same, high-quality education *and* they share diverse life experiences and viewpoints.
- *There are proven ways of designing and organizing a large school to reduce or eliminate the negative psychological/social effects.* The school-within-a-school (or "cluster," or "house") concept has been successfully employed in schools ranging from primary to high schools—but especially at the middle school level. Under this form of organization, a student stays within the same cluster, or house, throughout his or her years at the school. That provides a feeling of

continuity, and the limited size of the cluster prevents children from feeling overwhelmed, as they might within a very large school not broken down into these smaller units. Architectural design supports the cluster concept by carefully demarcating areas that belong to each cluster and those common areas shared by the entire school.

Fostering Positive Change: What Can Decision-Makers Do?

This is the hard part, because it not only calls for procedural changes and careful decision-making on the local level but also demands that all stakeholders press for fundamental changes on the state level.

Let's take the issue of educational specifications development. A good, thorough "ed spec"—one that will really help educators and designers implement the goals of a future-oriented mission statement, throughout the curriculum—is a very rare commodity. Why? Because to develop good ed specs, local boards of education often need expert guidance from consultants and architectural designers, and these kinds of services cost money that is usually very hard to come by during the planning stage. Boards of education, already financially squeezed, can seldom find money in their budgets to pay for adequate planning, and state departments of education provide no resources for this critical, up-front phase of the planning process.

What can be done? Well, on the local level, it may be incumbent on municipal legislators (town councils, etc.) to include such funds in their education budgets for years when a new school planning process is scheduled to begin. On the state level, three measures (at least) are sorely needed:

- State legislatures must be pushed to change the law regarding reimbursements, making money available to departments of education to distribute to local school districts *in advance of project submittals,* to assist them in developing ed specs;
- State departments of education must update their criteria for space use within the modern school facility and guide the evolution of school facilities by stipulating *proper* guidelines for funding and approval; and
- State D.O.E.s must be encouraged to develop a range of other resources to help individual districts plan new schools. These non-financial resources might include such things as comparative data on school buildings recently completed or now under design/construction around the state, sample educational specifications (for elementary, middle, high, and magnet schools), and a list of consultants offering help in developing ed specs.

It is, quite frankly, astonishing to us that such resources do not now exist in the state of Connecticut—which spent half a billion dollars on new school construction during 2000 (and not a single dollar on pre-submission planning!).

What else can local decision-makers do? As they plan a new school, they can focus on ways in which technology can help them control the size of the facility and thereby control costs. In this chapter, we've already suggested one area (stack space in media centers) in which creative thinking about the use of technology could help lessen the demand for space. And there are other ways—of even wider scope—in which the technologies that are already altering the learning process can also be used to cut the size, and therefore the cost, of the school of the future.

For example, the expansion of individualized programs of study utilizing online learning means that much classwork can be done away from the school building itself—and that there's no longer any real reason that *all* students must attend school during the same hours each school day. Instituting staggered or flexible schedules would reduce the number of classrooms and other learning spaces needed at any given time. Staggered/ flexible schedules would likewise reduce the size of school bus fleets, since buses would be operating throughout the day. (Current communications and navigational technologies could allow drivers to change routes as students' schedules change.) A smaller fleet would mean that school bus staging areas could also be reduced in size.

Utilizing (fully air conditioned!) school buildings year-round could likewise reduce overall space needs, especially if a trimester-type schedule were implemented in which each student would attend school for two of the three trimesters each year (meaning that only two-thirds of the total student body would be in school at any given time).

Are such ideas "radical"? They may at first seem so. But the fact is that communities across the nation are already making fundamental changes to the school day and school year—and that our school buildings are already becoming 24/7/365 facilities (or nearly so). What we're proposing is that this process of change be consciously coordinated with new-school planning and design. That's one way to discover how change can work for us—reducing the size of new schools, controlling the cost of school construction, and modifying school design in ways that truly serve educational methodologies of the present and the future.

Part II: The Middle School of the Future

Chapter 3

Creating Schools Collaboratively: Vision, Design, and Project Management

Successful, flexible, future-oriented facilities result when every stage of the planning, design, and construction process is marked by intensive collaboration and participatory decision-making. Below, we address each of these stages in turn: the development of the educational specification that will guide design, the design process itself, and the construction phase of the project. (A participatory process for achieving victory in school bond referenda is outlined in Chapter 15, "Passing Your School Referendum.") First, though, an essential definition:

Educational specifications, or program requirements, are the means by which educators describe the educational activities and spaces that need to be incorporated in a proposed new or renovated facility. These written statements serve as a vehicle of communication between the educator and the architect. Educational specifications concern themselves with the people and activities to be housed by the facility and with the school's program requirements, *not* with the specific architectural solutions that will be developed to meet programmatic needs.

Good "ed specs" are the foundation of a successful school building design. They effectively spell out objectives, activities, programs, and space requirements of the facility so that educational and other goals can be met. It seems safe to say that the most serious waste of public school funds occurs when a new building contains facilities that are not needed or when it omits those that are necessary. Educational specifications *include* what is necessary and *exclude* the things that are not.

Collaboration in the Development of Educational Specifications

There is no single method for producing a good, useful ed spec: different districts take different approaches, any of which might be successful. Some districts rely on the superintendent of schools to write the educational specification, and, if the superintendent devotes energy to the task, is a good writer, and is diligent in seeking others' input, this method may produce a superior ed spec. Many districts, however, hire consultants to guide them through this sometimes challenging process. Some architectural firms offer such consulting services, and, in an important sense, an architect is a natural choice, since many architectural firms can draw on a wealth of historical data and technical resources and because it is an architect who will ultimately have to use the specification to develop drawings. Although any of these approaches might work well, the one rule that *any* ed spec development process should follow is to invite the early and ongoing involvement of all of the new facility's "stakeholders"— that is, the members of the community who have an interest in the outcome of the project.

In fact, no matter who is writing the ed spec, it is crucial to turn to the educational staff and other stakeholders for information relevant to that particular school project. And there is no getting around the fact that soliciting their participation—and thereby generating their enthusiasm—is a lengthy and complex process that, to succeed, must be carefully managed. As we stress again and again in this book, democracy takes time and requires skilled leadership.

Step 1: The Vision. Don't make the mistake of dismissing the *vision* that guides the creation of a new facility as "the soft stuff." The facts and figures come later, but articulating a comprehensive vision of educational philosophy and of the facility's role in the life of the wider community is *the absolutely essential first step in producing a successful ed spec.* Drafting a vision statement helps the community to see where it is headed, to organize its priorities, to investigate new approaches to education and curriculum design (and to decide which of these will best serve its children), and—at its very best—to boldly address the challenges that the community believes the future will bring. In a sense, everything else—from the size of the gymnasium to the openness of the school to the wider community of users—follows from the vision guiding the building's planning, design, and construction. The best vision statements are extremely thorough, addressing virtually every aspect of the curriculum and the building's non-education-related functions *but stopping short* of specifying the numbers and kinds of spaces necessary to implement the vision.

Although the language of the statement itself is likely to be drafted by a small group of people or even by a single individual, it should represent the work and collective thinking of the entire community. Gathering that knowledge is best accomplished through a series of conversations and meetings with the various constituencies—students, principal and administrative staff, faculty, other school staff, taxpayers and community groups, and so on. There's no hard-and-fast requirement regarding the format of such conversations and meetings: some might be set up as "town hall"–type hearings that the entire community is invited to attend, others might be intensive focus groups with limited numbers of staff or parents, others might be one-on-one conversations between the superintendent and the school principal and faculty members. Consultants generally come equipped with strategies for gathering this input effectively, but it's clear that such methods should be tailored to the needs of the specific community and school and the working styles of superintendent, principal, and faculty. What's also clear is that—for the entire community's wishes, needs, desires, and insights to be genuinely represented in the final vision statement— many separate meetings may be entailed.

There's no easy way to categorize (or limit) the kinds of questions that might be considered during such exchanges, except to say that they should be somewhat broad and general in scope. Here are just a few examples:

- What are our projected enrollments for five, ten, and fifteen years from now? Are the community's demographics changing, and how? Should we anticipate a greater (or lesser) need for ESL programs, for example, or cultural orientation programs for recent-immigrant students? Is the demand for special education–related components likely to grow more intense in the coming years?

- How much technology is desired at the middle school level—and is this consistent with technology plans for the district's elementary and high schools?
- To what extent should the community's cultural diversity, or lack of it, influence the curriculum?
- How should the school be organized? At the middle school level, answering this question is likely to involve coordinating the "house," or cluster, concept with the specific "learning options" the district wants to explore: single grade/single year, looping, multi-age education, or a combination of these strategies.
- How will the wider community use the building? Will it be a place where town meetings will be held? Will the media center be open to the general public during certain hours? Will community arts groups be using the auditorium or other spaces? (And so on.)

Step 2: The Program. Once the vision statement has been prepared, it's time to begin translating the broad agenda that it lays out into the specifics of spaces, the numbers of students (and other facility users) who will occupy them, and the key relationships among spaces that will best achieve the vision statement's curricular and other programmatic goals. (By "key relationships," we mean things like adjacencies: for example, should the media center be contiguous to the main lobby in order to facilitate use by the wider community?)

Of course, the superintendent or ed spec consultant (perhaps working hand in hand with a "vision committee") will already have begun to gather some of this kind of information: it's inevitable that the vision of the new school facility will have been shaped by an awareness of the character and size of the student body, for example. But, until now, the process should have steered clear of developing specific programmatic solutions.

The key to devising these programmatic solutions successfully is, once again, collaborative process. The principle motivating a collaborative approach is a simple one: the stakeholders in any given curricular or extracurricular area are not just the people who have the greatest investment in that area; they're also the people who have the greatest knowledge about what it will take to implement the vision statement's agenda in that area. Thus, particular faculty and administrators knowledgeable in specific areas contribute ideas to help answer questions like the following:

- What is our special education strategy?
- Should we have a separate, dedicated cafeteria and auditorium, or a combination "cafetorium"?
- How much emphasis will we place on the arts? And how should art instruction spaces be coordinated with the team clusters? (Should they be within the clusters or should they be separate, shared facilities located in a place that's equally accessible from all the clusters?)

- What about science? Will science be taught within the cluster (perhaps in a special classroom-laboratory, or "CLAB"), or will the building contain a special, dedicated science area shared by all the teams?

During this phase of the ed spec's development, the vision statement should guide the approach to the "operational realities." But efficient use of the *entire* physical plant should be a goal, since no community will want to pay for an overdesigned facility (a "Taj Mahal") or one in which all program areas are accorded too much space.

Despite the fact that any new middle school building will be "customized" to meet a given community's specific educational needs and vision, those charged with the development of an educational specification may find it very helpful to have some sort of model to work from, or to play their own ideas off against. This book provides such a model—a somewhat generic, though comprehensive, middle school ed spec (see Chapter 7).

Step 3: From the Abstract to the Concrete. Once the programmatic details of the ed spec have been developed, it's time to begin assigning "numbers" to the project—first, square footages; then, dollar estimates of the cost of the facility as outlined in the spec. If the district has retained an architect to help develop the ed spec, this stage represents a continuation of the process; if not, this is the moment when an architect must be brought on board to begin translating the desires embodied in the ed spec into the actualities of size and budget. In plain terms, it's probably a waste of time for anyone but an architect to assign square-footage numbers to the project's components, so the person or committee developing the ed spec should resist the temptation to pencil in numbers until an architect has been hired to design the building.

It may be somewhat surprising to those unfamiliar with the process, but, once the architect has been given a list of desired spaces and probable occupancies, it's a fairly routine matter to determine the probable square footages of each of those spaces and, in turn, the probable gross and net square footages of the entire facility. (The "net" consists of all the space that will be used for programmatic purposes; the "gross" includes the net *and* all the other space—corridor space, infrastructure space, and so on — that will be needed to make the facility function.) An experienced architect will draw on a wealth of historical data to make these determinations.

From there, it is again a fairly routine process to come up with a ballpark cost for the building. Here, it's a matter of applying historical data *plus* comprehensive knowledge of the construction market in a given area or region, and any good estimator—whether the estimator is part of the architect's team, or a construction manager, or an independent estimating firm—will be able, once the square footages have been calculated, to apply the necessary formulas and to work out a fairly accurate construction budget, both for the entire facility and for each of its major components. These numbers won't be perfectly precise, of course, and a budget at this stage of development typically includes a "design contingency" line item to cover unknowns. (Estimates will become much more accurate after design has been performed, when estimators will be able to calculate amounts of building materials needed, labor time for specific trades, and so on.) But these "rough" numbers will be good enough to guide further decision-making.

What *further* decision-making? Well, experience shows that the specific programmatic desires articulated in an ed spec often outdistance the amount of money that a community can actually afford—or the amount that the voters are likely to approve in a referendum. It isn't until this point in the process—when the "rough" construction cost estimates are in—that decision-makers can begin to adjust the ed spec's program to the financial realities that the community faces.

Often, the community's governing body or town leaders will have begun this whole process with a certain maximum budget in mind. If that figure is, say, $25 million and the rough estimate comes in at $35 million, then it's necessary to return to the ed spec and begin prioritizing, distinguishing between "needs" and "wants," culling less-essential program elements, and looking for ways in which spaces can be put to multiple use—anything, in other words, that will reduce the amount of space and therefore the construction cost while maintaining as much of the desired program as possible.

This, too, is a collaborative process, and there's often some room for negotiation between the building committee or board of education and the community's political leadership. It may, in other words, be possible to salvage at least some of the elements that cause the envisioned facility to exceed the original budget limit. And it bears pointing out that this kind of negotiation is made all the easier *if* the process has been collaborative from the very beginning, since all the stakeholders—including those who hold the purse strings—will have been involved in envisioning the new school building and will want it to match as closely as possible all the accumulating expectations and hopes.

In fact, that's a *key* insight—and a good way to end our discussion of educational specifications. One of the chief reasons to do the ed spec right is *to generate excitement and enthusiasm for the new facility throughout the community.* If all the stakeholders feel that they've participated in the ed spec's development—and if they all have some understanding of the new facility's potential benefits to the entire community—they'll be much more willing to go the extra mile to make the building as good as possible. When they've been an integral part of the process, members of the town regulatory body are more likely to understand the need for a particular program element and to increase the allowable budget accordingly. And voters will be much more likely to respond positively when the matter is put before them in a referendum. A good ed spec is good politics. *It builds community.*

A Collaborative Approach to Design

Tomorrow's educational environments must accommodate new approaches to teaching and learning while serving the needs of all of a facility's stakeholders. Thus, the importance of continued community support over the life of a project cannot be overemphasized. Neither should we underestimate the pressures placed on municipal governments and local school districts with regard to costs and the performance of their facilities. Today, better-informed, better-educated voters are holding building committees and municipal and school officials accountable for both first-time costs and long-term performance of construction projects.

To maximize *project value* and to minimize maintenance and operating costs, important decisions regarding cost and overall quality must be made early in the design process and must be clearly communicated to all participants. The goal, here, is to minimize the need for changes late in the design process, when such changes are decidedly less effective and may compromise the project's quality or scope.

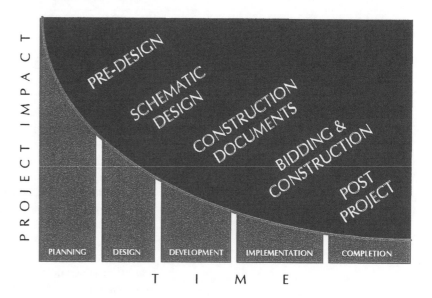

The beginning of a project provides the rare opportunity to make sure that potential problems are correctly identified and that they will be creatively solved. The beginning of a project is also the best time to solicit input into the design and planning activities from the entire community of users. A new middle school facility is certain to have quite a diverse set of stakeholders. Stakeholders are likely to include the following (and possibly others):

- Students
- Building committee members
- The Board of Education

- The superintendent and district administrators
- Municipal government agencies and officials
- The principal and school administrators
- Faculty and staff
- Parents
- Taxpayers
- Local businesspeople
- Community groups
- Community leaders

Because of this diversity, Fletcher Thompson utilizes an interactive process designed to address the needs and concerns of the broadest possible spectrum of stakeholders. The goal of this collaborative process is to achieve "buy-in" on the part of all participants. Sharing the "authorship" of the project strengthens the sense of community and contributes to a successful building project.

Involving the entire community of users requires an open exchange of ideas within a variety of forums, including workshops and focus groups. Some of these mechanisms may already be in place if the community has been effectively consulted during the drafting of the ed spec. The goal of ongoing meetings should be to broaden and extend stakeholder participation throughout the design phase.

The first priority for the design team is to *listen* carefully to what is being said. Community members rightly have strong feelings about their public schools and need to know that their concerns are being heard. As the dialogue progresses, it will be necessary to establish a common frame of reference, including a vocabulary of materials and furnishings. This can be facilitated through the use of study tools and deliverables such as presentation materials and renderings, simplistic models for critical design issues, 2-D diagrams and computer-generated 3-D images to document key programmatic relationships, site visits to comparable facilities, and samples to illustrate materials and aesthetic considerations (e.g., color consistency). No matter how carefully conceived such presentation materials are, however, the team must remain open to ongoing dialogue about design alternatives.

An orderly, structured process can help to sustain community engagement and avoid problems down the road. Specific meeting agendas, meeting minutes, and monthly status reports are essential. Key milestones should be identified early in the process and progress should be reviewed regularly. Finally, design goals must be balanced with budget criteria throughout all stages of project development. Continuity of the core team is of course desirable and will help to ensure that design ideas are implemented successfully and within budgetary restrictions.

Collaborative Project Management

Throughout the design and construction process, thousands of decisions are made that affect the quality, cost, and completion date of the final product. To successfully manage a project and communicate information to the members of the team in a timely fashion, Fletcher Thompson utilizes customized project management tools, including a *Task Schedule* and a *Master Control Budget*. These tools help answer the important questions:

- What is to be done?
- Who will complete the task?
- When must it be done?
- How much will it cost?
- What happens if work isn't completed on time?

Task Schedule. The Task Schedule lists and schedules tasks to be accomplished throughout the project process. This allows team members to remain focused on the big picture while clarifying the steps necessary to get there.

Meeting the aggressive schedule imposed on a school construction project necessitates a clear and organized decision-making process. The Task Schedule shows when all the necessary decisions must be made in order to meet project goals.

One of the first tasks on the schedule is the *Project Kick-Off Workshop*. In this meeting, the roles and responsibilities of all team members are established and the decision-making process is defined and agreed to. This consensus is critical to ensure the seamless flow of information and approvals necessary to move the project forward expeditiously.

The schedule is a dynamic document that also tracks the tasks as work progresses, allowing for proactive management to keep the project on schedule to meet the project's goals.

The sample Task Schedule included here shows the major milestones that would occur in virtually any school construction project. Of course, such schedules are tailored, expanded, and developed for specific projects and their integral components, incorporating the input of all the project team members.

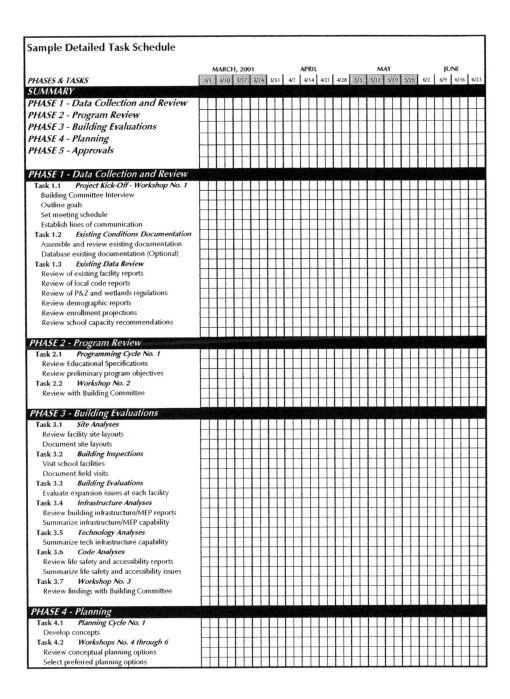

Sample Detailed Task Schedule

PHASES & TASKS	MARCH, 2001					APRIL				MAY				JUNE			
	3/3	3/10	3/17	3/24	3/31	4/7	4/14	4/21	4/28	5/5	5/12	5/19	5/26	6/2	6/9	6/16	6/23
SUMMARY																	
PHASE 1 - Data Collection and Review																	
PHASE 2 - Program Review																	
PHASE 3 - Building Evaluations																	
PHASE 4 - Planning																	
PHASE 5 - Approvals																	
PHASE 1 - Data Collection and Review																	
Task 1.1 *Project Kick-Off - Workshop No. 1*																	
Building Committee Interview																	
Outline goals																	
Set meeting schedule																	
Establish lines of communication																	
Task 1.2 *Existing Conditions Documentation*																	
Assemble and review existing documentation																	
Database existing documentation (Optional)																	
Task 1.3 *Existing Data Review*																	
Review of existing facility reports																	
Review of local code reports																	
Review of P&Z and wetlands regulations																	
Review demographic reports																	
Review enrollment projections																	
Review school capacity recommendations																	
PHASE 2 - Program Review																	
Task 2.1 *Programming Cycle No. 1*																	
Review Educational Specifications																	
Review preliminary program objectives																	
Task 2.2 *Workshop No. 2*																	
Review with Building Committee																	
PHASE 3 - Building Evaluations																	
Task 3.1 *Site Analyses*																	
Review facility site layouts																	
Document site layouts																	
Task 3.2 *Building Inspections*																	
Visit school facilities																	
Document field visits																	
Task 3.3 *Building Evaluations*																	
Evaluate expansion issues at each facility																	
Task 3.4 *Infrastructure Analyses*																	
Review building infrastructure/MEP reports																	
Summarize infrastructure/MEP capability																	
Task 3.5 *Technology Analyses*																	
Summarize tech infrastructure capability																	
Task 3.6 *Code Analyses*																	
Review life safety and accessibility reports																	
Summarize life safety and accessibility issues																	
Task 3.7 *Workshop No. 3*																	
Review findings with Building Committee																	
PHASE 4 - Planning																	
Task 4.1 *Planning Cycle No. 1*																	
Develop concepts																	
Task 4.2 *Workshops No. 4 through 6*																	
Review conceptual planning options																	
Select preferred planning options																	

MASTER CONTROL BUDGET

	Quantity	Units	Cost/SF	Total	Eligible Cost	32.00%
I. CAPITAL CONSTRUCTION COSTS (HARD COSTS)						
1.1 Site Development		SF		$	$	
New Construction		SF		$	$	%
Field Repair				$	$	%
1.2 Off Site Improvements				$		%
1.3 Building Construction				$	$	
New Construction		SF		$	$	
Lower Level		SF		$		
Level Two		SF		$		
Level Three		SF		$		
Renovations		SF		$	$	
Lower Level				$		
Level Two				$		
Level Three				$	$	%
1.4 Change Order Allowance	%			$	$	%
1.5 Contingency	%			$	$	%
1.6 CM Fees/Reimbursables	%			$	$	%
SUBTOTAL CAPITAL CONSTRUCTION COSTS				$	$	%
II. OTHER CAPITAL COSTS						
2.1 Land Acquisition				$	$	%
2.2 Furniture and Furnishings		student		$	$	%
2.3 Computer Station Hardware		each		$	$	%
2.4 Front End Equipment, Servers				$	$	%
2.5 Telephone, Computer Wiring				$		%
2.6 TV Distribution Wiring				$	$	%
2.7 Security System Wiring				$	$	%
2.8 Miscellaneous Equipment				$	$	%
SUBTOTAL OTHER CAPITAL COSTS			$	$	$	%
III. EXPENSES (SOFT COSTS)						
3.1 Architectural and Engineering Fees				$	$	%
3.2 Specialty Consultants				$	$	%
3.3 Testing/Special Inspections				$	$	%
3.4 Surveys and Borings				$	$	%
3.5 Reimbursable Expenses				$	$	%
3.6 Full Time CA, Clerk of the Works				$	$	%
3.7 Moving and Storage				$	$	%
3.8 Bid Printing and Advertising				$	$	%
3.9 Rendering, Models				$	$	
SUBTOTAL OF EXPENSES			$	$	$	%
IV. BUDGET SUBTOTAL				$	$	
4.1 Legal, Admin, Bonding, Finance	%			$	$	%
V. PROJECT CONTINGENCY/ESCALATION	%			$	$	
VI. TOTAL PROJECT BUDGET				$	$	

Allowable Reimbursable Square Footage: sf

Adjustment for State "Allowable Square Footage Per Pupil" Calculation: %

To Be Paid By Town

Master Control Budget. Fletcher Thompson maintains a high level of commitment to managing the cost of its projects throughout the design process. To ensure that the budget reflects the most up-to-date and accurate cost data available, we typically draw from the firm's historical construction cost database, reference published cost-estimating resources, and seek the help of regional estimating experts in both general construction and mechanical and electrical trades to adjust the unit costs used in our estimates. Doing so allows us to be sensitive and responsive to the cost-control side of the design equation while still being able to develop highly creative and exciting solutions to a community's needs.

Success in cost control starts with the development and ongoing refinement of a realistic and comprehensive project budget. The Master Control Budget that we have developed not only lists a project's "Capital Construction Costs" but also includes "Other Capital Costs" (i.e., "soft" costs) and "Expenses." (Examples of these kinds of costs include architectural and engineering fees, testing, special inspectors' fees, moving and storage, bid printing and advertising, renderings, models, computer-generated "fly-throughs," and construction management.) Building committees find this to be a valuable tool for continually evaluating and managing the total cost of their projects.

Like the detailed Task Schedule, the Master Control Budget is a dynamic document that tracks costs and is further refined as work progresses. This framework facilitates timely, proactive adjustments to keep the project within its budget guidelines. The sample Master Control Budget included here would, of course, be customized for a specific project.

As must be very clear by now, collaboration—in planning, design, and construction—is a very complicated process. To make sure that everything that needs to be covered actually gets covered, a master schedule and master budget essential tools. Multifaceted, problem-solving discussions too often focus on one problem (or a limited set of problems), to the detriment of other agenda items that also require close attention—and there's no way to keep on track without a schedule and a budget, which can themselves be refined and added to as the process proceeds. The schedule and budget we provide in this chapter aren't meant to be complete or exhaustive, but to show you the range of areas and specific action items that such documents might very well include.

Now, let's turn to an example of collaborative process at work. Though the middle school that resulted from this process is not a Fletcher Thompson–designed project, we feel that the highly participatory, future-oriented process that created the educational specification for the new East Lyme Middle School in Niantic, Connecticut, provides an exemplary case study well worth emulating.

Chapter 4

A Case Study of Collaboration: East Lyme Middle School

[Editor's note: The planning and design process that led to the creation of the new East Lyme Middle School in Niantic, Connecticut (opened September 2002), was a model of cooperation and collaboration. The process began with the formation of a Vision Committee that included middle school teachers, middle school parents, middle school students, administrators, representatives of the board of education, and even a few teachers from East Lyme district elementary schools. (One of the project's more controversial proposals involved moving the district's fifth graders into the new middle school; though initially resisted by some members of the committee, the plan eventually gained universal, enthusiastic acceptance by committee members.)

According to East Lyme Middle School principal Jerome R. Belair, the committee's work began with a comprehensive look at the current literature on middle-grades learners. Committee members read widely in the field, studying (among other works), Turning Points 2000: Educating Adolescents in the 21st Century *(Jackson and Davis 2000),* This We Believe . . . and Now We Must Act *(National Middle School Association 2001), and a document prepared by the Connecticut state Department of Education, "Doing What's Right in the Middle: Promising Practices in Schools with Middle Grades (Connecticut DOE 1999).*

"The key for us was to come to a common ground. We started with the background on young adolescents, and then we developed the program," says Jerry Belair. We had to have that common knowledge before we could begin discussing the facility."

The research conducted by the committee went far beyond the information members could glean from books. An equally important part of the vision process was to make field trips to a variety of New England middle schools, where committee members could witness the ideas they'd been reading about put into practice (or not, as the case may be). "We looked at a number of 'state-of-the-art' facilities," recalls Belair. "Some had the program we wanted; others had the facilities; a few had both the program and the facility."

Using all the knowledge it had gained, the Vision Committee developed its report, parts of which are excerpted, below. But this was hardly the end of the process. Adamant that the Vision Statement should not just be filed away and forgotten about, those involved in creating the new East Lyme Middle School ensured continuity of vision through all the stages of the planning, design, and construction process by designating certain Vision Committee members to serve on the subsequent Design and Building Committees. "They became the keepers of the vision," says Belair. "The vision remained on the table every time a space was designed. They were the ones who asked the architects, 'How are the attributes [outlined in the Vision Statement] being incorporated into the space?' They made sure that the product looks like the process.

"The vision drove the design, and now we're living it," concludes Belair, who couldn't be more enthusiastic about the new facility. "I'm hearing all the parents say, 'This is alive! This is real!'"

The materials generated during East Lyme Middle School's planning process that we present here include an overall "Vision for Learning" developed by the Vision Committee; a long excerpt from the Vision Committee's report, emphasizing the general attributes that the new facility would be expected to possess in order to implement the Vision for Learning; and several extremely interesting and useful documents designed to help committee members evaluate competing firms during the selection of the construction manager and architect for the job.]

Vision for Learning

East Lyme Middle School provides a curriculum that requires students to be active participants in learning. Subject matter is integrated and organized into thematic units of study. Units are organized around essential content and formulated by consideration of students' questions about themselves and their environment. Themes are connected to the problems which the world poses for students. These themes, relevant because they incorporate real issues, draw on the past to help students understand the present while planning for the future. Students learn the essential content through provocative, open-ended questions commonly used to provide a purpose and focus.

Students are required to demonstrate their achievement through authentic tasks. These tasks require higher-level thinking; draw on student experience, knowledge, and skill development; and necessitate some form of performance or product to demonstrate their competence. Students also demonstrate communication skills, facility in social interaction, analytic capabilities, problem-solving skills, decision-making, civic responsibility, skill in developing and maintaining wellness, and skill in using technology as a tool for learning.

Students frequently work with one another in cooperative learning situations, assuming the role of worker and performer rather than passive recipient. They engage in thought-provoking content, ideas, and activities in which the process of learning is valued as much as the final product. The learning environment reaches beyond the school campus, bringing the world to the school and taking the student to the community whenever possible.

The context for learning drives teacher decisions about the types of instructional strategies to employ, the design of student-learner activities, and the means of student assessment. As a result of this curriculum the teacher serves as the director, coach, or facilitator depending on the learner tasks. In addition, varied teaching strategies and learning activities address the multiple intelligences of all students.

Report of the East Lyme Middle School
Vision Committee May 11, 1999
(Excerpts)

Introduction

In a communication dated November 10, 1998, Superintendent Jack Reynolds charged the East Lyme Middle School Vision Committee to develop images of Grade 5–8 education in East Lyme through the year 2020. He wrote, "We have to make program assumptions and decisions. We must develop ideals, images, parameters, and criteria to ensure that this project provides a building that is truly responsive to the educational and community needs of not only the present but more importantly of the future." The charge of the committee was to dream, to put aside limits, and focus only on educational ideals.

Committee membership included representatives from the middle school students, elementary and middle school faculty, elementary and middle school parents, middle school administration, and the board of education. The superintendent of schools participated as an ad hoc member of the committee.

In response to the superintendent's charge, the committee researched the best practices for young adolescent learners and visited a number of middle schools, which not only included Grade 5 but also showed excellence in education in a number of areas. Several newly constructed schools were visited to glean design ideas and to hold them up to the educational practices that had been seen. In all of these visits, interviews were conducted, and programmatic and facility components were captured on videotape.

The committee sought input from various members of the middle school community, including the custodial, kitchen, and secretarial staffs as well as the teaching faculty. In addition, faculty meeting time at the elementary schools was devoted for the superintendent, the middle school principal, and the respective school representative to provide a Vision Committee update and to solicit input from the various staffs. Conversation at the elementary meetings focused on the nature of the fifth-grade learner and the inclusion of the fifth grade into the middle school educational experience. Videotaped input from fifth-grade students themselves was combined with a middle school overview provided by the student representatives on the committee. Each committee meeting was open to the public, and the community was welcomed; the first agenda item at each meeting was dedicated to community feedback and questions.

The committee shared information through a number of vehicles. Minutes and meeting agendas were posted in each of the three elementary schools, the middle school, the town hall, and the town library. Newsletter updates were published periodically from each of the four schools. In early March

[1999], the Vision and Design Committees met to exchange general thoughts and programmatic ideas and to consider the ways in which architecture could effect education. At this meeting, highlights of the collected video footage were shared. First Selectman Wayne Fraser was invited and attended a meeting in April to discuss community use and access as well as other community needs as they related to the expanded and newly renovated East Lyme Middle School. As a result of the April meeting, it was concluded that the Design Committee would provide opportunities for the community to come together and comment on additional facility needs.

Returning to its charge, the Vision Committee is confident the documentation that follows describes the best educational program for East Lyme's young adolescents. It describes a school and articulates a vision that will allow this program to become reality.

Executive Summary

The goal of this committee is to design an educational program that addresses sound strategies for the middle school learner, that challenges conventional learning assumptions, and that encompasses future developments in technology. The design presented in this document considers present practice, current research, and future needs. It describes a school that is unique to East Lyme, a learning signature that will reflect our spirit and give coherence to our best ideas about education.

The program successfully brings together 1,200 fifth through eighth-grade learners into small, closely knit learning communities. The makeup of these communities varies, providing choice to families. Some integrate multiple grade levels; others contain single grades. The program reflects a philosophy that includes a three-part learning experience for students: individual, cooperative, and large-group learning. The program integrates subject matter and assesses learning through real-world demonstrations.

Understanding that architecture effects learning, the design of this facility enhances this educational program and brings it to life. Team learning areas are the heart and soul of the learning communities. Adjacent classrooms are flexible, serving small-group meetings or large-group instruction. A shared space called a *kiva* is central to each team and facilitates team projects, presentations, networking, and creative learning. Teachers have office and work space within the team. Spaces serve multiple functions and are inherently flexible to meet our current variety of needs as well as the changing needs of a dynamic learning environment.

This vision captures all that is essential for the middle-level learner. It addresses an educational program, many and various learning areas, and multiple support and extended services necessary to meet the needs of the whole adolescent. It describes a school that values and celebrates, as it educates, each unique child.

I. Educational Program
The Grade 5–8 middle school is made up of small learning communities (teams).

- Each learning community is a network of students, teachers, parents, and other significant adults to which each child belongs.
- Families are provided a choice in team arrangement. They may select from a single grade, multi-grade, or multi-age arrangement. In some cases, teams stay together for more than one year while other teams of students change from year to year.
- Teams vary in size with two to four teacher members and 44–90 students.
- Classes are balanced in terms of grade level, gender, and individual needs to ensure a diversity of roles and abilities.
- Class size is maintained at a level which assures enactment of the vision.

At the heart of the learning community is the student.

- Young adolescents experience different stages of physical, emotional, intellectual, and social development. The school provides educational and social stimulation within a safe and secure environment.
- In order to develop into responsible individuals, students need opportunities for intellectual stimulation through a variety of experiences; the development and refinement of basic skills; challenges to their curiosity and creativity; interaction with adults and peers; exploratory experiences that provide for service, citizenship, counseling, and social, performing, creative and physical activities.
- There are high expectations for all students.

The educational program is moving from transmission of knowledge to discovery of knowledge.

- Learning experiences reflect skills important to the Information Age.
- Technology is used effectively to enhance, expand, and monitor learning.
- The curriculum is challenging, integrative, and exploratory.

The educational program is moving from an emphasis on knowing to an emphasis on searching.

- Each learner must actively search for, discover, learn, and apply information.
- Each learner must be able to clearly identify and strengthen his/her individual learning skills.
- There are varied teaching and learning approaches.

The educational program integrates subject matter and is process-oriented within the context of common fields of knowledge.

- Science, Math and Technology
- History and Social Sciences
- The Arts, Language, and Literature
- Physical, Health, and Life Skills Education

Learning is assessed by a variety of authentic methods that include methods related to "real world" demonstrations. Assessments engage learners in applying knowledge and skills in the same way they are used in the world outside of school.

- Presentations
- Portfolios
- Written products
- Technology products

The use of time is flexible, and scheduling maximizes time for students to think through and complete projects in meaningful ways. A variety of learning experiences is provided that include, but are not limited to, field experiences, distance learning, individual and group work, project-based learning, guest speakers, and community outreach opportunities.

Learners are required to think creatively and critically; develop communication skills; cooperate with others; use appropriate resources to seek, access, and apply knowledge; function independently; take risks to succeed; exhibit self-confidence; create options; and make choices.

Co-curricular, extracurricular, interscholastic, and intramural experiences are an integral part of the total educational experience.

Programs and policies foster health, wellness, and safety.

Developing sustained partnerships with community organizations adds invaluable dimensions in the educational process and fosters a sense of community.

Family involvement is a central function of the school. Enlisting the input, counsel, and involvement of families in all aspects of the school program ensures continual improvement and successful learning for all students.

II. Middle School Project Mission

[The mission is] to create a facility that is aligned with the East Lyme Middle School Vision, that supports educational programs well into the future, and that facilitates interaction among students, faculty, and staff. The design fosters a sense of belonging that enables students to fulfill their learning potential and accommodates virtually any type of subject matter and any form of instruction. This facility is a town center that supports community-based programs, activities, and events for the citizens of East Lyme.

III. Facility Design Guiding Principles

- Design will support the East Lyme Middle School Educational Program, Education Specifications, East Lyme Middle School Vision for Teaching and Learning, and the East Lyme Middle School Mission Statement.
- The design of the facility will support smaller communities within the full community.
- The facility will accommodate projected enrollment through 2010.
- Spaces will accommodate student-driven, interactive, project-oriented learning experiences.
- Facilities and spaces should be easily adaptable for dynamic and changing educational programs.
- All spaces need to serve multiple functions.
- Various sizes of meeting spaces should be distributed throughout the facility for ease of access for students, staff, and teams.
- The facility will support the use of contemporary technology as well as be easily adaptable for new technology developed in the future.
- Design will incorporate new and existing facilities resulting in appearance, feel, and function of one facility.
- All spaces within the facility will be welcoming and provide a sense of comfort for students, staff, and community.
- Design will facilitate free-flowing, safe, easy movement throughout the facility.
- Indoor facilities will allow for maximum exposure to natural light in appropriate areas.
- All furnishings need to be durable, high quality, age-appropriate, and supportive of the educational program.
- All areas will include acoustical treatment and should be designed to minimize transmission of sound.
- All finishes, systems, and components should be durable and easily maintained.
- The building will be designed for efficient use of energy.
- The facility will maintain a temperature of 69°–73° F year round.
- The facility will allow for ease of community access and use that minimizes disruption to school and educational activities and spaces.
- The facility will serve as an emergency center for the town.
- Outdoor space will be an extension of the educational, athletic, and community program.
- The design will meet the principles of universal design.

Construction Manager and Architect Evaluation Forms

[Editor's note: For many vision and/or building committee members, interviewing prospective architectural and construction management firms is one of the most challenging parts of the school planning process. Most if not all the firms vying for a project will be experienced and competent, so how does a committee select the best candidate? To assist its members in the evaluation process, the East Lyme Middle School Vision Committee developed lists of issues and questions to which interviewees would be asked to respond during their presentations, a list of construction manager

evaluation criteria, a list of attributes that the selected architect should be expected to have (and of things to listen for during the interviews), as well as a Construction Manager Interview checklist and an Architect Scoring Grid on which committee members could note their reactions during the interviews. We think these documents are extremely useful, and so we reproduce them here for other vision/building committees to emulate and adapt for their own purposes.]

Construction Management Interview Issues

1. Experience of firm:
- Volume of work—with construction management
- For public schools—with construction management
- On major alterations and additions projects—with construction management

2. Experience of key staff to be assigned, and extent of involvement of each:
- Principal-in-charge
- Project manager
- Project engineer
- Project superintendent

3. Experience in local [Connecticut] construction market:
- Relationship with general contractors
- Relationship with subcontractors
- Relationship with unions

4. Proposed staffing:
- During design
- During construction phases

5. Principal office location:
- Local office location and staffing
- Relationship between local and main office

6. Joint venture partners/consultants:
- Past experience of the proposed team

7. Total annual volume of construction management fees

8. Total annual billings of general construction work

9. Current work and backlog

Construction Manager Interview: Evaluation Criteria
- Expect everyone to claim they walk on water, unfrozen. How they feel about themselves will give you an indication of how flexible they may be when you are dealing with them. It is their job to represent you first; their need to finish the job as easily as possible comes second.

- [E]xpect the construction manager to have a good grasp of the scope of your project.
- [E]xpect the construction manager to involve the school administration, faculty, parents, local officials and students [in planning] a safety program. Look for details and breadth of scope in the plan this construction manager would propose.
- The people [on the CM's staff] who would work on our project should be identified and should be present at and participate in the interview. This gives us the chance to check references.
- During the pre-construction phase the entire scope of the project will be determined. Once this phase is finished, design and construction are relatively simple and straightforward. [We] want a construction manager who is proactive, one who can make constructability suggestions and quick cost estimates.
- The construction manager and general contractor know more about the performance of architects and engineers than anyone else, because they build from the plans and specifications. Good plans and specifications save time and money in the bidding and construction process. Construction managers, [however,] are reluctant to evaluate architects [with whom they may end up working]. We need frankness here!

Architect Interview: Questions for the Architect
How can the goals for learners be translated into architecture so the resulting environment is a true learning environment?

**EAST LYME MIDDLE SCHOOL
PROJECT DESIGN COMMITTEE**

Construction Manager Interview

Suggested Questions:	*Exc.*	*Good*	*Fair*	*Poor*
1. What is special about your firm that indicates we should employ you for this project?	___	___	___	___
2. Give a brief description of the project.	___	___	___	___
3. What procedures do you use to establish a safety program for this type of project? What safety program do you recommend?	___	___	___	___
4. Who are the staff members you would assign to our project? What qualifies them?	___	___	___	___
5. What services do you provide the committee during pre-construction?	___	___	___	___
6. What services do you expect to provide us in the selection of an architect?	___	___	___	___
7. What questions do you have for us?	___	___	___	___

Other questions you may wish to consider if we have time:

What was your best job? Why?

What was your worst job? Why?

After you sketch out the learning concepts we hope are captured in the facility design, how will you determine if they work? How can we measure the learning implications? How will you know if the facility reflects the educational goals?

How should the design of the learning space reflect and support the information age?

In your opinion, what kinds of spaces does the school need to prepare students for the real world? What does the new building require? How did you determine that?

Describe an effective planning process you've used to design an age-appropriate middle school that looks ahead to the future. Which school was that?

What is the role of the architect with the various committees (Vision, Design, Building)?

How can you help pare down the cost yet not lose the concepts and attributes we desire for a state-of-the-art middle school environment?

There will be two full years between design and the completion of construction. In the interim, many technological advances may occur. What do you suggest we do regarding the design or purchase of technology?

How could our middle school serve as an intergenerational community center?

Which middle schools have you recently designed? Successes? Obstacles?

What was your best middle school design? Why? Your worst? Why?

In order for this project to be successful, what needs to occur? What will your role be?

The Attributes of a Good Architect
- Is a good listener
- Understands middle school students and their developmental needs
- Understands middle school philosophy
- Is future-oriented (technology, flexible learning environment)
- Consults with the users of the facility
- Reflects vision of committee in the design of the facility
- Ensures good communication among all future users
- Has good planning process for designing an appropriate middle school
- Proposes reasonable fee
- Has process in place for keeping to schedule
- Understands and has experience with the State Department of Education Facilities Unit

Architect Interview: Things to Listen For
- Schools are learning environments—act as teaching tools.
- A flexible learning environment provides an important tool for interdisciplinary teaching and for facilitating self-selection among the users.
- Design addresses the need to study the students' ideas (developmental needs/like and dislikes) about learning and educational programming.
- Presentation incorporates program elements, educational specifications, and curriculum into the facility design.
- Communication—the architect has a planning process that works.
- The architect considers more than just the number of classrooms needed.

EAST LYME MIDDLE SCHOOL
ARCHITECT SCORING GRID

Grid

Attributes		A	B	C
a. Competence and expertise of firm's staff	a.			
b. Dedication to this project	b.			
c. Commitment to quality	c.			
d. Effective planning process	d.			
e. Process to keep on schedule	e.			
f. Open to input	f.			
g. Can deliver design with Vision Committee's Guiding Principles	g.			
h. Future-oriented (technology, community use, flexible space)	h.			
i. Knowledgable about young adolescents and their learning environment needs	i.			
j. Understands middle school philosophy	j.			

Total score (maximum 50)   _____ _____ _____

Score each attribute with a maximum of 5 points:

5 = Very Strong
4 = Strong
3 = Adequate
2 = Weak
1 = Very Weak

Priority Decision Grid
Circle your choice

1. A   A
    B   C
2.   B
       C

Total Number of Circles (tallies)

A.

B.

C.

Chapter 5

The Middle School of the Future: Design Principles

by Daniel M. Davis, AIA
and Patricia A. Myler, AIA

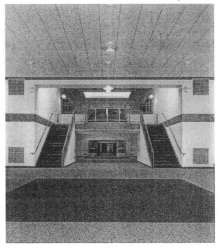

Public school teachers are generally very creative, inventive, resourceful people. And when it comes to many public school buildings—even some newer buildings—it's a good thing that most teachers are as ingenious as they are, since they're so often required to teach "around" the architecture, which insists on getting in the way of the learning experience. This unfortunate truth leads us to state what should be the *very first* principle in the design of schools of the future, middle schools included:

• *Architectural design must foster and enhance learning,* not impair or hinder it. In fact, the school building must be conceived as a *teaching instrument* in its own right.

Quality school environments enhance, even improve, attitude and achievement, and a well-designed middle school is one that carefully integrates the curriculum and the educational environment.

In a sense, everything about the design of the future middle school flows from this basic principle. But there are three other principles—closely related to the first and every bit as important—that must also be stated right up front, because they, too, should shape every aspect of middle school design, now and in the years to come:

• The school building should be *an expression of the values and goals of the community that builds it.* Ensuring that this happens requires just the sort of intensively *collaborative planning, design, and construction process* outlined in Chapters 3 and 4 of this book.
• The future *will not be static,* and a new school's design must strive, in every possible way, *to be flexible enough to accommodate the educational changes that will certainly occur over the life of the building.*
• Every aspect of a new school building should be *program-driven.* That's an up-to-date way of restating American architect Louis Sullivan's famous maxim, "Form follows function," and it involves making sure not only that everything that's necessary to accomplish a given program—determined by the project's many stakeholders—is included in the building's design, but also that elements that are extraneous to the program are strictly controlled or eliminated entirely.

Those are the absolute basics. Let's turn, now, to an exploration of how they get applied to specific aspects, or areas, of middle school design. (Note: Some of the principles intrinsic to designing schools of the future—those involving site design, security, acoustics, indoor environmental quality, sustainability, and accessibility—are covered in detail in Part III of this book and need only be mentioned here.)

"Making Big Schools Feel Small"

One of the foundational premises of the middle school movement has already been mentioned several times in this book, but it bears repeating again here, since it's become so integral to the way that middle schools are conceived and designed:

- The middle school provides an appropriately transitional environment between the intimate, homelike atmosphere of the elementary school and the larger, more self-directed environment of the high school.

The building itself must play a part in helping young adolescents deal with the great intellectual, emotional, physical, and social changes that occur during early adolescence. On the most general level, that means that building design must foster the "communities of learning" that it houses, which in turn requires that the building incorporate strategies for "making the big school feel small."

Usually, the desired intimacy of scale—and the strong sense of group identification that ensues when students feel that they have "a place of their own" within the larger school environment—is achieved through some sort of team arrangement, with the teams clustered in "neighborhoods." There are a variety of ways this can be done, some of which are graphically illustrated in the following chapter, "The Middle School of the Future: Conceptual Drawings." Suffice it to say here that the design of an individual team area, as well as its relation to its neighborhood and to the school as a whole, needs to be closely tied to—*needs to grow out of*—the particular model or models of learning that the project's stakeholders have decided to adopt, and yet the design also needs to be flexible enough to accommodate a variety of different learning models and grouping scenarios.

For instance, a middle school might initially be designed based on a program that envisions a "traditional" team-based teaching model, in which each of the school's three neighborhoods comprises five regular classrooms and one science room and in which a grade level (5, 6, 7) is assigned to each neighborhood. As the educational program grows, however, astute educators may decide that they can strengthen the school community by distributing grades 5, 6, and 7 more or less evenly throughout each neighborhood. Now, students enter the neighborhood in grade 5 and stay there through grade 7—increasing the opportunities for experimenting with "looping" or multi-age learning models. In fact, fluctuations in enrollments often necessitate a great deal of flexibility in configuring teams. It's rare that a population of students is evenly distributed across grade levels, so a traditional model in which neighborhoods are organized around grades doesn't address a situation in which, for example, grade 5 requires 11 classrooms, grade 6 requires ten, and grade 7 needs only eight.

A Facility Built *for* Change

Middle school educational practice today is built on the premise that exploration and experimentation are *inherently good things*: A variety of approaches should be tried, and those that work should be adopted and refined over the course of time. (The corollary, of course, is that approaches that don't work should be shelved.) Middle school advocates reject a standardized, "one size fits all" approach to education, and reform is conceived not as a "goal" but as an ongoing process. Because of this, it's not just *likely* that middle school education will change during the coming years; it's a *certitude.* The middle school of the future, therefore, must go far beyond grudgingly accommodating change. It must be *built for* those changes that will certainly occur.

Moreover, flexibility isn't just something that will be needed in the future. A very high degree of flexibility is required *right now,* to accommodate all the nonstandardized (and highly flexible) aspects of middle school education that are already in place, including:

- Decentralized authority and horizontal (not "top-down") communication.
- Teaming and group decision-making, with teachers acting as facilitators or "coaches."
- Exploratory, project-based learning in which students "learn to learn" by engaging in a very wide range of activities.
- An ever-shifting combination of individual and small- and large-group learning experiences.
- Block scheduling.

Achieving truly flexible design—design that *welcomes* change—can require a delicate balance. On the one hand, flexible design runs counter to the rigidly institutional design of, say, yesterday's junior high schools. Color, light, air, texture, and organization are all consciously manipulated to produce a sensorily stimulating, "noninstitutional" environment. By the same token, however, designers must take care not to "overdecorate" that environment. The middle school belongs, first of all, to the students who attend it, and student-centered learning demands that the school function as a stage on which the students are the central players—or as the *backdrop* against which they perform.

We'll return to that theme in just a moment. But, first, let us point out that maximizing flexibility requires paying scrupulous attention to *each and every component* of facility design, including things like classroom furniture, storage spaces, movable partitions, and connecting doors between rooms.

Flexibility should be *the* most important criterion in furniture selection. It's obvious that the rigid grids of desks and chairs that characterized the traditional classroom are totally inappropriate for a middle school approach that emphasizes constantly changing patterns of interaction, each driven by the nature of the subject being explored and the kind of project being undertaken. What may not be so obvious, though, is that large round tables also make for relatively inflexible classroom environments. (A round table takes up a lot space; it's heavy and therefore difficult to move about; and its size predetermines the size of the group that can use it.) One furniture solution that many newer middle schools are employing involves the use of smaller, trapezoidal tables, each capable of accommodating one or two students, that are lightweight and easily movable and that can be "pieced together" in a very wide variety of arrangements that lend themselves to different kinds of learning—larger and small circles for group interactions, "amphitheater"-type patterns for performances and presentations, and so on. (They also accommodate individual or one-on-one work, of course.) Other furniture components that enhance flexibility include movable shelving units that, besides being used for storage, can double as dividers separating noisy group activities from quieter kinds of research and study.

Adequate storage is always an issue in school design. Usually, attention focuses on the amount of storage or the size of various kinds of storage spaces. These will always remain important considerations, but an equal amount of attention has to be paid to the *flexibility* of storage—and to how well it matches the kinds of educational activities it's meant to support. There's no reason, for example, that student lockers can't be clustered in or near the various team areas, so that they're conveniently accessible throughout the school day. There's no reason that lockers must conform to the traditional (tall, narrow) locker shape, especially since the large back-packs that many students carry to school these days don't fit into traditional lockers very easily. (By the same token, maybe other storage options—checkrooms, for example—should be considered.) And—to take just one more example—there's no reason that resources that are ordinarily concen-trated in a school's media center can't be distributed into a variety of storage/access locations throughout a facility.

It may seem odd to claim that design should positively interact with the *methods of assessment* used by a school, but it's true. For example, if a middle school employs a "portfolio" method for assessing students' progress, it's very important that there be storage spaces capacious enough to safely store—perhaps on a long-term basis—the projects that individual students and groups produce and accumulate over time. These might take the form of easily accessible, specially designed shelves or cabinets capable of holding both the two- and the three-dimensional "products" that students create.

Finally, a genuinely flexible facility is one that addresses the possibility that the building may be put to a different use at some point in the future if a district's needs change. Today, it's not uncommon to see former high schools being renovated to serve as middle schools to serve growing middle-grades enrollments (the Sarah Noble School, featured in Chapter 1, is just such a project), and it's possible that a middle school built today to serve three grades may, in the future, house two (or four) grade levels.

"Bumping into Things"

Children should bump into things. Does that sound strange? We don't mean, of course, that they should physically injure themselves. Rather, we mean that the school environment should give them plenty of opportunity to *encounter and explore* the world around them. Children are naturally resourceful, curious, competent, and imaginative, and they want to interact and communicate with others. They can best create meaning and make sense of their world in rich environments that support "complex, varied, sustained, and changing relationships between people, the world of experience, ideas and the many ways of expressing ideas" (Cadwell 1997, p. 93) rather than from simplified lessons or learning environments. Moreover, they're most likely to learn from "peak experiences" that are discrepant, surprising, active, and have a strong emotional element. "A handful of profound learning experiences requiring analysis and synthesis is vastly more lasting and meaningful to students than weeks spent skimming reams of superficial facts for memorization and recall" (Christopher et al. n.d.).

Translating these attributes of powerful, effective learning experiences into architectural terms is a bit of a tall order, requiring creativity and even a bit of humility on the part of the designer. But in early 2002, we had an experience that led us to do some serious thinking about designing spaces for the kinds of hands-on, exploratory learning experiences—some experts have called them experiences of active, or "muscle," learning—that allow children to "bump into things" in the best sense of the phrase. We happened to pay a visit to the new Aerospace Research Labs at the Massachusetts Institute of Technology, in Cambridge. What especially impressed us about the facility were the *studios* where engineering students gather to build, present, and critique projects. Unlike so much other educational architecture that we've seen, these studios were intentionally designed in a *nonprecious* manner. They were, in other words, real, hands-on workplaces—*easy to mess around in and difficult to mess up* in the sense of causing permanent damage to the facility.

We think that's an idea that's widely applicable in educational environments on *all levels*—perhaps especially at the middle school level, where such strong emphasis is put on exploratory, project-driven learning. Why not design at least some learning spaces in this intentionally nonprecious way? That doesn't mean that design doesn't have to be *meticulous*, because it's utterly important that such spaces provide everything that's needed, architecturally and in terms of services, to accomplish the projects that will happen there. There must be flexibility in the location of power and data lines and water sources (for power and data, an overhead grid that can be accessed throughout the lab may be a good option). It's also crucial that such spaces be easy to clean—and/or that they be organized in such a way that it's not necessary to clean up everything at the end of a given session if the project isn't yet finished. It's important that storage be adequate and appropriate for the work that goes on. And, of course, it's critical that the furniture and finishes in these spaces be especially durable, to withstand the wear and tear of real, hands-on work.

Based on what we saw at MIT and on conversations we've had with educators—including Dr. Christine Casey, an educational consultant who contributed her thoughts to this book—we've begun to feel strongly that all new middle schools ought to incorporate one or more such "nonprecious" spaces—labs or studios where kids can "work with *stuff*." Such lab/studio spaces might be totally generic in character *or* they might be devoted to different kinds of hands-on projects and be shared by various teams on a rotating basis throughout the school year.

Built to Last

We've just mentioned the importance of durability in the selection of furniture and finishes for "nonprecious" studio/lab spaces, but, really, durability should a primary criterion in choosing furniture and finishes for the school as a whole. Durable finishes not only look better longer, but—as is explained in detail in Chapter 9, "Middle School Security: Closed Yet Open"—there's a significant security-related value in selecting especially durable materials because they're relatively impervious to vandalism damage. (And, as that chapter shows, vandalism tends to beget more vandalism, so there's a great deal of wisdom in nipping it in the bud.)

Especially durable materials tend to be more expensive in terms of first costs than do less-durable alternatives. It's our strong feeling, though, that this is the wrong place to be penny-wise, since it's often the case that durable materials will pay for themselves many times over during the life of the building because they're easier to maintain, don't have to be replaced so often, and are resistant to vandalism. Take the example of flooring: The installation costs of terrazzo floors (at $10–$12 per square foot, the most expensive option) are significantly higher than those of vinyl composite tile (VCT) flooring (the least expensive, at about $1–$2 per square foot). But terrazzo is likely to last the life of the building; with a minimum of upkeep, it continues to look handsome; and it's *very* difficult to damage. VCT, on the other hand, can wear out—and begin to look bad—relatively quickly. It's labor-intensive to maintain, needing to be buffed weekly and given a new coat of wax two or three times a year—but even that's not perfect, since dirt can become embedded in VCT flooring during the waxing process. The lesson isn't just that "you get what you pay for;" it's that you'll continue to pay (and pay) if you choose the less durable and *seemingly* less costly option. (There is, by the way, an intermediate, "compromise" option: ceramic tile, which generally ranges between $7 and $8 per square foot.)

Before making any decision on a particular finish, it's therefore essential to understand its longevity and its maintenance requirements—and to predict the amount of wear and tear that a particular finish is likely to be subjected to in a particular location. Sheetrock may be an appropriate wall material in some corridors; other corridor applications may be better served by impact-resistant drywall or by CMUs (concrete masonry units). (We should also note, here, that durability isn't the only criterion guiding the selection of materials; a finish's acoustical properties or its degree of moisture-resistance may, in certain spaces, trump durability. For more on these issues, see Chapter 10, "Improving School Acoustics—A Systems Approach," and Chapter 11, "Indoor Air Quality—Problems and Solutions.")

"Invisible" Technology

Our public schools' relationship to educational technology has, we think, matured far beyond the point when the computer station was the showpiece of the classroom. Though it's doubtless the case that technologies to assist and enhance learning will continue to proliferate—and that the use of high-tech devices and systems will become an ever more essential component in learning of every kind—we believe that it's about time we begin thinking of high technology as "just another tool" in education's toolbox, and that we design school buildings in ways that seamlessly integrate technology into learning spaces. (Portable, wireless technologies will definitely help in this regard.)

As a design principle, seamless integration means avoiding "over-celebrating" or overemphasizing technology—even as we create learning spaces that flexibly accommodate technologies of many different sorts. Technology, in other words, should be "invisible": always there, always ready to use when needed, but just a plank in the stage on which learning takes place. That's just another way of saying that in our enthusiasm for educational technologies we shouldn't lose sight of the fact that it's the student—not the electronic device or the technological system—who's the major player here, and that it's the relationship between students and teachers and among students themselves that ought to be the main focus.

One cautionary note, we feel, needs to be voiced about the future of educational technology and its potential impact on the design of school buildings. Elsewhere in this book, we talk about some ways in which expanding opportunities for "virtual learning" may have a profound impact on school design—for example, by reducing the square-footage needs of media centers and science lab/classrooms. And there's been a lot of speculation about how certain kinds of computer- and Internet-based learning activities can be performed *anywhere*, raising the possibility (though admittedly an outside one) that the public school building itself might someday become a "dinosaur"—a no-longer-necessary artifact of education's past.

Our caution is a simple one: that we shouldn't allow our enthusiasm for virtual learning—which has some very real uses—lead us to forget that hands-on, *physical* experiences as well as *social* experiences of group interaction are equally legitimate, equally important aspects of education. In a society where decisions are made democratically and where work is increasingly team-based, the school building will *always* be necessary as *the* place where socialization and education in group decision-making can occur. Moreover, the school building's importance in educating students for creative worklives is underscored by the fact that real creativity depends on hands-on learning experiences and interaction with a wide diversity of other human beings (see Florida 2002). Not only is the public school building *not* going away anytime soon; it *shouldn't* go away, and our aim should also be to strike a careful balance between those kinds of learning that students can do alone, off site, and those that require *non*virtual, real-world spaces.

A Colorful, Well-Lighted Place

Daylight is *the* standard for lighting quality in educational environments—
which means not only that natural daylighting should be maximized but also
that artificial lighting should emulate the attributes of daylight to the
greatest extent possible through the use of "full-spectrum" fixtures. Studies
have demonstrated a positive correlation between daylighting of interior
spaces and academic performance. For example, a 1999 California Board for
Energy Efficiency study, which tracked 21,000 students in three states,
found that over a one-year period students in classrooms with the most
daylight improved 20 percent faster on math tests and 26 percent faster on
reading over those students in classrooms with the least amount of daylight
(Zernike 2001). (Teachers, by the way, also perform better in naturally daylit
environments.)

The days of the harsh, fluorescently lit classroom are *gone for good.*
"Historically, classroom lighting levels have been determined by two
significant factors: foot candles and cost" (Frey 1999), but these criteria
need to be reexamined based on the *quality* of the light provided. Daylight,
which contains a continuous spectrum of all light wavelengths, is the
standard measure for color quality in lighting, with a Color Rendering Index
(CRI) of 100. (By contrast, most fluorescent lighting gives off a discontinu-
ous spectrum: a flickering light with spikes of color and a CRI range in the
low 50s to 86.) And because it's free, daylight is the most energy efficient
source of illumination; maximizing daylight can have an extremely positive
effect on a school's utility bills.

Designing for daylighting can be a complicated undertaking, however, since
the penetration of *direct* sunlight into learning spaces is usually *not*
desirable, for a number of reasons including the burden that the extra heat
from direct sunlight can put on cooling loads and, of course, the glare that
direct sun can cause. Controlling glare is especially important in spaces
where computers are used, since reflected glare can bounce off computer
screens into the eyes of the user. Some of the strategies commonly employed for maximizing daylight while minimizing glare are the use of
full-spectrum filters, clerestory windows, skylights, and lightshelves.

That, by the way, is also a reason to strictly limit the use of direct artificial
lighting, especially in flexible spaces where furniture is likely to be
reconfigured often (and where, therefore, the placement of computers is
unpredictable). Indirect light provided by pendant fixtures is generally
preferred, though there's a problem with indirect lighting, as well: its visual
monotony. (It's often advisable to counteract that monotony, and provide
some visual relief, through the use of task lighting and/or accent lighting at
displays.)

Designing for daylighting involves paying attention to the overall orientation of a facility and the spaces within it. Generally, a north-south
orientation—with windows concentrated on the east- and west-facing walls
of interior spaces—is best, for it allows spaces throughout the facility to
enjoy a shifting pattern of light throughout the day. By contrast, north- and

south-facing windows receive more or less even amounts of light—too little or too much, respectively.

Unfortunately, a concern for compass orientation has waned in recent decades, with the development of heating and cooling systems that can effectively control interior climate conditions no matter how much—or how little—sunlight is entering a space. When the quality of light changes over the course of the day, however, the occupants of a space feel a greater connection to the outside world, and it's been shown that an awareness— even a subconscious awareness—of that daily rhythm of changing light can, like daylight itself, be a boon to performance and creativity. (We return to the theme of interconnection between outdoors and indoors below, but— while we're on the subject of light—let's mention that providing window seats in classrooms, media centers, and other learning spaces is one way of bolstering the connection between indoors and out-of-doors.)

The *colors* used in furniture and on interior finishes are another consideration too often neglected in the past. "A change of color is the least expensive and fastest way to improve a school's environment. Bright colors stimulate brain activity and respiration. Cool colors promote muscle relaxation and reduction in blood pressure—good for calming budding teenagers in the middle grades" (Zernike 2001).

Middle schools being designed today employ a greater range of color than was traditionally used in the past. It's important not to use too much of any single color. Rather, the palette should complement the activities that occur in a given space: mild (neutral) colors are recommended for walls and floors to minimize glare; restful colors are best for reading areas; and stronger, bolder colors should be reserved for areas that demand attention—for instance, the "teaching wall" behind the markerboard. Other considerations in choosing colors include their interaction with natural daylight (how do they appear on bright, sunshiny days versus cloudy, overcast ones) and their long-term viability or "endurance" in terms of fashion or style. It's probably wiser to limit the use of especially "trendy" colors to small areas that can easily be repainted.

Teachers Need Space, Too

Designing a building to foster learning requires paying attention to the needs of teachers as well as those of students, since faculty creativity and professionalism are so essential to students' success. To develop creativity and improve professional standards, teachers need private spaces where they can pursue individual work and common areas where they can meet with other faculty to discuss lesson plans, students' progress, and professional matters—as well as relax and enjoy one another's company. Faculty development can be pursued in one, centralized center or a number of decentralized centers dispersed throughout the facility (and reflecting the organizational structure of the school). Individual faculty offices should be large enough (and appropriately furnished) to comfortably accommodate private conferences with students and/or their parents.

A Balanced, Welcoming Facility

Before going on to the conceptual drawings that translate into concrete terms the sometimes rather abstract ideas that we've been discussing in this chapter, we need to mention two other aspects of good middle school design: overall *balance* and a sense of *welcome*.

Spatial "balance" is a difficult idea to communicate verbally, since it has to do with how well the facility works *as a whole, and from the perspective of those using it*: Do the pieces fit together well? Are the relationships between the classroom wings (or team areas) and core spaces carefully worked out so as to provide convenient access to shared areas from any part of the building? Are spaces sized appropriately? Are courtyards and other spaces easy to make effective use of, and do they provide the right amount and kind of interplay between the interior and the outdoors? (That is, is there an creativity-enhancing "osmosis" between interior and exterior spaces?)

A well-balanced school building has already traveled a fair distance toward becoming a *welcoming* facility—one that invites users in, invites them, in fact, to *use it*. By "users," of course, we mean *everyone* who uses it: students first of all, but also teachers, administrative and other staff, parents and other school-related visitors, and (very importantly) the whole gamut of after-hours community users who might enter the facility for a wide variety of purposes. (Of course, the school will want to restrict after-hours accessibility to certain areas of the building—a topic that's treated in greater detail in chapter 9, "Middle School Security: Closed Yet Open.")

One essential component of "welcoming" design is *visibility*. A user should always be able to find his or her way from point A to point B with relative ease. This aspect of circulation—which architects refer to as *wayfinding*—can be enhanced through clear, easily intelligible signage that's placed just where people will need it. (In middle schools, it's a good idea to punctuate clear circulation routes with colorful accents that appeal to adolescent vitality.)

Another way of establishing a sense of welcome is to use design to *celebrate* the school and the community. We said earlier that the building should, to the greatest extent possible, serve as a stage or backdrop for the students who are, after all, the school's central players. Celebrating their achievements is made easier when there are plenty of places—walls, boards, cases—to display the work that they have done. And the larger community is celebrated when designers take care to ensure that the building "fits" the community. That doesn't mean being stodgy or old-fashioned. It means that the building design should somehow incorporate references to the community's life and history. It should *visibly belong* to the community.

Now, let's see how all these principles might play out in practice.

Chapter 6

**The Middle School of the Future:
Conceptual Drawings and
Cluster Plans**

The middle school design principles discussed in the previous chapter can be successfully implemented in many different ways. The conceptual drawings on the following pages present a variety of alternative floorplans for the middle school as a whole (pp. 68–73), as well as for team areas, or "clusters" (pp. 74–76). The cluster plans reveal, in a detailed way, the various possible relationships between classroom spaces and shared learning spaces (agoras, kivas).

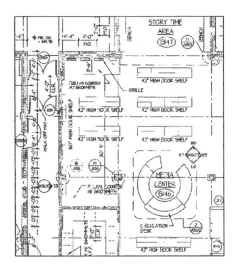

Floorplan Options

COURT/FIGURE 8 CONCEPT

- Multiple entry opportunities
- Loop circulation eases congestion
- Creates two courtyards
- Core facilities dispersed throughout building

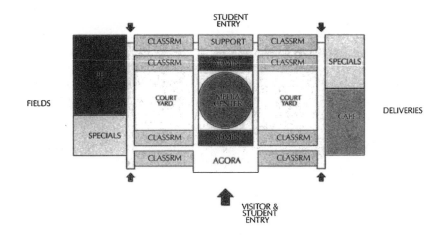

COMPACT LINEAR CONCEPT

- Central entry/arrival area
- Central core facility
- Facility divided into two classroom areas
- Limits length of corridors
- Creates four definable courtyard areas
- Easily expanded core facilities

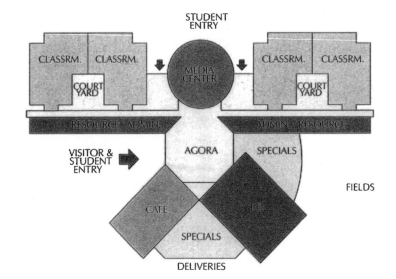

EXPANDED LINEAR CONCEPT A

- Subdivision of classroom areas creates more intimate scale
- Hierarchical circulation allows a variety of experiences
- Good separation of public and private areas
- Easily expanded classroom areas
- Easily expanded core areas

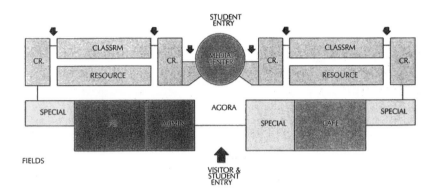

CENTRAL PAVILION CONCEPT

- Continuity of classroom areas allows good grade flexibility
- Loop circulation eases congestion
- Compact footprint
- Easily expanded classroom areas
- Good distribution of core facilities throughout school

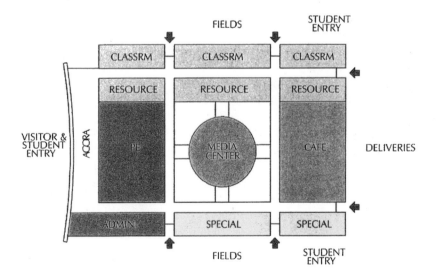

Chevron Cluster Concept

- Two separate entry areas: one public and one private
- Separation of public and private areas
- Expandable classroom areas
- Hierarchical circulation allows a variety of experiences
- Classroom facilities divided into two areas
- Creates small definable courtyard areas

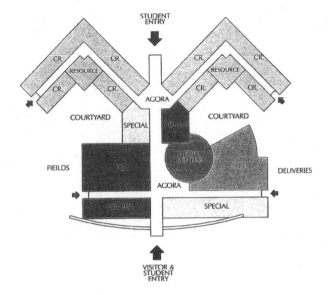

Pinwheel Concept

- Central entry/arrival area
- Central core facility
- Easily expanded classroom areas
- Facility divided into four classroom areas
- Limits length of corridors
- Creates four definable courtyard areas

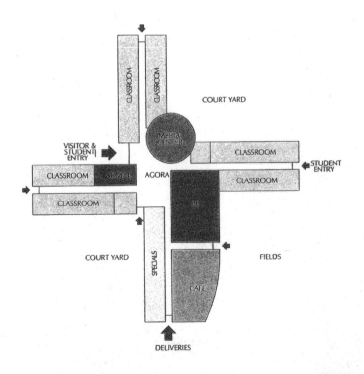

Chevron Concept

- Central entry/arrival area
- Central core facility
- Easily expanded classroom areas
- Facility divided into two classroom areas
- Simple/understandable organization
- Creates definable front and back site areas

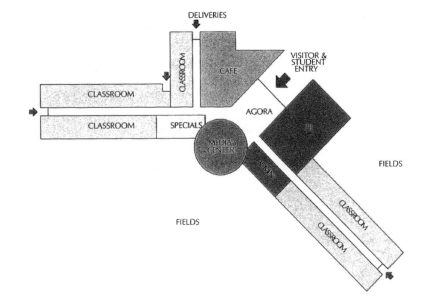

Academic Cluster Concept A

- Continuity of classroom areas allows flexibility
- Separation of public and private areas
- Loop circulation system eases congestion
- Compact footprint
- Easily expanded core facilities
- Expandable classroom area

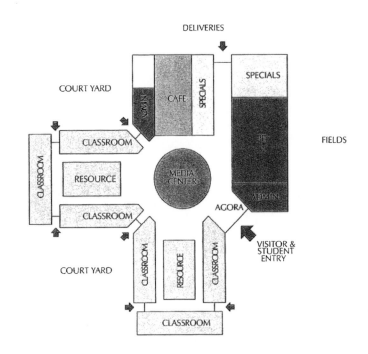

EXPANDED LINEAR CONCEPT B

- Subdivision of classroom areas creates more intimate scale
- Continuity of classroom areas allows good grade flexibility
- Simple/clear organization
- Good separation of public and private areas
- Easily expanded classroom areas
- Easily expanded core areas

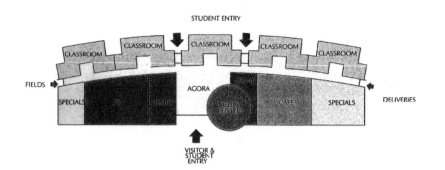

ACADEMIC CLUSTER CONCEPT B

- Continuity of classroom areas allows flexibility
- Separation of public and private areas
- Loop circulation system eases congestion
- Compact footprint
- Easily expanded core facilities
- Expandable classroom area

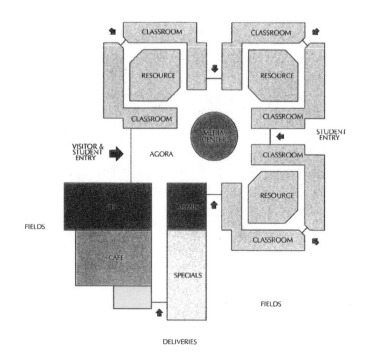

COURT/CORE CONCEPT

- Continuity of classroom areas allows flexibility
- Separation of public and private areas
- Loop circulation system eases congestion
- Compact footprint
- Easily expanded core facilities
- Expandable classroom area

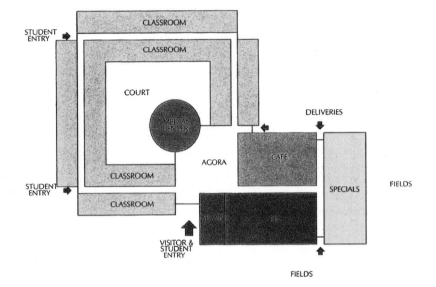

PRECIOUS/NONPRECIOUS CONCEPT

- Continuity of classroom areas allows flexibility
- Separation of public and private areas
- Loop circulation system eases congestion
- Compact footprint
- Easily expanded core facilities
- Expandable classroom area

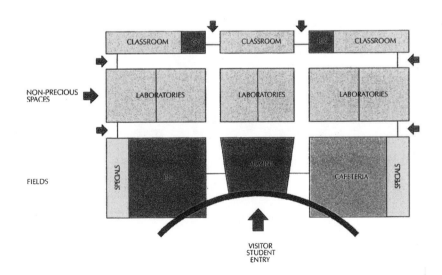

Cluster Plans

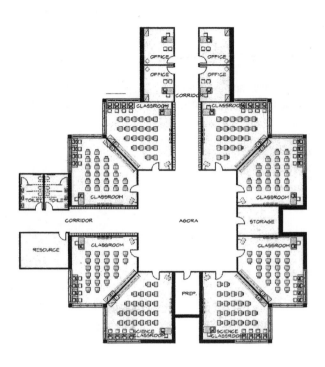

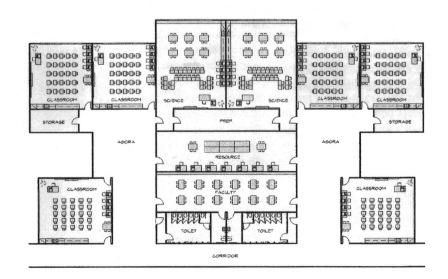

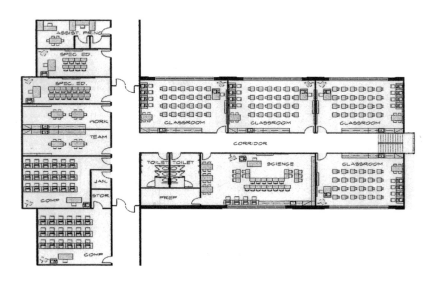

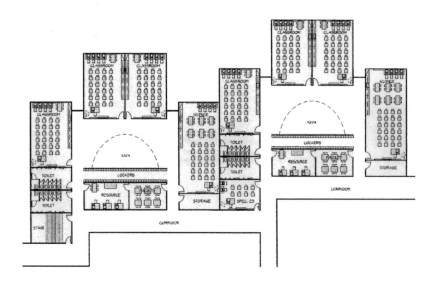

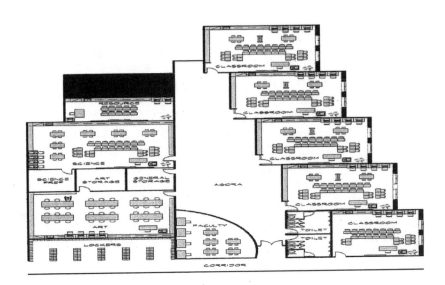

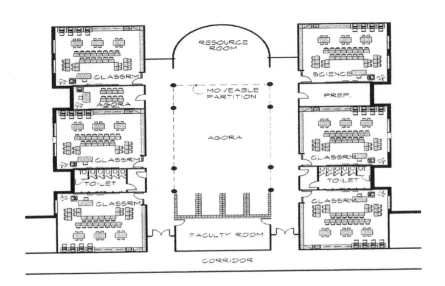

Chapter 7

The Middle School of the Future: A Draft Educational Specification

At root, a good educational specification—or "ed spec"—grows out of a well-developed philosophy of education. Moreover, the long-term success of a facility being planned and built today requires that the people responsible for creating the ed spec do some serious, informed thinking about what the future is likely to bring. So before delving into the specifics of what an educational specification for the middle school of the future might contain, let's spend a little time reviewing the basic educational principles in which such a specification should be grounded, and then take a glance at just a few of the many issues and trends that may influence educational facility design in the years to come. (School design–related issues that may potentially arise in the future are treated in greater detail in the Epilog to this book.)

Educational Philosophy

The primary commitment of the middle school of the future is to offer an educational program of excellence designed to meet the special needs of early adolescents. These youngsters are entering a new stage of development, a time of life when they experience rapid physical, emotional, social, and intellectual changes. The middle school of the future must strive to provide all students with an equal opportunity to develop their maximum potential, recognizing that each student is truly an individual with unique abilities and needs.

The middle school of the future must also aim at helping students acquire the skills necessary for success in the complex, rapidly changing, information-based world of the 21st century. Built on the belief that each child can and should experience the pleasure of learning and creating, the middle school of the future will provide ample opportunities for students to:

*   Acquire the ability to think and to solve problems cooperatively as well as independently, and to use imagination and creativity to solve problems, create new knowledge, respond to new and unexpected information, and forecast consequences.
*   Acquire advanced knowledge and develop specific skills in a variety of academic areas, including reading, writing, calculating, and thinking.
*   Experience personal success, develop self-esteem and respect for others, and acquire interpersonal skills and habits of personal health and fitness.
*   Learn constructive and creative use of the tools of modern technology
*   Acquire the skills necessary to become effective, problem-solving citizens of their changing communities and world.

With the home and community, the middle school of the future shares the responsibility for the education and growth of each student, and should strive wherever possible to assist each student in achieving his or her goals. The school's own goals and strategic objectives need regular review to encourage the continuing professional development of administrative and teaching staff and to ensure that student performance improves and that students continue to excel. These goals and objectives should be consistent with state and federal statutes, should take into consideration the desires of the community, and should be defined in such a way that the nature and degree of student achievement is understandable and measurable on both a short- and long-term basis. Let's turn, now, to these goals and strategic objectives.

Goals

The goals of the middle school of the future include:

- To help students develop the essential skills of lifelong learners.
- To offer students academic, exploratory, and activity programs designed to meet the specific needs of early adolescents.
- To provide an organizational pattern that includes small communities for learning, interdisciplinary teaming, flexible grouping, and integrated approaches to instruction.
- To foster an educational atmosphere that stimulates the growth of each student's personal responsibility, creativity, talents, and gifts.
- To assist students in learning, developing, and practicing effective interpersonal skills.

Strategic Objectives

To establish effective policies and maintain a positive learning environment, the middle school of the future needs to develop a set of strategic objectives that help educators focus attention and action on those areas where policy decisions are most critical. The following strategic objectives are not intended to be all-inclusive, but they do represent areas that are key to the continuing excellence.

Meeting Student Needs
- To provide a program in which each student receives fair treatment and support in his or her quest for personal educational development.
- To provide an atmosphere that motivates each student to realize his/her learning potential.
- To provide a program in which each student can acquire a beneficial general education, including, but not limited to, competency in English, mathematics, science, and social studies.
- To encourage students to participate in the full range of co-curricular activities.
- To provide each student with an opportunity to attain the skills of effective communication, including the expression of ideas and feelings, through reading, writing, speaking, and listening.
- To provide a program in which each student can develop skills in critical and objective thinking, and in research, analysis, planning and evaluation processes.
- To encourage in each student a feeling of pride in work and accomplishment and a sense of self-worth and personal dignity, and to develop an awareness of physical and emotional growth.

- To encourage each student to learn the values of good citizenship and character, social cooperation, physical development, and aesthetic appreciation, and to appreciate a pluralistic society.
- To provide an opportunity for each student to gain an awareness of the opportunities offered by a variety of careers, and to offer appropriate preparation and guidance.
- To be attentive to the unique educational needs of all students, including those requiring special education.
- To provide counseling services to students with special personal needs.

Curriculum and Program of Instruction
- To provide a comprehensive, interdisciplinary educational program that includes a range of learning opportunities and develops competencies in life skills.
- To provide a cost-effective program of instruction suitable for each student, with academic counseling furnished as needed to plan and implement that program.
- To provide opportunities beyond curricular and structured programs for students at all levels to develop special interests, whether physical, intellectual, or creative.
- To continue to raise the standards of education through systematic review and evaluation of all programs.
- To utilize current technology such as computer science/practical arts in a manner that will help prepare every graduate for employment or further education in a rapidly changing world.

Educational Staff
- To treat employees fairly and encourage open communication and mutual support for respected endeavors.
- To encourage staff members to continue their professional growth and the enhancement of their skills and competencies, as well as offering opportunities for such professional growth.
- To encourage staff members to participate in developing the educational program and measuring its effectiveness.
- To encourage in-service training programs designed to assist teachers, administrators, and guidance counselors in dealing with the social, emotional, and academic needs of students.
- To encourage teachers and administrators to meet regularly and discuss educational and professional areas of mutual interest and concern.
- To encourage communication between and among grade levels, schools, and departments.

School-Community Communication
- To encourage community participation in school programs.
- To offer staff, students, parents, and the wider community access to information concerning school affairs, so that common purposes may be understood and common strategies implemented.
- To encourage the establishment of a Program Advisory Committee (PAC) consisting of parents, teachers, administrators, and students

(where appropriate). The PAC will make recommendations concerning goals, objectives, and curriculum projects.

- To foster the understanding that schools exist for the benefit of all members of our society and that the whole community has an interest in the effectiveness of our schools.
- To review annually the goals and objectives with the community and the school staff to be sure that the goals and objectives are still viable and to promote measurable progress toward their achievement.

Environment and Resources

- To develop a comprehensive, long-range plan for the most effective use of the schools and grounds.
- To encourage the community to provide the resources necessary to meet the demands of a suitable program of education consistent with the Board of Education's goals.
- To provide that the physical condition of the schools supports the Board of Education's educational and instructional objectives.

Looking Toward the Future

When planning a new school facility, a community faces what in many cases may be the largest expenditure in its history. The need for such a project is usually related to deteriorating facilities and/or increasing enrollment, both existing and projected. Much time is spent reviewing the need, but—beyond trying to project enrollment trends—little time is spent thinking about what the future might bring.

When it comes time to develop a specification for the new school, in some cases a school administrator develops the spec; in other instances, an architect, working with staff, develops it. Sometimes, the community reaches out to a professional specification writer. In all cases, however, the writer or writers of the ed spec rely on the district's teacher-leaders for input and direction. Unfortunately, these teachers are seldom equipped to respond in a way that's truly future-oriented.

Why not? Well, for the most part, teachers rely on their national subject-matter associations for pragmatic standards to guide their input thinking. National associations, for the most part, do not use futurists to develop guidelines; rather, they rely on experienced teacher-leaders and professionals from teacher preparation institutions. That's understandable, but in the process the future is being sold short.

It is difficult to look 20 or 30 years into the future. The nation's best futurists are associated with well-funded corporate "think tanks" and high-level university projects and are not generally available to help local communities plan their new schools. And teachers have, in general, spent very little time listening to futurists' prognostications. Hence, when teacher-leaders are asked for their input on schools of the future, they generally limit themselves to correcting existing deficiencies related to climate control, storage, and their own comfort—including a focus on lavatories and faculty lounges. Again, this focus is completely understandable, but it does nothing to address the potential changes—technological, medical, social, etc.—that may exert a profound influence on the way educational environments work in the years to come.

The creation of the middle school of the future is, of course, circumscribed by what is possible within the constraints of today's approval processes and today's ways of thinking. Working within the process can at times be frustrating because probing the future reveals so much more than today's process is willing to entertain. But let's take a moment to step beyond what today's process allows and to sketch out some of the developments that may influence education—and therefore school design—over the next few decades.

Ethics

Private schools teach ethics. As public money goes to private schools (through voucher plans that have now won approval by the U.S. Supreme Court), public schools will in all probability respond by also teaching ethics—if for no other reason than to compete with private and parochial school alternatives.

While American public school teachers have long been teaching ethics as "discipline" or as part of a value system presented by example, to actually teach a system of ethics or morals has been difficult, because educators fear crossing the delicate and somewhat vague "church-state" line. Various movements have nevertheless attempted to skirt the church-state issues and have suggested that a system of ethics should be adopted by and taught in the public schools. Three decades ago, a "moral maturity" curriculum hit the market; its pragmatic focus declared that what was good for the general public provided a good-enough definition of what a personal/school code of ethics should be. And the U.S. Congress continues to support the "We the People" program, which is aimed at helping students understand the Constitution and Bill of Rights. This program's materials place a heavy emphasis on understanding democratic principles.

It bears pointing out that codes of ethics, if instituted, stand a much better chance of success if their rationales—and the consequences of violating rules—are well understood by students. This takes time, and might involve having students help craft the code, analyzing the proposed rules and developing in-depth justifications for their use.

Spiritual Growth

Issues involving the separation of church and state are even more clearly in evidence when we think about the place of "the spiritual," or religion, in public school education. American public school students today come from a wide variety of religious backgrounds, and, especially as they reach middle school age, are likely to be wrestling with their own definitions of God and other spiritual matters. Inevitably, they bring their spiritual beliefs, questions, and struggles to the classroom. Moreover, as recent events have powerfully demonstrated, it is impossible to understand today's world without having some grasp of world religious traditions.

These unavoidable realities raise complex challenges for educators—not only because of the tradition of church-state separation in American public education but also because of the extreme practical, intellectual, and emotional difficulty of dealing with different—and often competing—religious systems in the classroom. What's clear is that teachers need much more training in how to deal with such situations—and in how to assist students who are struggling to develop their own spiritual selves. To do so, they may well have to spend time and effort nurturing their own spirituality. The degree to which American public school educators are taking this challenge seriously can be gauged from the fact that the American Association of School Administrators devoted the entirety of the September 2002 issue of its magazine, *The School Administrator,* to the theme of "Spirituality in Leadership."

Interestingly, contemporary school design is already being molded, to a certain extent, by concepts that might be termed "spiritual." For example, the central gathering spaces, or atriums, that are being used in many school buildings today are often somewhat church-like in character and serve a community-building purpose that could be described as spiritual in nature. More comprehensively, author Susan Frey has, through her several popular books, outlined a holistic method for "cultivating spirituality in the classroom" (see Frey 1999). Her approach, which has been enthusiastically received by many educators and school facility designers, integrates curriculum, nutrition, exercise (breathing, stretching, and movement), and multiple aspects of the learning environment, including light, color, and spatial configuration. Design principles like those developed and articulated by Frey can certainly be applied in a nonsectarian way, but architects must always be cognizant of church-state limitations even as they strive to create environments conducive to spiritual growth and well-being.

School-based Courts
Schools of the future will need space to house a judicial system, complete with courtroom space and room for counselors, prosecutors, judges, and other court-related functions. While student courts now exist, teachers play a minimal role in their operation. That will change as ethical codes are adopted and consequences for violating a rule become more severe. One of the challenges that will be faced in the implementation of intra-school judicial proceedings will be how to allow for participation by family members. Most likely, the adoption of school-wide codes of ethics will be effected—and legitimized—through a democratic, one person–one vote process. (This is one of the ways that teaching about citizenship can be put "into action.") Unfortunately, in most school buildings being designed and built today, it's not easy to accommodate forums for democratic decision-making by the

entire student body and their families. Auditoriums large enough to host community-wide debates and legislative processes simply are a rarity—they simply cost too much, and they're not used often enough to justify the expense. In a similar vein, the large auditoriums that do exist are often poorly equipped, technically, and aren't set up for electronic voting. These uses ought certainly to be considered when designing and outfitting a new school auditorium.

Capacities and Abilities

Technologically, it's foreseeable that we will reach a point where we will be able to perform genetic scans on students, allowing us to identify the strengths and weaknesses of their capacities and abilities through DNA analysis. Relatedly, on the medical front we are rapidly approaching a time when we will be able to prescribe designer drugs to enhance and strengthen each student's capacity and ability.

Whether we will actually implement such technologies, of course, remains to be seen, and their introduction into American public education is sure to be surrounded by controversy. Nevertheless, it's possible to imagine a future middle school that will house a technological system with sufficient storage capacity and access speed to allow genetic counselors and medical doctors and their assistants to assess and adjust individual student educational prescriptions and provide an associated drug support system. These functions—the drawing of blood, the analysis of DNA, and the prescribing and dispensing of educational drugs—will require specialized spaces and equipment.

Physical Education

Physical education will move in a similar direction. It's possible to imagine a scenario in which a genetic specialist, a medical assistant, a counselor, a nutritionist, and the physical education teacher will work together to develop individual educational prescriptions, which will require specialized training activities. Today's free weight and aerobic facilities would be supplemented with training stations that relate to the enhancement of all the senses and all physical abilities. For instance, there would be stations focusing on flexibility, strength, visual acuity, perception of color, smell, taste, touch, strength, endurance, mental toughness, hearing (tone perception), and so forth. Designers would devote much more space to individualized phys ed programs and associated record-keeping, so that students could understand the specifics of their personal progress.

Classroom Concept and Design

Democracy requires an understanding of group dynamics and effective socialization for participation in democratic decision-making, and the classroom of the future will be, first and foremost, the place where such socialization will occur and such decision-making processes will be taught.

Classrooms will function as homes-away-from-home and as teacher-supervised social centers.

Designers of the future will create classrooms that will function, in effect, as "family rooms." (There will also be a need for bigger family rooms, which might be created, for example, by the combination of smaller rooms ordinarily divided from one another by movable partitions.) The separation of students by grade level will disappear, and grade levels will be replaced by individualized instruction levels, structured for each student based on his or her needs, capacities, and motivation, and to some extent on chronological age and developmental stage.

Activities in the family room–style classroom will focus on group interaction, helping students from diverse backgrounds learn how they can understand, benefit from, and celebrate one another's strengths and support each other in dealing with weakness.

As we imply in the section on spirituality, above, aesthetic considerations—born of a more complete understanding of the effects of light, color, music, and art on learning and social interaction—will come more strongly to the fore, and we can imagine a time when taxpayers will grant designers much more artistic license and be willing to foot the bill for aesthetic enhancements because they understand the positive effects that such considerations have on their children's development. Line-items supporting commissioned works of art in public school buildings will become more common.

Basic Skills

As we're indicating, it's likely that academic instruction will mostly occur outside the classroom. Students will learn research skills and subject-matter content primarily on their own. Laboratory-based learning—including experiences in science, art, language, math, social studies, music, and career-related subjects—will be scheduled on an as-needed basis. The laboratory spaces themselves will be interdisciplinary, capable of accommodating a wide range of subjects.

Each student will be trained in the empirical, laboratory data-collecting process. He or she will treat life (in school at least) as a laboratory experience in which personal data is systematically recorded and analyzed. Experiments will be set up in accordance with data collected. The educational process will, in effect, become a chain of personal experimentation.

Scheduling Logistics

School schedules are also likely to undergo a sea-change, and the traditional school day (in which all students are expected to be on school grounds for the same number of hours each day) will become a thing of the past. Students will come and go in accordance with their individual schedules. Each student will be in touch with his or her families (the members of the school "family" as well as family members at home or at work) at all times and will carry an identification device that will constantly track his or her whereabouts, much as a cell phone can do now. The Global Positioning System will be used to keep track of everyone in the school community. Transportation will be scheduled on an individualized basis, with bus drivers receiving regular updates scheduling pickups and drop-offs and providing the necessary directions.

The Environment

Heavy emphasis will be placed on creating "green" building designs. The public will insist on buildings that are cost-effective, that are environmentally sustainable, and that provide high-quality comfort control systems. (Issues related to sustainable design are covered in detail in Chapter 12, "A Sustainable Approach to Middle School Design.")

Security and Safety

The attitude that the school community is a family will be supported by the school's safety and security system. All the members of the community will be connected to one another, and, in effect, the community will protect itself. "Bubbles of caring" will invisibly surround the facility so that security personnel will be alerted instantly when a problem arises. The technology for this kind of networkable system—in which security is based on individual alert buttons worn by all staff and students—already exists and has been implemented at some colleges.

The World of Work

The connection between the world of school and the world of work will be increasingly seamless. At appropriate times, students who have specific career focuses in mind will participate in after-school workplace experiences.

Business leaders will be chosen to assist the school and will in turn support the school financially, instructionally, and with their presence—in person or virtual.

The Future Is Already Happening

Do these ideas seem far-out or unrealizable? If so, just think about how strange many of the aspects of today's schools would have seemed from the perspective of 20 years ago. In fact, we're already well on our way toward implementing at least some dimensions of the kind of program we've just been outlining. New middle schools now commonly feature things like the following:

- Wireless Internet access for everyone and full-building cable infrastructure with large servers and personal digital devices (laptops, PDAs, etc.) for each student.
- Flexible-use plans utilizing movable walls in classrooms and in the auditorium to adjust space when needed.
- Some "virtual" science laboratories built alongside traditional labs.

- Teacher offices and teacher-student conference areas, which permit higher classroom utilization rates.
- Cost-effective, environmentally friendly "green design" features.
- Air conditioning enabling year-round facility use.
- For the physical education and athletics programs: field houses, swimming pools, concession stands, and press boxes.
- Natural daylighting of interiors; operable windows.
- Smart boards; ceiling-mounted computer projectors in every classroom; voice amplification systems in classrooms; and flexible studio desk and teacher "cubby" configurations.
- Central coat and instrument storage in lieu of lockers. (In the future, it's likely that individual student brief cases will replace large backpacks and will provide adequate personal storage for the school day.)
- Electronic-book circulation systems and movable chairs and table units in the media center (with less media center space devoted to book stacks).
- A cafeteria that offers a wide variety of healthy foods available on an 18-hour basis.
- Counseling and special education areas that accommodate specialists and conferencing.
- Distance learning and teleconferencing capability.
- Sophisticated fine arts performance spaces, both large and small.
- New technology spaces equipped to provide training for a wide range of careers, ranging from infrastructure wiring, to website design, to broadcasting.

A Draft Educational Specification

The detailed draft specifications that follow are for a middle school facility housing 1,000 students in Grades 6 through 8. This specification is not meant to be rigidly copied but rather to serve as a model of a thorough, workable specification—but one that does not necessarily serve the needs of any particular district or community. (In other words, it is highly generic in nature.)

General aspects of the building not covered in the specifications below include the following:

- The school will be designed based on green building principles to achieve a sustainable facility compatible with the environment and cost-effective to operate.
- All core facilities, including the gymnasium, cafeteria, large-group instruction area. library/media center, and auditorium will be designed for full use during the school day and community use after hours.
- The building will be *extensively used,* and designed in such a way as to permit each student to experience learning and follow his/her interests to the extent of his/her capacity and ability.
- The school will be *universally designed,* meaning that the environments and equipment it contains are usable by the widest range of people. All technology will be usable by people with a range of disabilities.

Academic Subject Areas

Nonspecialized Classrooms: General Considerations

We suggest that nonspecialized academic classrooms include movable trapezoidal desks of a large enough size to hold a student's laptop computer, personal digital assistant, and/or electronic reader, as well as hard text material and papers and pencils. The teacher stations should be much like modern corporate "cubbies," with room for individual student conferences and with excellent computer and peripheral support including room for a computer/monitor, scanner, printer, and CD burner.

For each grade level, there should be at least one "combinable" pair of classrooms to provide for flexible grouping. The partitions must be movable, soundproof, and of high quality.

Art Education

1. Program Objectives

To help students develop an awareness, understanding, and appreciation of art techniques and processes, art media, and art history, and to emphasize aspects of visual communication and critical thought.

2. General Description

Students in grades 6 through 8 receive one or more hours of art instruction each week during the school year. Art education introduces students to the basics of art, including a variety of media, the fundamentals of design and color, the execution and application of design principles, decision-making, and critical thinking.

3. Activities to be Housed

Drawing, painting, printmaking, working with clay, sculpting, two-and three-dimensional assemblage, photography, and computer-generated artwork, etc.

4. Persons to be Housed

One art teacher and up to 25 students per class.

5. Furniture and Equipment

Furniture and equipment in all classrooms should include student tables with impermeable surfaces, stools, a teacher demonstration work table, an emergency eyewash station, a kiln with vent systems, clay storage shelves in a lockable enclosure, three trough sinks with drain traps in an island or peninsula, and stackable drawer files containing 300 shelves for storage of student work. Also needed are open shelving for three-dimensional artwork, movable drying racks, a paper-cutting table, easels, movable pedestals for still life, potters' wheels, a press for printmaking, large rolling mirrors, bookshelves, display boards and cases, blackboards and whiteboards, a recessed projection screen, computer terminals with printers, computer tables, a wall-mounted video screen, and darkroom facilities.

6. Special Requirements

Art classrooms should be located near English, social studies, world language, and music rooms. They should have plenty of natural light, suitable artificial light, and easy access to the outside. Each room should have a walk-in, lockable storage area and a comfortable, quiet, and easy-to-clean floor surface.

English

1. Program Objectives

To develop students' skills in effective oral and written communication; to develop an awareness and appreciation of literature and the ability to critically evaluate it; and to further an understanding of the integral role of language and expression in all studies.

2. General Description

Students in Grades 6 through 8 receive approximately four hours of instruction in English per week for the entire school year. The English curriculum encompasses the study of literature; English grammar, usage and vocabulary; composition; and oral presentation. Skills emphasized include reading, writing, critical thinking, presentation, project development, individual teamwork, and active inquiry. The content and skills emphasized in English are often included in an interdisciplinary approach to instruction, which also includes aspects of social studies, world language, art, and music. Ten classrooms should be dedicated to instruction in English.

3. Activities to be Housed

Large- and small-group instruction and class work. Students will discuss, read, write, word process, present, dramatize, and conduct research, applying skills and content learned by utilizing material available in the classroom as well as through the technological resources of voice, video, and data.

4. Persons to be Housed

One English teacher and up to 25 students per classroom. A special education teacher or paraprofessional may share instruction of small groups or individuals within the regular classroom.

5. Furniture and Equipment

Furniture and equipment should include student work tables and chairs, a teacher work table and chair, blackboards and whiteboards, display boards, a recessed projection screen, a wall-mounted TV monitor, networked computer terminals and printers, computer tables, open shelving, lockable cabinetry with file drawers, and a lockable storage closet. The English program requires ample book storage space, as well.

6. Special Requirements

All classrooms used for the teaching of English will be wired for voice, video, and data retrieval. All English classrooms should be located near social studies, world language, art, and general music rooms. English and other teamed subjects require sufficient flexibility in classroom design to move walls and combine two or more classes for large-group instruction and other activities.

Family and Consumer Sciences

1. Program Objectives

To help students develop knowledge and skills in the areas of nutrition and good health, consumerism, home arts, and home management.

2. General Description

Students in Grades 6 through 8 receive between one half-hour and one hour of instruction in family and consumer sciences each week for the school year.

3. Activities to be Housed

Large- and small-group instruction and class work. Students will discuss, read, write, observe demonstrations, compute, research, and engage in food preparation, textile arts, etc. Students will utilize print materials stored in the classroom, as well as access technological resources of voice, video, and data.

4. Persons to be Housed

One family and consumer science teacher and up to 18 students in each class.

5. Furniture and Equipment

Furniture and equipment in all classrooms should include student tables and chairs, blackboards and whiteboards, display boards, a recessed projection screen, a teacher work table mounted with demonstration mirror, networked computers with printers, computer tables, and a wall-mounted video monitor. Food labs should include cabinetry, sinks, counter space for food preparation, a refrigerator and freezer, stoves, microwave ovens, dishwashers, and small appliances.

Furniture and equipment in the textile lab should include cabinetry, sewing machines, a computerized sewing and embroidery machine, a washing machine, and a dryer.

6. Special Requirements

Special requirements include large, lockable storage areas in each classroom for supplies and equipment, and access to parking area for easy transport of supplies. Family and consumer sciences labs should be located near health education rooms and physical education areas. All family and consumer sciences classrooms should be wired for voice, video, and data retrieval.

World Languages

1. Program Objectives

To help students develop Level I language proficiency, an awareness of global interconnectedness, and an appreciation of other cultures.

2. General Description
Students in Grades 6 through 8 have approximately four hours of world language instruction each week for the entire school year.

The three-year sequence in Grades 6 through 8 comprises Level I of the chosen language (German, French, or Spanish). Emphasis is placed on listening skills and oral proficiency with instruction in grammar, vocabulary, sentence structure, and cultural awareness.

3. Activities to be Housed
Large- and small-group instruction and class work. Students will speak, listen, read, write, word process, present, dramatize, and conduct research. Cultural projects include cooking, artwork, music, audio and video recording, puppet theater, poetry readings, and presentations.

4. Persons to be Housed
One language teacher and up to 25 students per classroom.

5. Furniture and Equipment
Furniture and equipment should include student tables and chairs, a teacher work table and chair, whiteboards and blackboards, display boards, a recessed projection screen, a recessed map rack, open shelving, lockable cabinetry with file drawers and storage closet, a sink with water fountain and adjacent counter space, networked computer terminals with printers, computer tables, and a wall-mounted video monitor.

6. Special Requirements
All classrooms used for world language should be wired for voice, video, and data, as well as hookups to the district's master language lab. Special requirements include at least one soundproof, movable door between a world language classroom and an adjacent classroom for the purpose of combined activities or large-group instruction. World language classrooms should be located near English, social studies, art, and general music rooms.

Health Education
1. Program Objectives
This program provides opportunities for students to develop the knowledge, attitudes, and skills necessary for maintaining good personal health.

2. General Description
Students in Grades 6 through 8 receive an average of one hour per week in health education instruction. Health education prepares students for the physical, emotional, and social changes experienced during adolescence by encouraging a healthy self-concept and providing relevant health information needed to make constructive decisions about issues such as mental health and substance abuse.

3. Activities to be Housed
Large- and small-group instruction and class work. Students will discuss, read, write, word process, present, dramatize, and conduct research, applying skills and content learned by utilizing print materials stored in the classroom as well as by accessing technological resources of voice, video, and data.

4. Persons to be Housed
One teacher and a maximum of 25 students per classroom.

5. Furniture and Equipment
Furniture and equipment should include student desk/chair combinations, student work tables and chairs, a teacher's work table and chair, a blackboard and a whiteboard, a recessed projection screen, display areas, networked computer terminals with printers, computer tables, open shelving, lockable cabinetry with file drawers, a lockable closet, a sink with water fountain, and a wall-mounted video monitor.

6. Special Requirements
All classrooms used for health education should be wired for voice, video, and data retrieval. Health education classrooms should be located near family and consumer science rooms and physical education areas.

Mathematics
1. Program Objectives
To help students develop computational and problem-solving skills and to apply these skills to real-life situations.

2. General Description
Students in grades 6 through 8 receive approximately four hours of instruction in mathematics each week for the entire school year. Mathematics includes a range of studies from basic operations through pre-algebra, algebra, and geometry. All mathematics courses emphasize logical thinking, problem-solving, and application of skills learned.

3. Activities to be Housed
Large- and small-group instruction and class work. Students will discuss, read, compute, write, present, problem-solve, research and otherwise practice and apply mathematics skills learned.

4. Persons to be Housed
One mathematics teacher and up to 25 students per classroom. A special education teacher and/or paraprofessional may share instruction of small groups or individuals within the regular classroom setting.

5. Furniture and Equipment
Furniture and equipment in each classroom should include student work tables and chairs, a teacher work table and chair, blackboards and

whiteboards with graphing grids, display boards, a recessed projection screen, open shelving, lockable cabinetry with file drawers, a lockable storage closet, networked computer terminals and printers, computer tables, and a wall-mounted video monitor.

6. Special Requirements
All classrooms used for the teaching of mathematics should be wired for voice, video, and data retrieval. Math and other teamed subjects require sufficient flexibility in classroom design to move walls and combine two or more classes for large-group instruction or other activities. All math classrooms should be located near science classroom/labs and technology education labs.

Music
1. Program Objectives
To help students develop an appreciation and knowledge of music to increase their enjoyment, critical analysis, creativity, and cultural awareness.

2. General Description
All students in Grades 6 through 8 have approximately one and one-half hours of music instruction per week for the entire school year. Music students learn to perform vocally and instrumentally (string, bass, woodwind, and percussion) in both large and small ensembles. For those not involved in performing music, the curriculum includes the study of keyboards, guitars, and rock music. Computerized keyboard labs are a growing aspect of the program. Two rehearsal rooms are needed. An instrumental rehearsal room should be large enough to house up to 100 students per rehearsal. A choral rehearsal room should be large enough for up to 75 students per rehearsal. One general music classroom will house up to 25 computerized keyboards for up to 25 students. One small ensemble room is needed for small-group ensembles and lessons.

3. Activities to be Housed
Singing, listening, and instrumental playing in large and small groups, as well as composing, recording, acting, dancing, discussion, and lecture.

4. Persons to be Housed
Up to four full-time instructors with up to 100 students per teacher in large-group rehearsal areas and up to 25 students per teacher in general music and small-group ensemble classrooms.

5. Furniture and Equipment
Furniture and equipment should include movable risers, stackable or folding student chairs, student tables, blackboards and whiteboards, display boards, a recessed projection screen, teachers' work tables, divided shelving for sheet music storage, pianos, music stands, musical instruments, portable and lockable percussion cabinets, networked computers and keyboards, and sound systems. There should be an office area for music teachers with desks

and chairs, networked computer stations, telephones, and lockable filing cabinets.

6. Special Requirements
Choral, instrumental, and general music instruction and small-group lessons are often scheduled simultaneously, necessitating separate rehearsal rooms and instructional spaces. Music instruction areas should be soundproofed. Also needed are lockable storage for instruments and small electronic equipment. One room should be equipped with a sink. During musical performances, large groups of students must be moved efficiently and quickly to and from the stage passing through the spectator seating area. General music classrooms should be located near art, English, social studies, and world language classrooms.

Physical Education
1. Program Objectives
To develop students' health and well-being by helping them to acquire lifetime physical fitness, recreation, sports, and adventure-based activity skills.

2. General Description
All students in Grades 6 through 8 have approximately one and one-half hours of physical education (PE) per week for the entire school year. The PE curriculum emphasizes physical fitness, individual and team sports, and adventure activities. Adaptive PE and occupational and physical therapy should be delivered in suitably equipped spaces adjacent to the gym. Four teaching stations are needed.

Two full-size playing fields adjacent to indoor instructional spaces are needed for outdoor PE activities. A desirable component for outdoor education is the addition of a quarter-mile, all-weather track whose infield is marked for various track and field activities.

3. Activities to be Housed
Aerobics, basketball, field hockey, fitness workouts, floor hockey, gymnastics and tumbling, lacrosse, soccer, softball, team handball, track and field, volleyball, weight training, wrestling, health and safety instruction, co-curricular and extracurricular activities, adaptive PE, changing clothes, and personal hygiene.

4. Persons to be Housed
Four PE teachers, each with a class of up to 25 students. Support staff include an occupational therapist and a physical therapist, both of whom work with students outside of regularly scheduled PE classes.

5. Furniture and Equipment
Furniture and equipment should include teachers' desks and chairs for PE

offices, lockable storage in offices, gymnastics equipment, game equipment, movable "Project Adventure" equipment, assorted balls, racquets, and other small equipment, aerobic machines, and weight-training equipment.

6. Special Requirements
Physical education spaces should have ready access to playing fields; sufficient storage for both large and small equipment; a wood or composite floor; acoustically treated ceilings; solid or fabric-covered movable room dividers; padded walls from floor to 8 feet above floor; boys' and girls' locker rooms with secure, individual lockers; changing areas, lavatories, and individual showers; fresh air ventilation; and staff offices with showers. PE areas should be located near health education and family and consumer science classrooms.

Science
1. Program Objectives
To help students develop skills and knowledge about the physical, biological, and earth sciences.

2. General Description
Students in Grades 6 through 8 receive approximately four hours of science instruction each week for the entire school year. Science instruction focuses on biological, physical, and earth sciences. The content and skills taught in science are often included in an interdisciplinary approach to instruction, which also includes aspects of mathematics and technology education. All science rooms should include two distinct areas: one for classroom instruction and one for lab activities.

3. Activities to be Housed
Large- and small-group instruction and class work. Students will read, write, compute, problem-solve, research, observe, demonstrate, experiment, and otherwise practice and apply science concepts learned, utilizing material available in the classroom as well as accessing technological resources of voice, video and data.

4. Persons to be Housed
One science teacher and up to 24 students per classroom. A special education teacher or paraprofessional may share instruction of small groups or individuals within the regular classroom setting.

5. Furniture and Equipment
Furniture and equipment in each classroom should include student work tables and chairs or desk/chair combinations, a teacher worktable and chair, permanent lab stations with impermeable surfaces, a special portable lab station for disabled students, a teacher demonstration area, lockable cabinetry and a storage closet, blackboards and whiteboards, display boards, a recessed projection screen, a wall-mounted video monitor, networked computer terminals and printers, computer tables, sinks with hot

and cold water in all lab and demonstration spaces, chemical shower/eye wash with drain, adequate ventilation, and required safety equipment.

6. Special Requirements
All science classroom/labs should be wired for voice, video, and data retrieval. In addition to classroom storage, science requires a separate storage and materials preparation area. This space should include the following: a sink with vented hood; lockable, vented cabinets for the secure storage of acids and other hazardous materials; lockable chemical storage cabinets; open shelving for instructional materials; and a refrigerator. All science classrooms/labs should be located near math classrooms and technology education labs.

Social Studies
1. Program Objectives
To help students develop knowledge and understanding of world cultures and an increased awareness of the individual's role in society at large.

2. General Description
Students in Grades 6 through 8 have approximately four hours of instruction in social studies per week for the entire school year. The social studies curriculum encompasses the study of geography, history, sociology, economics, and current events. Skills emphasized include reading, writing, critical thinking, presentation, project development, individual teamwork, and active inquiry. The content and skills emphasized in social studies are often included in an interdisciplinary approach to instruction, which also includes aspects of English, world language, art, and music.

3. Activities to be Housed
Large- and small-group instruction and class work. Students will discuss, read, write, word process, present, dramatize, and conduct research, applying the skills and content learned by utilizing print materials stored in the classroom as well as accessing technological resources of voice, video, and data.

4. Persons to be Housed
One social studies teacher and up to 25 students per classroom. A special education teacher or paraprofessional may share instruction of small groups or individuals within the regular classroom setting.

5. Furniture and Equipment
Furniture and equipment in each classroom should include student work tables and chairs, a teacher work table and chair, blackboards and whiteboards, display boards, recessed maps, a recessed projection screen, open shelving, lockable cabinetry and a storage closet, a sink with drinking fountain and adjacent counter space, networked computer terminals and printers, computer tables, and a video monitor.

6. Special Requirements
All classrooms used for the teaching of social studies should be wired for voice, video, and data retrieval. Social studies and other teamed subjects require sufficient flexibility in classroom design to move walls and combine two or more classes for large-group instruction or other activities. All social studies classrooms should be located near English, world language, and general music rooms.

Technology Education
1. Program Objectives
To help students develop an understanding of technology through the study and application of materials, tools, and processes in solving problems in communication, manufacturing, construction, and transportation systems.

2. General Description
Students in grades 6 through 8 have an average of one hour of technology education each week for the school year. The technology education program will focus on application of knowledge, skills, insights, and tools to solve problems in communication, manufacturing, construction, and transportation systems.

3. Activities to be Housed
Computer applications, engineering and manufacturing technologies, inventing, graphic design production, simulations, and other activities that apply and integrate math and science skills.

4. Persons to be Housed
Three technology education teachers and up to 24 students in each technology education lab.

5. Furniture and Equipment
Furniture and equipment should include student work tables and chairs, teacher work tables and chairs, blackboards and whiteboards, display boards, a recessed projection screen, lockable cabinetry and a large storage area, sinks, a safety shower/eyewash with drain, exhaust hoods, a spray booth, a soldering bench, networked computer workstations with printers, computer tables, and other equipment necessary for an up-to-date technology education program.

6. Special Requirements
Technology education labs should be located near science and math classrooms. Disabled students will participate in tech ed through the use of electronic resources located in these labs.

Shared and Common Areas

Special Education Resource Room

1. Program Objectives

To provide special education services to identified students who remain in mainstream classes so that they may learn to function successfully in a regular school setting.

2. General Description

Students with identified disabilities that preclude their continuous participation in the regular classroom are scheduled into a resource class for assistance and support as specified in individual education plans established by the Planning and Placement Team.

3. Activities to be Housed

Individual and small-group tutoring, other independent and small-group learning activities, individual testing, computer-assisted instruction, and conferences with individuals or small groups of students.

4. Persons to be Housed

One special education teacher, one instructional paraprofessional, and groups of between six and twelve students.

5. Furniture and Equipment

Furniture and equipment should include student work tables and chairs, a teacher work table and chair, blackboards and whiteboards, a recessed projection screen, display boards, open shelving, lockable cabinetry including file drawers and a storage closet, computer terminals with printers, computer tables, a wall-mounted video monitor, and a sink with drinking fountain and adjacent counter space.

6. Special Requirements

All special education rooms should be wired for voice, video, and data retrieval. Special education resource rooms should be centrally located and have basic furnishings and equipment similar to those in the regular classroom.

Special Education Self-Contained Program

1. Program Objectives

To enable students with multiple disabilities to learn an individually prescribed curriculum at rates and depths appropriate to their potential, and, where possible, to help them develop prevocational skills.

2. General Description

Students with identified disabilities that preclude their continuous participation in the regular classroom are scheduled into the self-contained program for instruction. Their program is delivered as specified in their Individual Education Plans established by the Planning and Placement Team.

3. Activities to be Housed

Individual and small-group instruction, tutoring and enrichment activities, development of life skills (eating, personal hygiene, prevocational tasks, playing), physical therapy routines, and activities that develop gross motor skills.

4. Persons to be Housed

One special education teacher, one instructional paraprofessional, and small groups of students.

5. Furniture and Equipment

Furniture and equipment should include student work tables and chairs; a teacher work table and chair; blackboards and whiteboards; display boards; open shelving; secure cabinetry including file drawers and a lockable storage closet; a quiet area with cots; a kitchenette including a sink with drinking fountain, a cooktop, upper and lower cabinets, and counter space; a computer terminal, a computer table, and a wall-mounted video monitor.

6. Special Requirements

The self-contained special education classroom must have easy access to a fully equipped handicapped bathroom; ceiling height must be ample to allow gross motor activities such as ball throwing.

Teaching Teams

1. Program Objectives

To provide coordination of curriculum and instruction, to maximize supervision of students' overall progress and achievement, to problem-solve, and to communicate efficiently with other groups and individuals both within and outside the school.

2. General Description

Teaching teams will be created based on curriculum and grouping practices.

3. Activities to be Housed

Teaching teams deliver coordinated, curriculum-based instruction to groups of students, as well as planning and aligning instruction to maximize effectiveness.

4. Persons to be Housed

All students and teachers will be assigned to teams in Grades 6 through 8. Teams are balanced in terms of grade level, gender, and individual needs to ensure a diversity of roles and abilities.

5. Furniture and Equipment

Although teamed teachers and students function within regular teaching spaces, teamed teachers require common workrooms to facilitate and encourage collaboration. Storage space for student work, supplies, equipment, and instructional materials are necessary, as are shared teacher computer stations within the workroom (see "Staff Workrooms," below).

Team Learning Areas/Agoras

1. Program Objectives

To provide a large space and central location where students from two to six adjacent classrooms can come together for group instruction and learning.

2. General Description

A large enough space to accommodate an entire team of students is needed. This area should be immediately adjacent to or within the team area, which includes from two to six classrooms.

3. Activities to be Housed

Team meetings, group work and group projects, presentations, group lectures, and guest speaker presentations.

4. Persons to be Housed

Up to an entire team of students (two to six classes) and teachers (two to six).

5. Finishes, Furniture, and Equipment

Finishes, furniture, and equipment should include a combination of carpeted and tiled flooring areas, bench seating, soundproof movable dividers, whiteboards and blackboards, a projection screen, public address speakers, a telephone and intercom system, a sink and counter space, water fountains, male and female restrooms, furniture for displays and group work, multiple computer stations, a storage area, and a shared teaching-team office area.

6. Special Requirements

The size of this area must accommodate a variety of instructional methods and equipment, and should have direct access to an outdoor learning environment

Staff Workrooms

1. Program Objectives

To provide spaces for teachers to prepare and store materials, to prepare lessons, to confer with colleagues, and to communicate by telephone with parents.

2. General Description

Workrooms should be available to all members of teaching teams. Common teacher workrooms encourage discussion about and collaboration on matters of student progress and achievement, curriculum, and instruction. Teacher assignments to specific workrooms should reflect planned organizational patterns.

3. Activities to be Housed

Activities to be housed in teacher workrooms include preparation of lessons, conferences with colleagues, storage of materials, and telephone communication with parents.

Activities to be housed in the material preparation center include researching and downloading from electronic databases, word processing, graphic design, production of paper copies or transparencies, duplication, laminating, and creation of display materials.

4. Persons to be Housed
Each teacher will be assigned to a curriculum cluster and to a particular cluster workroom. In general, about eight teachers will be assigned to each teacher workroom. Two materials preparation centers shall be strategically located.

5. Furniture and Equipment
Each teacher workroom should include a desk and secure file cabinet for each teacher, secure built-in cabinetry and storage cabinets, blackboards and whiteboards, display boards, two networked computer terminals, a wall-mounted video monitor, a private telephone area, and an intercom.

Each materials preparation center should include large worktables, networked computer terminals with color printers, large-capacity copying machines, a laminating machine, a typewriter, paper cutters, a letterpress machine, one overhead projector with recessed projection screen, a wall-mounted monitor with VCR/DVD for previewing, a secure materials supply closet, an intercom, and a telephone.

6. Special Requirements
Teacher work areas should be soundproofed to ensure quiet conditions for lesson preparation, personal calls and telephone conferences, etc. They should be located near clustered classrooms.

Large-Group Instruction Space
1. Program Objectives
To provide space for large-group instruction and other large-group activities, such as meetings, presentations, plays, etc.

2. General Description
The area should accommodate small groups of 100 and large groups of up to 450 people.

3. Activities to be Housed
Grade-level and team meetings, dramatic presentations, assemblies, staff meetings, community meetings, etc.

4. Persons to be Housed
Students, staff, and community members.

5. Furniture and Equipment
The large-group instruction area should include a presentation area; a stage; tiered, amphitheater-style seating; and a full public address system.

6. Special Requirements
The area should be easily accessible to community members as well as the school population. This area might be created in the auditorium with movable partitions (if an auditorium is included in the spec).

Auditorium
1. Program Objectives
To provide a venue for assemblies bringing together nearly the entire school community, as well as large-scale community meetings, dramatic and musical performances, etc.

2. General Description
The auditorium is a fully equipped performance and meeting space with raked orchestra seating, a balcony, and a stage. It seats up to 850 people and is fully disabled accessible. The balcony area can be partitioned off for separate use as a lecture hall, chorus practice/vocal training area, or staff development space, or for other functions.

3. Activities to be Housed
Schoolwide assemblies; musical and dramatic performances; larger-scale academic gatherings and staff-development meetings; community uses including performances, town-hall meetings, lectures, etc.

4. Persons to be Housed
When fully utilized, up to 850 spectators, as well as onstage musicians, performers, etc.

5. Special Requirements
Sound and lighting equipment for professional-level theatrical and musical productions; appropriate acoustical treatments; movable soundproof partitions for balcony; electronic hookups for sound reinforcement for hearing-disabled audience members.

Library/Media Center
1. Program Objectives
To help students and staff develop the ability to use information effectively by fully integrating print and nonprint resources into all curricular areas.

2. General Description
The library/media center provides students and teachers with ongoing access to desired information through printed books and periodicals as well as online and other electronic research resources such as the Internet, databases, etc. Further, it assists them in the development of their own media production skills.

All students in Grades 6 through 8 receive regular instruction in the use of facilities and resources in the library/media center. In addition, all students are guided to become increasingly independent in their use of the library/media center.

3. Activities to be Housed
Materials processing, storage, and circulation; classroom instruction; technology production and television production; administrative and clerical tasks.

4. Persons to be Housed
Up to two library/media specialists, up to two technology technicians, up to four clerical and instructional paraprofessionals, and up to 100 students at one time.

5. Furniture and Equipment
Furniture and equipment should include student work tables and chairs (and/or carrels), staff desks and chairs, computer tables, computer terminals with printers, open shelving for the print collection, lockable storage, blackboards and whiteboards in instructional areas, recessed projection screens, display boards, materials processing counters, a copy machine, a laminating machine, and kiosks for downloading electronic books, book trolleys, and display cases and boards.

6. Special Requirements
The library/media center may require specialized equipment to support media production projects.

Other Shared Learning Spaces
The middle school building will also contain three Computer Education Labs, designed to house computers that are more powerful and sophisticated than those available in the classroom, as well as a Gifted and Talented Resource Room, which houses a variety of resources available to students on an as-needed basis.

Administrative and Support Areas

Administration
1. Program Objectives
To provide leadership, coordination, and support for the instructional program and related services.

2. General Description
General office space is required for the school principal and other administrators and clerical staff. Conference spaces for two groups of between six and 20 people, a materials preparation area, and a staff room are also needed. The public reception area must be large enough to accommodate the normal traffic of visitors, students, and staff.

3. Activities to be Housed
Activities to be housed include telephone responses and personal reception; preparation and distribution of materials; filing and record-keeping; schoolwide communication; conferences with students, staff and parents; and preparation of refreshments for meetings, etc.

4. Persons to be Housed
Individuals to be housed include a principal, up to four other administrators, one principal's secretary, main-office secretaries, a telephone receptionist, a bookkeeper, and one office paraprofessional.

5. Furniture and Equipment
Furniture and equipment should include office and visitor furniture, storage, files, office machines including one networked computer at each desk, a public address system, a telephone system, an alarm-system control panel, a copying machine, supply storage, teacher mailboxes, and a kitchenette with sink and storage.

6. Special Requirements
Requirements include male and female restrooms, natural light and ventilation, the ability to have secure storage of records and petty cash, a coatroom or closet, and direct, fully visible access to the front entrance area. All administrative personnel should have access to a central database of student information as well as other networked software.

Cafeteria and Staff Dining Room
1. Program Objectives
To serve lunch daily to up to 1,000 students in a pleasant, low-stress environment that encourages good nutrition and appropriate social behavior. To provide a useful large-group meeting area for both school and community use.

2. General Description
The cafeteria must accommodate up to 400 students simultaneously. The school cafeteria will also be used as a large-group meeting place for school- and community-related special events. Also, the staff dining room must accommodate up to 70 adults per sitting.

3. Activities to be Housed
Daily lunch for students, large-group meetings of students, students' social events, and general community uses. The staff dining room will house daily lunch for staff members.

4. Persons to be Housed
For meals, the cafeteria should accommodate up to 400 students and four to six supervisory personnel per sitting. When used as a large-group instructional meeting place, the cafeteria should accommodate seating for up to 500 people.

5. Furniture and Equipment
Furniture and equipment in the cafeteria should include removable, multipurpose seating for up to 500 students or community members,; round tables for cafeteria seating; vending machines; sufficient general lighting; water fountains; intercom, public address and telephone systems; and lockable

storage. The staff dining area should be equipped with comfortable, versatile furniture; a kitchenette with sink, counter space and lockable storage; sufficient general lighting; and intercom and telephone systems.

The kitchen will be designed and constructed in accordance with applicable guidelines and in adherence to health codes. There will be office space for the manager and locker/toilet space for the staff. The kitchen will be adjacent to the receiving area. All surfaces will be washable. The following will be included: a combined walk-in cooler/freezer; separate storage for food and cleaning supplies; separate sinks; fire extinguishers; one microwave oven; one double-stack convection oven; a two-compartment pressure steamer and a steam-jacketed kettle; a commercial stove with fire-suppression hood system; a computer and printer; food preparation tables including some with butcher-block surfaces; pots, pans, and other utensils; and serving counters for hot and cold food.

6. Special Requirements
Special requirements include acoustical design to minimize noise (special interior finish materials, acoustical treatments). Design should facilitate ease of circulation for serving, dining, and waste recycling.

Guidance and Pupil Personnel Service
1. Program Objectives
To assist students in their academic and personal development and to serve as consultants to staff and parents.

2. Activities to be Housed
Enrollment and registering of all students; cumulative record-keeping; individual, small-group, and large-group counseling and conferring; individual, small-group and large-group instruction and activities; academic planning and scheduling; and individual and small-group testing.

3. Persons to be Housed
Up to four guidance counselors, up to two school psychologists, one social worker, one speech and language specialist, one English as a Second Language teacher, up to two remedial instructors (or "Chapter I") parapro-fessionals, other specialized service providers, two secretaries, one attendance clerk, one data coordinator, student counselees, parents, and other visitors.

4. Furniture and Equipment
Furniture and equipment should include office and visitor furniture, fire-proof files, office machines including one networked computer at each desk, a telephone and intercom system, a copy machine, display racks for student and parent information, and supply storage.

5. Special Requirements
All guidance offices should be soundproofed for privacy. The guidance

office, main office, and health office should be near each other for coordination of functions and sharing of facilities and equipment.

All guidance personnel should have access to a central database of student demographic information as well as other networked programs.

Health Office
1. Program Objectives
To provide quality health care and assistance to ill students and staff and to offer preventive health services as required by the state.

2. General Description
The health office will serve the entire middle school population. It must be staffed daily by licensed registered nurses, who dispense general health care to students in need and conduct screenings and other preventive programs as required. School nurses collaborate with administrative, guidance, and pupil personnel staff on a daily basis and participate in individual students' planning meetings as needed.

3. Activities to be Housed
First aid and emergency care, special physical examinations, record-keeping, and screening services including vision, hearing, height, weight, and scoliosis (curvature of the spine) tests.

4. Persons to be Housed
Persons to be housed include up to two full-time nurses, one health paraprofessional, ill students and staff.

5. Furniture and Equipment
Furniture and equipment should include separate and secure cabinets for medications and supplies, secure cabinets for charts and records, a refrigerator, an examining table, emergency equipment, nurses' desks, resting cots, two sinks (as required by OSHA), a telephone, an intercom connected to all areas of the building, a network link to the administrative computer system, and any special equipment needed to conduct the screenings listed above.

6. Special Requirements
Special requirements include a location adjacent to administrative offices and within view of the students' pick-up and drop-off area at the front of the building. Bathroom facilities for handicapped students, separate treatment rooms, an isolation area, and partitioned areas for ill students are necessities in the school health office.

Parent Resource Room
1. Program Objectives/General Description
To provide a place where parents can meet informally; receive information about the school, its staff, and its curriculum; and participate in one-on-one or small-group meetings with faculty and other school personnel.

2. Activities to be Housed
Meetings and informal interactions among parents; educational programs designed to help parents assist their children in learning activities; conferences between parents and teachers; PTA planning sessions.

3. Persons to be Housed
Small groups of parents and school personnel.

4. Furniture and Equipment
A conference table and chairs, as well as additional seating for larger-group meetings; magazine and brochure racks for information display and distribution; a telephone and intercom; a computer and computer station; a blackboard or whiteboard.

Custodial and Maintenance Service
1. Program Objectives
To provide an aesthetically pleasant, operationally safe, healthy, and economically efficient environment to enhance the learning process.

2. General Description
The custodial office and workspace should accommodate the custodial and maintenance staff of the middle school. Office and work space should accommodate a desk and file cabinet for the head custodian, a desk and file cabinet for maintenance workers, secure lockable cabinets for small and valuable custodial tools and supplies, and secure lockable cabinets for maintenance tools and parts. The custodial workspace should be in close proximity to the school's delivery dock and to the fire alarm annunciator panel.

3. Activities to be Housed
Small repairs, furniture assembly, repairing and cleaning of custodial equipment, changing clothes, eating lunch, and completing paperwork.

4. Persons to be Housed
Anticipated number of custodians would reach 11 (on two shifts) and two maintenance mechanics.

5. Furniture and Equipment
Furniture and equipment should include desks, files, benches, storage cabinets, clothing lockers, a lunch table, a telephone, an intercom, a washbasin, toilet facilities, and two deep service sinks.

6. Special Requirements
Ample storage space (fire-rated for combustible materials) must be provided for a minimum of three months' worth of custodial supplies. A separate, lockable secure area must be provided for maintenance supplies such as plumbing, electrical, and hardware sundries. The loading dock serving the custodial area must also be in close proximity to the kitchen, but, for sanitary

reasons, a provision must be made so that custodial/maintenance supplies and material do not have to be unloaded through the kitchen for sanitary reasons.

The custodial and maintenance shop will have ample ventilation, lighting, and numerous electrical outlets on several circuits. A floor drain should be provided in each custodial workroom. Custodial closets should be placed appropriately throughout the building. Storage space is required for chairs, desks, tables, cabinets, and other equipment not in use. Separate storage space, readily accessible by staff, is required for instructional supplies, books, paper, etc.

Table 7.1 shows probable net square footage (nsf) requirements for program-related spaces described in the foregoing draft specification. It does not include non-program–related spaces such as faculty and administrative restrooms, mechanical and electrical rooms, building storage rooms, receiving/custodial spaces, and other spaces, which count toward total gross square footage (gsf). In general, it is possible to estimate gsf by applying a multiplier of 1.5 to nsf. Thus, gsf for this hypothetical facility would probably be about 265,000 square feet.

Table 7.1 Summary of Net Square Footage Requirements

Description	Number of Spaces	Square Feet per Unit	Square Feet per Program Area
Art	4	2,000	8,000
English	12	900	10,800
Computer Education Labs	3	2,000	6,000
Family/Consumer Science	3	1,200	3,600
Foreign Language	9	900	8,100
Health Education	1	900	900
Library Media	1	10,000	10,000
Mathematics	9	900	8,100
Music			
Instrumental Rehearsal &	2	40,000	8,000
Choral Rehearsal	1	2,000	2,000
Vocal/Electronic/Theory	2	1,600	3,200
Small Group Room	3	640	1,920
Physical Education			
Four Station Gym	1	9,600	9,600
Small Exercise Room	2	2,500	5,000
Gym Storage	1	1,000	1,000
Gym Locker Rooms	2	1,300	2,600
Learning Strategies Support	4	450	1,800

Table 7.1 Summary of Net Square Footage Requirements, Continued

Science Lab & Instruction	9	1,500	1,3500
Science Preparation Room	2	250	500
Social Studies	9	900	8,100
Special Education Resource Room	9	400	3,600
Special Education Self Contained	2	1,050	2,100
Technology Education	3	1,800	5,400
Grade Level Core Team Teacher Rooms	4	800	3,200
Special Area Teacher Workstations	3	400	1,200
Large Group Instruction	1	10,000	10,000
Gifted & Talented Resource Room	1	1,000	1,000
Cafeteria	2	4,500	9,000
Kitchen/Serving Expansion	1	2,000	2,000
Auditorium			
Stage Area	1	3,700	3,700
House (Seating Area)	1	11,000	11,000
Wheelchair Locations	10	180	1,800
Reception & Secretarial	1	1,300	1,300
Principal's Office	1	400	400
AP/House Administrators	3	350	1,050
Guidance Counselor Offices	5	200	1,000
Psychologist's Office	2	200	400
Social Worker's Office	1	150	150
Work/Copy/Storage	1	450	450
Main Conference Room	1	400	400
8-Person Conference Room	1	300	300
Nurse's Office/Exam Room	1	1,000	1,000
Staff Dining Room	1	1,400	1,400
Book Storage Rooms	2	600	1,200
Parent Resource Room	1	900	900
NET PROGRAM AREA			**176,670**

Systems

Integrated Electronic Communication System
The communication system shall include the following:

- Each normally occupied teaching space, office, staff lounge, administrative space, boiler room, kitchen, and receiving area shall be linked by a telephone and speaker, providing public address, emergency, outside line access, and internal private communications.
- All spaces shall receive emergency call announcements.Data Infrastructure

Data Infrastructure
The building will feature a sophisticated technology infrastructure, allowing for "on demand" individual wireless word processing and Internet access in all spaces. In addition, each classroom will have computer network drops, and wiring should also permit connection to the teacher's station in each classroom. Capacity for expansion must also be included.

Clocks and Bell System
All normally occupied areas shall have a clock showing hours and minutes connected to a master clock that also controls bells and/or chimes. The master clock shall automatically correct and adjust all clocks to the correct time. Clock system may be integrated with the other communications systems. Clock system shall be state-of-the-art equipment.

Fire Alarms and Security
The middle school of the future shall be equipped with state-of-the-art, fully code-compliant fire detection, alarm, and sprinkler systems. Remote annunciator panels showing location of the source of the alarm shall be located near the administrative area and front door of the school and the custodial office. Upon activation of an alarm, an evacuation signal shall be transmitted throughout the school and a signal transmitted to a central station monitoring service. The alarm shall signal until manually reset. Sprinkler heads shall be carefully located and positioned to prohibit tampering. Alarms shall be easily heard throughout the building and visual alarms shall be proved as per code.

The systems will be integrated so that one monitoring agency protects the entire structure.

All required fire extinguishers shall be placed into recessed cabinets with the doors to such cabinets equipped with audible local alarms.

Heating, Ventilating and Air-Conditioning (HVAC) System
The HVAC system shall be carefully and thoroughly studied so that only the most reliable, flexible, and energy efficient system is provided.

In addition to a boiler plant, there must be standby reserve capacity and redundancy to provide heat and hot water if the primary source fails or requires service during the heating season. An alternate source of hot water for domestic use shall be provided for summer operation so major boilers may be shut down during non-heating season.

Connection to external emergency power sources shall be provided (including all code-required automatic transfer switches) to keep vital building components and areas functioning in an emergency.

The school will be fully air-conditioned.

Plumbing
Building shall exceed all minimum code requirements for number of toilet fixtures, sinks, and drinking fountains.

All fixtures shall be heavy-duty and of vandal-resistant design. Local service valves and isolation valves shall be provided. Toilet partitions shall be heavy-duty and vandal-resistant, with high-quality hardware. Fixtures shall be wall-hung. The building shall be divided into sections with isolation and drain valves in each section.

Electrical Distribution
Each normally occupied space shall be furnished with numerous electrical convenience outlets located throughout the space to permit flexibility of room layout and eliminate use of extension cords. Power in each classroom shall be from two sources, one for exclusive use of computers and the other for general use. Outlets in corridors and storage areas shall be located on centers no greater than twenty-five feet to permit easy use of vacuums and floor machines.

Each electrical distribution panel shall have a twenty-five percent expansion capacity.

Hardware
All hardware shall be heavy duty. All panic devices shall be rim type with removable mullions rather than vertical rod type. All doors—stairwell doors, corridor smoke doors, etc.—shall be held open with magnetic devices connected to the fire alarm system.

Elevator
The elevator will be of the size and capacity to accommodate an automatic floor scrubbing machine, as well as the moving of desks, furniture, and large equipment.

Site Development

Parking and Traffic Flow

* There shall be adequate parking space for facility, administrative staff, custodial/maintenance staff, visitors, and volunteers. Extensive community use of the school on evenings and weekends should be anticipated in the design of parking areas.
* Parking areas and traffic-flow patterns should be designed to accommodate buses during loading and unloading, delivery vehicles and access to loading dock, employee parking, and visitor parking.
* The bus queuing area should be separate and distinct from parking areas and the parent pickup area and shall accommodate the full complement of buses servicing the school. There should be a separate parent pick-up area.
* Traffic flow shall have adequate and safe sight distances. Walking patterns shall be designed to minimize crossing vehicular traffic.

Accessibility, Safety, and Aesthetics

* Adequate lighting shall be provided for evening use of the building along all sides of the school, walkways, and parking areas.
* Disabled access shall be provided per code.
* All levels of the school shall be above grade. Windowless interior spaces should be avoided to the extent possible.
* All sides of the school shall be designed to be aesthetically attractive and accessible.
* Interior courtyards shall be designed and landscaped to be reasonably maintenance-free, and must be fully accessible.
* The entire site shall be landscaped to be pleasing for the school's occupants and neighbors as well as to be easily and efficiently maintained.
* Provisions shall be made to accommodate snow plows and resultant snow piles.

Outdoor Physical Educational/Athletics Program

* The site shall accommodate the physical education program of the school and appropriate community use during after-school hours.
* Fields shall accommodate a variety of sports, including soccer, field hockey, and track.
* Indoor restrooms shall be easily accessible from the field.

Academic and Recreational Uses of Site

Given a relatively secure site made safe by fencing, surveillance, location, and other means, the site can potentially contain a variety of academic and recreational areas, including:

* Gardens (including butterfly gardens)
* Walking trails

- Outdoor environmental classrooms
- Fish pond
- Weather measurement and prediction stations
- Specialized recreational areas, including dance courts, volleyball courts, bocce and shuffleboard courts, large chess and checker boards, model car racing inclines
- Message boards and kiosks
- Art display areas
- Musical performance areas
- Memorial spaces
- Flag poles with specialty flags

Environmental Considerations

To ensure that the environment for learning and working is safe, effective, efficient, and aesthetically pleasing, the building shall have an open, inviting atmosphere, characterized by natural light, adequate ventilation, open spaces, and functional effectiveness in all design features, furnishings, and equipment.

General Considerations

Every entryway shall have a hard floor finish and recessed mats. The entrance and all visitors must be visible to main office personnel. All outer doors other than front entrance must prevent access from the outside during the school day as well as after school hours. The floorplan should minimize length of travel between team clusters and shared common spaces. To enhance security and help prevent theft, access to community areas such as gym, cafeteria, and auditorium must be segregated from rest of building.

Windows

All windows should be operable, with screens. Classroom windows should include room-darkening shades. Windows should abate loss of heat.

Lighting

All lighting shall be designed to maximize students' learning and personal comfort and minimize energy consumption.

Health and Safety

Every consideration should be given to prevention of "sealed building syndrome," exposure to radon gas, and other hazards. Adequate ventilation and air circulation, and use of nonallergenic interior finish materials should be priorities.

Aesthetics

The building should have a unified interior design with attention to appropriateness, functionality, and durability of structural elements and furnishings, pleasing and practical colors and textures, noise control, and many recessed display areas for student work.

Options

- If a school district wishes to reduce the number of square feet in the specification, an option would be to combine the technology and science lab spaces into a joint-use room. This would allow different technologies to be put into different science labs to allow for specialized instruction. In fact, a reworked curriculum of the future might provide for combined science and technology instruction.
- Likewise, a portion of the auditorium could be used as the 400-student large-group instruction area and also as a vocal/choral area, making for better utilization of space. Movable dividers can be included as needed to make this happen.
- The school as specified prescribes ample square footage in all areas. If necessary, specific areas could be cut back by shrinking square footage.

Part III: Issues in Middle School Planning, Design, and Construction

Chapter 8

Site Design and Landscape Architecture for the Future Middle School
by Barry Blades, ASLA

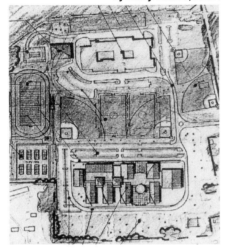

Like so many other aspects of school planning and design, the process of locating a site for a new school, designing that site, and providing an appropriate landscape architectural treatment has grown much more complicated over the past two decades or so. Today, landscape architects designing and landscaping the grounds of a typical middle school must respond to a very broad range of sometimes-conflicting needs, regulations, and contingencies, the most important of which are discussed below.

What will the future bring? That, of course, is always hard to say. But, to extrapolate from current trends, it is likely that the many forces now affecting the siting and landscaping of our schools will intensify and that their interaction will become even more complex in the years to come.

The Automobile

Americans love their cars. There's nothing new in that, but what we have noticed in recent years is an increasing tendency for elementary and middle school children to be taken to and from school by private car. Many parents seem to have gotten in the habit of picking their children up from school for after-school activities—and this, in turn, appears to have encouraged them to start bringing their kids to school by car, as well.

At suburban elementary and middle schools these days, it's not unusual to see a significant number of parents waiting in their cars for their children at the end of the school day. That alone puts additional pressure on the school site, but the situation can be worse at the middle schools because of the greater independence of middle school–age children. Some, of course, arrive at and depart from school on the school bus; others are driven by parents, older siblings, or the parents of friends; and still others come and go by foot. This can create tangled, intersecting vehicular and pedestrian traffic patterns. Though mornings are generally less problematic (everyone doesn't arrive at once, and cars don't wait around), the traffic congestion caused by this combination of school buses, private-car drop-offs, and pedestrian traffic can still be significant. Designers are having to accommodate this trend—that is, to develop strategies for relieving the congestion and lessening the conflict—in their designs for new middle school sites.

Additionally, although parking space is always at a premium on new school sites, the challenge of providing adequate parking has been exacerbated recently because of the increasing after-hours use of middle school buildings by the wider community. It's seldom, if ever, possible to provide all the parking space needed for after-hours users (or for visitors attending a special event), but designers try to accommodate such needs in their plans—for instance, by earmarking lawns and/or athletics fields for occasional drive-up parking, by identifying convenient off-site parking areas (in nearby parks or around nearby churches), or by designing paved areas that are used infrequently (e.g., bus queue lanes, maintenance roads, etc.) and that can serve as overflow, special-event parking.

Figure 8.1. Separation of vehicular circulation patterns.
In this site plan for Memorial Middle School, Middlebury, Connecticut, bus drop-off and staff parking are on the right of the building; parent drop-off and visitor parking to the left. (The existing building appears in white; the area with vertical lines is the addition.) In this scheme, the building entrance on the bus queue side is open only during arrival and dismissal times; all daily visitors are required to access the building through the main entrance, located near the parent drop-off and visitor parking.

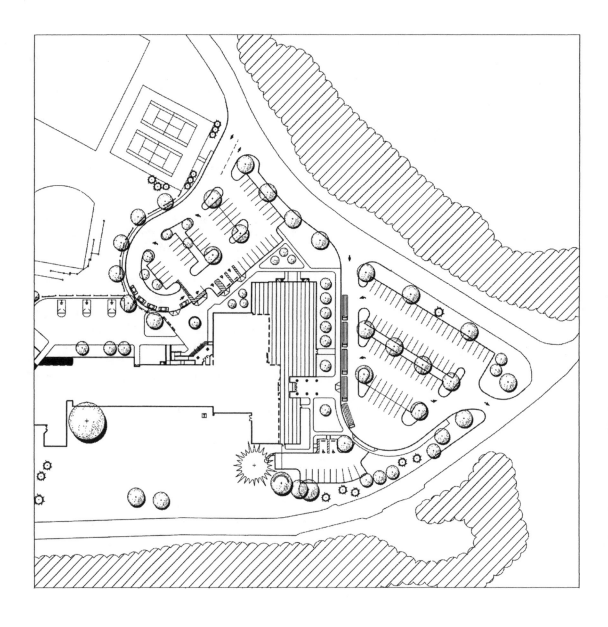

Beyond the adequacy of parking space, the issue of *convenient accessibility* of parking areas to school entrances has also become more problematic than in the past. Today, security concerns encourage administrators at many schools to maintain only one open entrance during the normal school day. Typically, both parent queuing and visitor parking areas are located near this entrance so that administrators can properly monitor the flow of these occasional users. Because of the lack of available space, the bus loop and faculty parking are then located to access other building entrances that can be locked down after the morning arrival and afternoon departure times. Even on a relatively large site, therefore, it's likely that some parking areas will be rather far from the entrance. When coupled with accessibility requirements mandated by the Americans with Disabilities Act (ADA) and other, similar laws and regulations, this can pose some thorny challenges to landscape architects.

Site Conditions

The relatively large sites required for new school construction are becoming increasingly rare commodities. U.S. suburbs are overbuilt, and the competition for desirable land for other uses (residential, commercial, etc.) is tremendous. Thus, there are fewer and fewer "perfect" sites on which to place a new school. Elsewhere in this book (see Chapter 2, "Cost, Change, and School Construction") mention is made of the impact that this situation is having on first costs because of the stepped-up need, in so many cases, to perform extensive site remediation (e.g., grading, rock excavation, etc.) before construction can begin. But the shortage of suitable sites is causing other side-effects, as well.

Among these are the site-design challenges that emerge when new-school sites are in close proximity to neighbors. Twenty years ago, a new school building could be plunked down in the middle of fields or a forested area, and designers did not typically need to be overly concerned with the school's impact on distant residential or commercial properties. Now, noisy, smelly, or "messy" areas—school bus queuing areas, athletics fields, and service areas with garbage-disposal facilities (which have grown larger because of recycling regulations mandating a number of dumpsters or bins for different kinds of waste)—must often be carefully screened so as not to cause consternation to nearby homeowners and businesses.

Situating schools in developed neighborhoods can cause yet another quandary for landscape architects. Zoning regulations and a community's desire to maintain a consistent neighborhood landscape aesthetic often necessitate extensive landscaping at school sites. Unfortunately, the operating budgets of many schools are inadequate for the level of maintenance such landscaping requires. The design challenge, then, is to successfully blend the school's landscape into the fabric of the neighborhood without putting a burden on operating budgets.

The shortage of suitable sites also means that there are few new-school sites today that do not contain environmentally sensitive areas within their boundaries. In the Northeast, this most often entails wetlands areas that are protected by federal, state, and municipal regulatory agencies. To obtain permits from these agencies for activities that might impact the wetlands, it is often necessary to develop strategies for wetland "mitigation" that will compensate for the loss of wetland functional value. This mitigation can take a number of forms: for example, the cleanup of degraded wetland areas, the introduction of new landscaping that will provide food and habitat for wildlife, or the creation of new areas that provide wetland value. One form of mitigation is the use of wetland areas as outdoor classrooms for schoolchildren studying biology, ecology, and botany.

But there are additional considerations when a school site contains environmentally sensitive zones: in some cases, wetlands and bodies of standing water must be fenced off for safety reasons. In almost all cases, stormwater management strategies (for example, biofilter pools and onsite detention basins) must be implemented to protect adjacent downstream properties. While wetlands and other bodies of standing water can be environmentally beneficial, they can also cause problems. If not properly designed and/or controlled, they can become breeding areas for mosquitoes—raising health concerns associated with these insects. Pesticides used for mosquito control can also cause concern.

Outdoor Classrooms

The designation of certain portions of onsite wetlands as "outdoor classrooms" has generally been well received by regulatory agencies. Of course, this kind of outdoor learning space is much more than just a "mitigation strategy" designed to secure agency approval. It's also a place where schoolchildren can observe the processes of nature close up and firsthand, and that can be especially important at the middle school level because of middle schools' focus on exploratory, hands-on, project-oriented learning.

Outdoor classrooms for the onsite study of environmental science—whether they're placed in wetlands or other kinds of interesting natural terrain—don't look much like "classrooms," and it's doubtful that they'd be recognizable as such by the lay observer. For example, they don't contain tables, chairs, or any of the other components one might expect to see in a learning space, indoors or out. Rather, they're distinguished by what they *don't* have: compared to other areas of the site, they're relatively un-landscaped, so that students can witness the natural cycles of local plant and animal life and can study the evolution of an ecological system over time. Preparation of such areas often involves the restoration of a degraded natural system, and we always consult with a school's biology and environmental science faculty before "designing" (if that's the right word) this type of outdoor classroom environment to make sure that it corresponds with the school's programmatic needs. Schools can make extremely creative use of such areas, the wetlands area was being overrun by an invasive plant species, and students helped monitor the invader's progress and even assisted in its eradication.

It should mentioned that the outdoor classroom concept isn't restricted to wetlands areas—nor to the study of environmental science. Because of the advantages of "loop" circulation patterns within a middle school facility, many middle schools include one or more courtyard spaces bounded on three or four sides by the building itself. These spaces can be designed for use as outdoor classrooms, though it's unfortunately our experience that such spaces, even when they're outfitted with tables, chairs, and other components, too often go unused in actual practice. The reasons for this are several: teachers and administrators worry about the noise that might be generated—and which might be amplified by sound waves' bouncing up against the walls of a courtyard, disrupting activities inside the building—or they're concerned about adequately supervising children in the outdoor space. It's clear that using such spaces well requires commitment and ingenuity on the part of a school's faculty and administration. One suggestion might be to link outdoor learning to the program of the adjacent interior spaces, and to make sure that the activities that occur in the outdoor space are relatively passive, non–noise-generating ones: for example, where an art room opens onto a courtyard, that outdoor space might be used as a place where students can sketch or paint in full natural daylight.

Athletics Fields and Community Use

At the same time that school sites have been getting tighter (smaller, more constrained by environmental regulations and by the concerns of close-by neighbors), the demands placed on these sites have been growing. Elsewhere in this book, much is made of the trend toward after-hours use of middle school buildings by the wider community. What's true indoors is true outdoors, as well. Just as middle school auditoriums are increasingly playing host to local theater groups, town hall–type community meetings, and so on, middle school grounds are doing double-duty: as play areas for children during the school day and as the venue for organized sports (both children's and adults') when school is not in session. Today, it's pretty much expected that a new middle school's site will include regulation- or near-regulation-size playing fields for a variety of sports (or fields that can easily be converted, on a seasonal basis, from one sport to another— baseball to soccer, for example). Some new middle schools' sites also include walking/running tracks intended for use not just by the school's phys ed program but also, during off-hours and non–school days, by adult joggers and even for charity fundraising walkathons.

There's no question that greater use of school grounds by the surrounding community is a good thing—it enables the fuller use of resources that, in fact, *belong* to the entire community and it plays a major role in helping develop taxpayer/voter support for a school construction project. But it can magnify the challenges faced by site designers. As flat, easily developed land has become scarce, towns have sometimes had to choose sites with more significant topographic changes. These steeply sloping sites often require the terracing of amenities such as parking and athletics fields to minimize construction cost. Unfortunately, this terracing makes it more difficult to accommodate athletics fields. Also, ADA-required accessibility to these fields can be more difficult to achieve. (As an aside, it's also important to note that spectator seating at athletics fields must be completely accessible to physically disabled people—a topic that's dealt with in some detail in Chapter 13, "Exceptional Kids Need More Feet.")

Just as we're witnessing an increasing need for regulation-size athletics fields (and more of them!) at the middle school level, we're also seeing a stepped-up demand for *better-quality* fields. Schools and the town parks and recreation departments that in many cases coordinate athletic fields' after-hours use want better turf, better irrigation and subsurface drainage systems, higher-quality infields for baseball and softball fields, and better furniture and amenities. The rationale is simple: not only is a high quality field better able to stand up to the wear and tear of nearly constant use, but a better field is also a safer field. If at all possible, enhancements like the ones just listed should be included in a new school's initial construction budget, since they'll help control maintenance costs over the long haul. Given how undependable maintenance budgets can be from year to year, that's an extremely important consideration.

Safety and Security

Middle school security is aided by so-called "passive" site design. The principle—which has been widely applied to urban schools and which is now being used in suburban settings, as well—is a simple one: avoid the potential for trouble by *not* creating spaces where trouble might develop. Building exteriors should be free from nooks and crannies that could serve as hiding places; plantings should either be minimal and low to the ground so as not to provide places to lurk, or composed of what is sometimes called "hostile shrubbery"—that is, thorny bushes that would make very unpleasant hideouts. The goal, obviously, is to maximize the ability to easily surveil the entire exterior. In suburban settings, that same principle mandates, where possible, that a school building be surrounded by a ring road that enables local police to conduct 24-hour surveillance of both the building exterior and adjacent athletics fields and that gives unrestricted access to fire department and other emergency vehicles in the event of an emergency.

So far, most middle schools are making only limited use of surveillance by closed-circuit television (CCTV) cameras. (The use of CCTV and other electronic surveillance and access equipment is much more common, and sophisticated, at the high school level.) Some middle schools are placing such cameras at their front doors and perhaps at a few locations scattered around the grounds. And concern for safety and security has led to an increase of outdoor lighting (also necessary for CCTV) on middle school sites. Outdoor lighting, however, once again raises the issue of the school's impact on adjacent residential properties. (Measures for improving middle school security, both interior and exterior, are treated in more detail in Chapter 9, "Middle School Security: Closed Yet Open.")

Maintenance

Finally, It would be irresponsible if we didn't return, at least briefly, to the impact of maintenance budgets on landscaping. We've already mentioned the fact that community-enforced landscaping standards and the heavy use of athletics fields can create dilemmas for the landscape architect who wants to make sure that ongoing maintenance doesn't outstrip a school's operating budget.

Funds earmarked for groundskeeping and gardening are—as every public school administrator is well aware—extremely limited, and those budgets are getting more pinched all the time. (The expense of cultivating flowerbeds that change from spring to summer to fall is simply too hard to justify in an era when districts are scrambling to find ways of reducing the number of children per class, raising teacher's pay, etc.,) Today, landscape designers who work on schools tend to cast a microscopic eye even on such issues as whether a particular patch of lawn can be mowed by a large-width riding mower or requires a hand-mower. Decisions regarding whether to plant evergreen or deciduous bushes and trees and whether to use grass lawns or some other sort of ground-cover in certain locations (especially courtyards) are also dependent on the long-term maintenance costs of the various alternatives.

Similarly, while no one denies that wood site furniture looks and feels terrific, few districts have the money to spare for the periodic sanding and refinishing that's needed to keep wooden furniture in presentable shape. From a design point of view, the situation is made more palatable by the fact that much of the new outdoor furniture that's being made from recycled plastics and other high-tech materials is not only durable but looks pretty good, too. Cognizant of the limitations of operating budgets, designers are encouraging building committees to consider more durable materials that may have a higher up-front cost (e.g., concrete curbing, which is more resistant to damage from snow plows than is bituminous curbing) but that will reduce maintenance costs down the road.

As mentioned at the start of this chapter, it is reasonable to assume that the future of landscape design for middle schools can be extrapolated from current trends. As suitable sites become even fewer, as environmental and accessibility regulations remain in force or intensify, as community use of school grounds expands, as concerns for children's safety and security heighten, and—assuming that the nation's oil supply remains unthreatened and Americans' love affair with their cars undiminished—as schools' need to accommodate private automobile traffic grows, site designers' and landscape architects' task will become ever more complex. Solutions will, undoubtedly, be found, even to the most difficult challenges. But arriving at those solutions will be a much smoother process if decision-makers understand all the forces at work, and the way they interact.

Chapter 9

Middle School Security: Closed Yet Open

by James A. Beaudin, AIA
and Jeffrey A. Sells, AIA

In recent discussion of school security, the needs of middle schools have received scant attention. Unlike elementary school pupils, middle-schoolers are old enough to heed warnings from their teachers, meaning that one central concern that guides security design in K-5 schools—the potential for kidnapping by estranged parents—becomes less critical. And, unlike high schoolers, children of middle school age are typically very communicative, which means that problems can often be averted by paying close attention to what children do and say. This demands an open environment, yet one that adequately protects children's safety and school property. Maximizing security at middle schools therefore requires achieving a delicate balance: imposing necessary barriers (whether physical, electronic or psychological) while doing everything possible to design an environment in which students and staff feel at home.

Team Spirit

Among the most prevalent internal problems that middle schools must deal with is bullying—especially the intimidation of younger, smaller children by those who are older and larger. The potential for trouble is exacerbated during the middle school years: children entering adolescence are subject to rapid growth spurts at the same time that they're first grappling with the rules of socially appropriate adult behavior. The way in which most middle schools are now being organized takes account of this unique stage in children's lives—and it's here that architectural decisions can have the most obvious effect in promoting safety.

Most middle schools today are being organized by "teams." (The precise term differs from district to district: "clusters," "pods," and "communities" are similar concepts.) Generally, each team—there may be several for each grade level—consists of a group of 80 to 110 students and the four or five faculty members who teach and supervise them. Intensive, daily interaction between children and the same core faculty enhances learning and promotes a sense of belonging that can be critically important to children of this age.

Just as important, however, is the careful, physical segregation of each grade level from the others—to inhibit any opportunity for cross-grade bullying. At the very least, the different teams are assigned to separate wings or corridors, with a special emphasis on keeping sixth graders apart from their older, sometimes much bigger schoolmates. At Fairfield Woods Middle School in Fairfield, Connecticut—a 1960s-era building that underwent full-scale renovation six years ago—Principal Lynda Cox explained that the simple strategy of painting each team's area a distinctive color has helped reinforce boundaries. Using different colors to mark off the teams' areas bolsters each child's sense of having a "home base," discourages wandering and underscores the team's connectedness. At some new middle schools, each team has its own separate wing—often with classrooms clustered around a shared hallway or resource area. A separate corridor leads to each cluster, and students from one team never travel into another team's hallway. Opportunities for the roughhousing that can occur in crowded hallways are further reduced when all of a team's lockers are located in that team's own corridor.

Effective communication among faculty is a key component of security, and this, too, can be enhanced architecturally. In some new schools designed according to the cluster concept, each cluster contains a faculty meeting room. Though such conference rooms primarily serve as spaces for curriculum planning, they are also useful as spaces where faculty can share information about students in private and prepare strategies to ensure that any problem is handled swiftly.

Other Architectural Strategies

Communication is also fostered through appropriate placement of guidance and administrative areas. Offices for guidance counselors and related personnel—the school nurse, the speech therapist—should be adjacent to one another *and* to the school's administrative offices, so that staff can quickly share information if a problem arises. Just as crucial, these suites should be centrally located, easily and equally accessible from each team's area. A central, accessible location facilitates the "open door" policy that so many middle schools have found to be an effective way of nipping potential problems in the bud.

As mentioned above, corridors are prime trouble spots—as are stairwells. Especially in larger schools, overcrowded conditions can occur at the beginning and end of the school day, during changes of classes and when groups of students are traveling to the gym, the cafeteria, the media center or other specialized areas of the building. Such overcrowding all but invites the pushing and shoving that can lead to something more serious. Because of this, in middle school planning and design a great deal of attention is now being paid to traffic control—to ensure that more than one route is available for travel to and from any part of the building. Also, many administrators have found that constantly maintaining separation of grade levels—in the gym, at lunchtime and when students assemble to board buses—helps reduce the opportunity for cross-grade bullying.

Controlling Vandalism

Aside from bullying, vandalism may be the commonest security-related problem that middle schools face. Preventing vandalism and limiting damage when it occurs require both savvy design *and* speedy (and ongoing) maintenance. The several middle school principals we talked to all empha- sized one point: vandalism inevitably worsens if the physical plant is allowed to deteriorate.

Fairfield Woods' Cox remembered that vandalism was rife at her school before the building was renovated; since then, she said, the school has not had a single incident of internal vandalism, in large measure because every aspect of the school's redesign and organization fosters students' common sense of respect for "their own place." Paul Porter, principal of the Seymour Middle School in Seymour, Connecticut, made the same point somewhat differently. According to Porter, "Kids tend to pick away at things like cracks in the wallpaper, or rips in a mural;" making repairs immediately is *the* critical element in checking vandalism's spread.

Some anti-vandalism measures are now "built into" every new school. For example, it's now common practice to finish off all interior walls in a school's public spaces with graffiti-resistant epoxy paints. There are, however, additional architectural anti-vandalism measures that merit consideration. It may be wise to avoid "soft" ceilings (i.e., acoustical tile) in toilets and stairwells, where students typically travel unsupervised. Hard, gypsum board ceilings are much less easily damaged and, unlike dropped ceilings, provide no places where items might be hidden.

In districts that have a history of vandalism to the exterior of school buildings, it may be worth considering substituting the transparent polycarbonate material called Lexan (used for bulletproof tellers' windows in banks) for glass in perimeter windows. Although this measure might double first costs for glazing, long-term savings achieved through *not* having to replace broken panes might render the measure cost-effective. In some urban areas, it may make sense to reduce overall exterior glazing and to use solid glass block, which permits daylight to enter the interior but is extremely difficult to damage, rather than window glass on certain exterior walls.

Keeping Outsiders Out

The middle school principals we've consulted report that security problems are as likely—if not more so—to originate from outside the school community as from within. Protecting the perimeter of a school's building and grounds is of critical importance. All outside areas used by schoolchildren—recreation areas, playing fields—should be fenced off. The entire perimeter of the building itself should be well lighted, and the lighting kept on all night long. (One district we're familiar with went so far as to completely encircle a middle school building with a patrol road so that local police could surveil the entire building without ever having to leave their squad cars.) Parking lots, too, should be well lighted, and parking lot fixtures should be protected against vandalism with Lexan lenses, which provide a shield that can't be broken by BB gun pellets or rocks.

Electronic Security

Although relatively few middle schools have yet to install elaborate electronic security measures—turnstiles, metal detectors, closed-circuit TV cameras, access card systems, and the like—many are contemplating adding such systems. If you are planning a new facility or an upgrade, one of the most important things you can do is to make sure that the necessary cabling/wiring infrastructure is put in place, so that electronic security devices can be easily added when and if you decide that they are necessary.

At some middle schools, after-hours use of the building by student or community groups presents a particular problem. Some schools are finding that "zoning" the building electronically—channeling after-hours users through certain entrances/exits; locking down sections of the building that are not in use; installing an electronic ID system that still permits authorized adults to access other areas of the building, as necessary; and establishing an alarm system that immediately alerts custodial staff if an exterior door has been left ajar—all but eliminates the chance that anyone will wander through the building unsupervised and significantly reduces opportunities for theft. (Methods of locking off certain areas of the building must be meticulously worked out to ensure that fire codes regarding egress are not violated.)

Decisions about closed-circuit TV cameras must be carefully considered. According Peter Orvis, a Wilton, Connecticut–based school technology consultant, a key decision involves whether cameras are intended for deterrence only—in which case it may not be necessary to record images—or for investigation and documentation in the event an incident occurs. If you do intend to record the images your security cameras capture, you may want to opt for one of the new digital systems. Unlike older, analog systems that employ VCRs, digital systems permit you to segregate a particular image—of an intruder, say—on a computer screen and to track that image automatically. By contrast, the videotapes of VCR-based systems (whose images are also much less sharp) must be painstakingly reviewed in real time.

Common-Sense Security

The best approach to middle school security ultimately relies on common sense. As we've indicated, experience shows that fifth, sixth, seventh and eighth graders are naturally much more open and conversational than their high school counterparts, and some middle schools are taking advantage of this fact of human development by adding security officers to staffs. These security officers are *not* "security guards"—they're teachers' aides, often employed on a part-time basis, reporting to work at lunchtime and staying through the end of the day. The children know who they are and what their function is, and they constantly interact with them in corridors, cafeterias and other shared areas of the school. Schools that have such staffpeople have learned that security officers can find out *a lot* about what's going on simply by observing students and listening to their unguarded conversations.

Technology consultant Orvis pointed out that most schools, middle schools included, have too many locks—and too many keyholders! Protection against theft can be augmented, dramatically and simply, by reducing the number of exterior doors that have key-opened locks and by restricting the number of people authorized to carry keys. Electronic access-control systems can also be helpful in this regard. Whereas it's impossible to effectively control the duplication of keys for mechanical locks, an electronic access system permits authorization to be updated as frequently as necessary.

Finally, our own educated hunch that middle school security is improved by the open, frequent exchange of information was corroborated by the principals we talked to. Fairfield Woods' Cox said that, in her opinion, the best way of protecting children against harm by their peers is to constantly bring home the message that "violence has real implications." And Seymour Middle School's Porter several times repeated his belief that open communication is the key to maintaining school safety—bringing people together to share news immediately whenever an incident occurs, dispelling rumors quickly, and never allowing the impression to develop that anyone is hiding vital information from students, faculty or parents.

Chapter 10
Improving School Acoustics—
A Systems Approach

Try reading the following paragraph:

Many educators feel is important to acoustics in classrooms by children with problems but unnecessary do so in used by students normal hearing. Yet populations of students normal hearing also from better classroom.

Difficult (or impossible) to understand, yes? Why? Because every fourth word—or 25 percent of the text—has been removed. That's the visual equivalent of a *speech intelligibility rating of 75 percent*, which the Acoustical Society of America says is the acoustical condition that prevails in many American classrooms today (Seep et al. 2000). A look at this unintelligible paragraph makes it easy to understand that there is a direct correlation between speech intelligibility and student performance.

What the paragraph above means to say is:

Many educators feel it is important to improve acoustics in classrooms used by children with hearing problems but unnecessary to do so in those used by students with normal hearing. Yet many populations of students with normal hearing also benefit from better classroom acoustics. (Seep et al. 2000)

Adding the ten missing words back in makes a clear and concise statement—demonstrating quite neatly the critical importance of speech intelligibility and the meaninglessness of a statement not fully communicated. Granted, there are other clues to understanding the spoken word, such as body language, gestures, lip movement, voice modulation, and so on. These clues are most effective in a live, in-person presentation, but today's instructional methods include many prerecorded presentations as well as live distance-learning interactions, and these and other high-tech instructional modes will come into even greater use over the years to come. A 75-percent intelligibility rating in the classroom of the future is therefore unacceptable, especially when one considers that raising the level of intelligibility is, with some thoughtful planning and design, a fairly simple matter.

Why Does the Problem Persist?

One of the major reasons behind the poor acoustics in today's classrooms is a simple lack of awareness of the problem—this despite a recent U.S. General Accounting Office (GAO) report that ranks noisy classrooms high on the list of educators' frustrations. Poor acoustics is not a glaringly obvious problem; it cannot be recognized by simply walking into a room. Only the users of the space can discern it, and then only when actively engaged in the educational process. The GAO's *Condition of America's Schools, February 1995* survey reports that more than 28 percent of schools have unsatisfactory or very unsatisfactory acoustics for noise control (GAO 1995). That's worse than the results for other environmental problems, including those involving ventilation, security, indoor air quality, heating, and lighting.

Given the total school-age population in the United States (47,200,000 pupils in 1999), this means that poor acoustics affects the learning process of *millions* of American students. And, unfortunately, the ill effects of poor speech intelligibility fall disproportionately on those who can least afford them. Overcrowding has a negative effect on classroom acoustics—and overcrowding is much more likely to occur in large urban schools and in schools that serve minority populations (Lewis et al. 1999). These are the same schools, of course, whose populations are most likely to include a high percentage of students for whom English is not their native language—and whose learning and performance are likely to suffer most from poor speech intelligibility.

Designs for middle school learning spaces still largely ignore the problem of classroom acoustics. New classrooms typically include acoustical treatments such as some carpet on the floor, acoustical tiles on the ceiling, gypsum wallboard partitions, and some batt insulation in the wall cavity between classrooms. Classrooms are also usually acoustically separated from adjacent spaces, but this typically represents the extent of acoustical design. Little, if any, consideration is given to specific acoustical criteria such as speech levels, background noise, reverberation times, or speech–to–noise ratios. And classrooms are typically designed repetitively: if there are no user complaints, the design is considered good, and so the next school project is designed in the same way the last school was. This method, however, ignores an important psychological reality—that users of a new facility are usually so gladdened by the opportunity to teach in brand-new spaces that they are hesitant to complain about "trivialities" such as classroom acoustics. After all, the thinking goes, the building was designed by experts. Assured that they have state-of-the-art learning spaces, teachers remain unaware that classrooms might be even better, acoustically speaking.

The problem persists for a few other reasons, as well. One is that until recently there have been no acoustical performance and testing standards for classrooms, so designers have had limited data on which to base their designs. A building code change, proposed to the International Code Commission (ICC) on November 14, 2001, adds a classroom acoustics section to the International Building Code (IBC). The proposed IBC is closely based on a draft ANSI standard (S12.60-20X). With ICC approval, classroom acoustic provisions become requirements in all states adopting the IBC. Obviously, every school design is unique, and each school has different programmatic needs, but careful use of guidelines and well-considered planning of all the spaces should go a long way toward solving the technical acoustical problems that are now so widespread.

Another reason for the problem's persistence has to do with the perceived cost of specialized design for acoustics or of remediating existing problems.

But these costs should be considered as *integral* to the unit costs of a new building or renovation, and acoustical design should not be subject to value-engineering cuts. The value of acoustical improvements becomes clear when one considers that initial costs are far outweighed by the long-term costs resulting from disadvantaged learning.

Poor Speech Intelligibility—Origins of the Problem

Speech intelligibility can be impaired either by unintentional noise or by intentional sound that, for one reason or another, is inadequate to convey meaning effectively or that interferes with other intentional sound.

Unintended Noise. Background noise from an unintended source can compete with desired or intended sounds. Most commonly, background noise arises from building systems or from a lack of acoustical separation between occupied spaces. Here are some sources of the unintended noise that commonly afflicts school buildings.

- *Mechanical systems.* The need for ventilation and temperature control in modern schools requires that a large volume of air be constantly moved in and out of classrooms. That movement—the rush of air through ducts, grilles, and diffusers—can create background noise, which is often compounded by sounds generated by the fans and motors used to drive the air. In some older school buildings, steam heat—the hissing radiators and the banging pipes—contributes to the problem during the heating season. Classrooms located directly below the roof are subject to low-frequency vibrations created by rooftop-mounted mechanical equipment such as air-handling units, chillers, and exhaust fans.
- *Lighting and electrical systems.* Because of its economy and efficiency, fluorescent lighting has become the standard for virtually all buildings except residences. This type of lighting requires electronic ballasts, and these ballasts create a distinct hum. Electrical transformers that step down voltage, usually located in electric closets throughout a building, also emit a constant hum. Even though this noise is of a fairly low frequency and volume, it nonetheless contributes to background noise in adjacent areas. (Electrical switchgear also creates a hum, but this equipment is generally located well away from instructional spaces and contained in fire-rated spaces whose walls, coincidentally, acoustically isolate those spaces.)
- *People.* Background noise often results from people carrying on their everyday activities—moving around, talking, interacting, working. One often hears teachers complain about the noise created by the shuffling of desks and chairs. (And, in rooms with tile floors, one frequently finds an ad hoc solution to this problem: tennis balls stuck on the feet of desk and chair legs.) Other occupant-generated noise is an acoustical separation problem. Any movement through corridors outside the classroom (not to mention the banging of lockers) generates noise. Sounds bleeding out into the corridor from classrooms whose doors have been left open to improve ventilation infiltrate nearby spaces.

Food service areas can be particularly troublesome, acoustically. The movement and conversations of workers, product deliveries, and the ordinary use of utensils and equipment in the food-preparation process can, together, produce quite a racket. Though kitchen areas are typically back-of-the-house spaces, the noise can easily carry through reverberant corridors, as can the din produced in the cafeteria at mealtimes. Crossover noise emanating from gymnasiums or caused by custodial activities can, especially when combined with sounds from other sources, create a significant background noise level.

- *Reverberation.* Large spaces (cafeterias, gyms) are generally noisy spaces—not by planning but by default. Ask any teacher who's assigned lunch duty about the din in the cafeteria. These spaces are outfitted (appropriately) with washable surfaces that are hard and smooth—exactly the kind of surfaces that reflect sound. In such a space, reverberation time is extended, and sound is constantly being regenerated to produce a very high, constant background noise level—the din. Too often, the cost of providing acoustical treatment to control such noise is perceived as prohibitive. If a gymnasium is noisy—so the thinking goes—that's okay because, after all, the gym is meant to house noisy activities. A gymnasium, however, isn't just a basketball/volleyball court with bleachers; it's also an instructional space, and the fact that physical education teachers, like all teachers, need to communicate information verbally should be considered when designing a gym.

- *Exterior noise.* Noises from the surrounding area—from vehicular or pedestrian traffic, from nearby manufacturing facilities or construction sites, or from lawnmowers and other onsite noise-generators—can infiltrate the school building. The sounds of students engaged in sports activities, especially where outdoor athletics fields are located very close to the building, and of school buses queuing up for the afternoon trip home occur each and every school day.

Intentional Sounds. Sometimes intelligibility problems are created by the desired sound source itself. For example, if the sound source is weak it may not be able to overcome background noises such as those described above. Here are some of the intelligibility problems related to *intended,* rather than unintentionally produced, sounds.

- *Teachers' voices.* Obviously, every individual has a different voice pattern. Some people project well, with plenty of volume and good, clear articulation, while others are much more soft-spoken (with an endless range in between). Some teachers have speech impairment issues; others have foreign or regional accents that may make it difficult for the students they teach to understand them. And, of course, everyone occasionally suffers from an illness—a cold, sore throat, or laryngitis—that affects his or her speech. Those teachers who have difficulty overcoming background noise levels are those who suffer the most from poor acoustics. They must strain to be heard, which may color their presentation of the material and cause them unnecessary stress—perhaps even putting them at risk for stress-related health problems.

- *Audiovisual sound systems.* The A/V equipment used in schools is sometimes not as good—or in as good repair—as it might be. Intelligibility problems can occur if, say, the speaker system in a video monitor used for presenting a prerecorded program is inadequate or damaged, or if the equipment used in a live distance-learning is malfunctioning. In fact, if a video system is not a state-of-the-art product designed specifically for the space, then it can be reasonably assumed that it will be inadequate. Certainly, we've come a long way from the shaky-voiced, 16mm instructional movies of yesteryear, and vast improvements have been made in the content and production values of audiovisual presentations. But sound quality can still be a problem, and designers still struggle with the question of how best to distribute a clear and properly attenuated signal to each and every individual, especially in spaces where seating is not fixed. Turning up the volume only leads to greater distortion of the signal, and intelligibility does not necessarily improve. In fact, high-volume sound may bleed into other spaces—adding to the background noise level and disrupting activities in adjacent classrooms.

- *Public address sound systems.* Schools are required to have public address systems as part of a their emergency response plan. PA systems are also great communication tools for disseminating broadcast messages. Unfortunately, PA systems are subject to cost-cutting: good systems are value-engineered away, replaced with systems whose capabilities barely reach the minimum required for code compliance. For the most part, such systems produce poor-quality, almost-unintelligible sound.

- *Learning activities.* The clatter of keyboards and the whir of fans in a computer lab, the chatter of students working in small groups—these can also create background noise. When a student group is large or there are multiple small groups, the conversations will blend together, magnifying the problem.

- *Gyms as performance spaces.* If you've ever attended a school band concert in a gymnasium you probably understand what bad acoustics are. Most gymnasiums simply don't work well as performance halls. Schools that do have the funds to build an auditorium usually build it correctly—meaning that an expert in acoustics is consulted during design. Auditoriums are generally acoustically separated from surrounding spaces and do not present crossover acoustical problems.

When background sound levels—whether produced by unintentional or intentionally produced sound—approach the level of the intended sounds in a classroom or other learning space, the message gets partially masked, resulting in a poor intelligibility rating.

The Systems Approach to Acoustical Design

The solution to poor speech intelligibility resides in a *systems approach* to acoustical design. Two basic principles underlie the systems approach:

- *People—the users and occupants of the building—are an integral part of the system: they are often the generators of the sounds, and they are always the receptors of the sounds.* This means that decision-makers must be convinced of the importance of good acoustical design—that appropriate acoustical design carries a positive cost/benefit ratio. Student performance will be enhanced by the proper acoustical design of instructional spaces. The stress that teachers feel will diminish, and there will be a corollary reduction in stress-related health problems.
- *All of a building's problems are in some way related to each another, so addressing only one problem without considering the overall system may well cause or exacerbate another problem.* An acoustical problem may be solved by adding a soft surface to a room, but that "solution" might provide an environment for mold growth. (This can cause problems not only for that space, but—because the mold spores can be distributed via the ventilation system—for the whole building.) Turning up the volume in one room may cause additional background noise in an adjacent room because of noise crossover through the adjoining ventilation-system ductwork; adding duct liners to reduce the crossover noise might, in turn, cause indoor air quality problems.

Some Design Guidelines

The following guidelines exemplify the systems approach.

Programming. In the programming phase, the acoustically critical spaces—particularly the core teaching/learning spaces—must be identified, and adjacency criteria must be established for them. Adjacency studies should be part of the programming task. These matrix-type studies have long been part of the programming phase of all kinds of projects, but as the design profession has become increasingly specialized many programming tasks have become "second nature" and thus no longer received the focused attention they once did. To ensure good building acoustics, acoustical adjacencies should be carefully considered. Such studies will reveal problem areas that need special attention or treatment, as well as non-problematic areas that can be ignored.

Site Selection. The design process begins with site selection. In choosing a site for a new middle school, diligent consideration should be given to the surrounding area, to identify both noise generators and sensitive receptors (because the school itself will be a noise generator). If at all possible, schools should be located far away from the following noise generators: manufacturing and industrial processing plants, warehouses/shipping facilities, retail facilities with frequent deliveries, landfills, emergency-vehicle stations (such as police, fire and ambulance stations), and municipal public works yards. Also to be avoided are sites near construction company yards where equipment is stored, and sites that are close to other sites where construction is scheduled or likely to occur. (Construction noise is, of course temporary, but keep in mind that construction on major projects can last for years.) Sites that are close to transportation infrastructure—railroads, light rail systems, airports, heliports, and highways (especially limited-access roads or major truck routes)—should be avoided. It's worth noting that many of the noise-generators listed here could also have a deleterious effect on other aspects of the school environment, as well—for example, vehicular exhaust from a nearby highway might have a negative impact on air quality inside and outside the school.

Site Design. Site designers need to consider the acoustical impact of areas where buses will queue and where parents will wait in their cars (with their motors running) to pick their children up from school. When deciding on the location of outdoor activity areas (outdoor classrooms, athletic fields, etc.), consideration should be given to how sound from those areas may affect activities within the building. Instructional areas inside the building should be located away from loading docks (which may have frequent truck traffic) and receiving areas.

Building and Learning Space Design. All spaces in the building—but especially instructional spaces—should be designed to specific criteria in order to enhance those spaces' acoustical properties. While design generally proceeds from the macro to the micro, the acoustics of classrooms and other learning spaces need to be considered early on as part of the overall building program to ensure that these learning spaces are acoustically efficient.

While there are multiple criteria for measuring and analyzing sound and the acoustical performance of spaces, most are too esoteric to be of practical value to educators. There are three acoustical criteria, however, that the decision-makers involved in school construction projects need to be aware of:

- Speech sound level
- Speech-to-noise (or signal-to-noise) and speech-to-reverberation ratios (S/N and S/R ratios)
- Reverberation time

These criteria are all expressed in terms of decibels (dB)—a measurement of sound pressure. The suffix "A" denotes the bandwidth of the measurement that closely approximates the normal range of human hearing. Reverberation time is measured in the number of seconds it takes for the reverberant sound to decay (or fade out) by 60 decibels. The criteria are as follows:

Speech sound level = 65dB(A) at all points in the room. This level can be attained through normal speech without amplification in a regular classroom with some acoustical treatments, such as acoustical ceilings and carpet on the floor.

S/N and S/R ratios = +15 dB(A) at all points in the room (background noise levels not to exceed 35 dB(A) as measured in an unoccupied room). This is a comparison of the desired sound to the background noise. Speech/

noise ratios (S/N ratios) express the difference between the sound levels of the speech and the noise. Since both the speech and noise are measured in dB(A), the S/N ratio, a relative measure, is simply the difference, in decibels, between the sound level of the signal (the speech) and the sound level of the noise. Speech/reverberation ratios (S/R ratios) are defined in the same manner as S/N ratios, with the A-weighted sound level of the reverberant sound substituted for the A-weighted sound level of the noise. A good S/N ratio for speech intelligibility is a minimum of +15 dB greater than the background noise.

Reverberation time = RT60 of 0.4–0.6 second. Reverberation times are defined as the time in seconds required for the reverberant sound to decay 60 dB.

Meeting these criteria will ensure acoustical properties that enhance communication within the classroom for the vast majority of students, including those with some hearing impairment.

Building Systems Design. Integrated systems reduce overall noise. As advances in design move our buildings toward greater environmental sustainability, building systems will, necessarily, become more and more integrated. Mechanical systems will "read" lighting systems to better control heat and cooling loads; natural daylighting systems will be integrated with artificial lighting; and lighting systems will be integrated with security systems—which, in turn, will comprise part of the overall "intelligent building" system. This integration will continue until each of our buildings—including our schools— is a single intelligent system supporting the needs and desires of its users. Much of this technology is available and already in use today, so the time is not far off when totally integrated, intelligent, environmental/sustainable buildings become the norm.

A Glimpse of the Future

What will middle school learning spaces of the future sound like? Sound-wise, these spaces will suit their purposes—with the furniture and finishes enhancing the spaces' acoustical properties. Acoustical treatments will include a mixture of reflective and absorptive surfaces that can be adjusted, or "tuned," to the needs of particular users and particular activities.

Acoustical ceilings will continue to be used, though their noise-reduction coefficients will be enhanced. As in today's classrooms, floor coverings will mix hard surfaces, such as tile, with soft, acoustically absorbent materials (including not only carpet but possibly other materials, such as cork-based products). The comfort systems—heating, cooling, and ventilation—will be acoustically transparent, as will the lighting systems.

The flexibility required in typical classrooms confounds most attempts to design an acoustically perfect classroom. Engineers—including acoustical consultants—rely on some constant to which they can apply variables in order to make, and test, assumptions about how a space will work in actual use. In middle school classrooms, the only constants are the physical dimensions of the space. The length and width of the room will not change (except where movable partitions are used), and the ceiling height is also constant. But classroom acoustical design that uses only fixed sound reflectors will be ineffective if the sound source is relocated—for example, if the room has been designed for a teaching station at an end wall but the teacher's desk is moved to a side wall. If, however, the designer strategically places adjustable sound reflectors/absorbers on the walls—treatments that can be easily manipulated by the users—the room can be acoustically tuned to changing configurations. The ceiling can be designed with a mixture of soft and hard surfaces by alternating high-NRC (noise reduction coefficient) tiles with hard, gypsum-type panels located so as to distribute the sound effectively to the entire room without excessive reverberation times. This concept is now being utilized in corporate conference room ceilings to help contain the sounds around a large conference table. The right mixture of hard and soft surfaces in the ceiling grid will reflect the sound of the teacher's voice to the opposite end while reducing the reverberation time to prevent reflected sound from muddling the primary source. The same principle can be used for the wall surfaces: adjustable reflectors can be placed on the center sections of the walls while the corners are treated with absorptive surfaces.

In typical middle schools of the future—like those of today—classrooms will be located along exterior walls to take best advantage of natural ventilation and daylight. In such an arrangement, at least one wall has windows, and the designer must keep in mind that glass is a sound-reflective material. Generally, some sort of shading device—usually a roll-up shade or adjustable blinds, either vertical or horizontal—is employed to control the amount of daylight entering the room. The opportunities for acoustic control that these shading devices provide are too often overlooked: if fabric curtains or fabric-based blinds are used, the room will also have an adjustable acoustical control device, much as one would see in a theater or auditorium but on a smaller scale.

The furniture should also play a role in enhancing room acoustics, and doors and partitions should be thoughtfully placed and constructed so as to reduce sound transmission from one learning space to another or from one side of a corridor to the other. Increasing the mass of a wall not only helps control lower-frequency sounds, it also augments the wall's value as a fire retardant.

The long-term switchover to renewable energy sources will have a beneficial side-effect, acoustically. Solar, geothermal, and fuel-cell systems, because they are relatively "passive," will reduce noise and thereby enhance speech intelligibility.

Acoustics versus Indoor Air Quality

No discussion of school-building acoustics would be complete without mentioning the ongoing debates between proponents of improved classroom acoustics and advocates of improved indoor air quality (IAQ). The IAQ advocates would like to eliminate materials that can support the growth of molds, mildew, fungi, or other microorganisms as well as those that contribute volatile organic compounds (VOCs) to the indoor environment. Unfortunately, these are typically the same materials that the advocates of good classroom acoustics would like to see added to rooms.

Carpet, for example, has some acoustical benefits. It absorbs higher frequency noise and provides a buffer between the furniture and the floor, reducing the noise created when furniture is moved around. But carpet can be a source of various biological and chemical contaminants that negatively impact the air quality of classrooms. If not meticulously maintained, carpet has the potential to become host to various molds, dust mites, and other biological contaminants. There is also a history of problems with new carpet releasing VOCs (either from the carpet itself or from the adhesives used to install it). The Carpet & Rug Institute has led the way to vast improvements in the off-gassing issue and makes stringent recommendations for maintenance. (For more information, visit the Carpet & Rug Institute's special education-related website, at <www.carpet-schools.com>.) If carpet is properly maintained it can provide the acoustical benefits mentioned above, but if poorly maintained it can pose serious health risks.

Sound attenuation treatments inside ductwork are also controversial. Sound attenuation is usually achieved through the use of glass-fiber duct lining. This insulation, however, provides an environment for the amplification of molds, mildew, and fungi, which contaminate the airstream. The exposed glass fibers can also break off and float into the breathing-air zone. Air distribution systems can be designed in such a way, however, to keep noise at an acceptable level without the use of duct lining—for instance, by proper sizing of ducts and terminals and by careful placement of sound attenuators throughout the system. In cases where some sort of duct lining is unavoidable, one of the alternatives to exposed glass-fiber duct liners should be used. (This, of course, does not come without a cost.)

The materials used in typical lay-in acoustical ceiling tile—starch and cellulose—can also provide a medium for the growth of molds, mildew, and fungi. Even when the tiles are made of glass fiber with an organic binder in the glass matrix, exposure to moisture or even excessive humidity can foster the growth of molds. Manufacturers do offer antimicrobial treatments, but the long-term effectiveness of this option remains untested. The solution here is to control moisture, which requires a properly designed, balanced, and maintained HVAC system. Once again, it's a systems approach that provides the best solution.

After all is said and done, some schools will also want to factor in the possibility of using amplification systems, which can be adjusted to meet each room's specific acoustical requirements.

Chapter 11

Indoor Air Quality— Problems and Solutions

Middle schools of the future will be housed in buildings both new and old. Indoor air quality (IAQ) problems show no preference for old or new construction—new buildings have problems just as older buildings do. The fundamental issue in all IAQ problems is the pollutant source. In this chapter, we look at the various sources of indoor air contamination, then describe some basic principles for improving IAQ in future schools.

Volatile Organic Compounds

In new buildings, IAQ problems often involve either chemical off-gassing or inadequate ventilation. Finishing materials used in new construction go through a curing process during which some of the chemicals used in their manufacture are volatilized into the air, yielding what are referred to as VOCs, or volatile organic compounds. (*Volatile* in this case refers to the material's instability in its natural state—solid or liquid—and its tendency to change into a vaporous state at room temperature.) These chemical compounds, some man-made and some naturally occurring, evaporate at varying rates, after which they are present in the air. Some compounds, like alcohol or acetone, evaporate very rapidly; others, like the oily substances used to create residues in spray pesticides or smoothness in alkyd-based paints, evaporate so slowly that they are referred to as SVOCs, or semi-volatile organic compounds. We usually recognize VOCs as odors, but they don't always have a smell. VOCs are not necessarily dangerous; their toxicity depends on the compound itself and the level of someone's exposure to it. Chemical compounds like benzene (carcinogenic) or formaldehyde (reasonably anticipated to be carcinogenic) are hazardous to human health, but perfumes, air fresheners, and citrus fruit oils are also considered VOCs.

There are many potential product sources of these chemicals in new buildings. The most common are paints, adhesives, sealants and caulking, resilient flooring materials, carpet, and some furniture components. (It should be mentioned that some indoor-air pollutants result from the activities that go on in school buildings every day. Among the VOCs that belong in this category are fumes and odors from consumable materials such as Magic Markers, cleaning fluids, and chemicals used in copying machines and printers.)

Careful and knowledgeable specification of finishing materials can reduce VOCs. Project specs should require sheet-type materials, such as carpeting, to be aired out prior to installation in the building. This process allows the majority of chemical residues to evaporate outside the new facility. The amount of off-gassing decreases very quickly in the first few days in most materials, but each material has its own requirements.

Another effective way to improve air quality is to air out the building itself. This involves setting the mechanical systems to maximum ventilation for a specified period of time prior to occupancy. (The heating system should never be used to "bake out" the building: this has a tendency to drive VOCs into other materials that can later release the chemicals after occupancy.) This airing-out period can present a problem, however, since school projects usually adhere to very tight schedules utilizing each and every day leading up to the beginning of a school year. But early planning—and a schedule that treats the airing-out period as an *essential* step in the construction process—can help to prevent IAQ problems.

Other Gaseous Pollutants

Other gaseous pollutants may originate from site-related causes. Radon gas, a naturally occurring, colorless, odorless, radioactive element, is a common problem in some areas of the U.S. Radon is easily mitigated with simple exhaust systems that use fans to pull the gas from the adjacent soil and vent it into the atmosphere above the occupied level. Soil gases may leach from leaking underground fuel tanks or previous site uses such as landfill or other disposal; such possibilities should be disclosed in the initial pre-selection site assessment work—and, as is mentioned elsewhere in this book, such land should usually be eliminated as a potential site for a middle school. Additional site-related pollutants include vehicular exhaust fumes and odors from trash containers that enter air intake systems.

Comfort System–Related Problems

A school's heating, ventilating, and air conditioning (HVAC) systems—also known as indoor comfort systems—are designed to specific criteria for ventilation rates and heating and cooling loads. Problems with such systems generally arise from their use rather than from their design. When working as designed, the systems create well-balanced comfort conditions within an occupied space. An appropriate amount of fresh (outdoor) air is supplied to the space and balanced with a certain amount of air exhausted from the same space. The fresh air brought into the space is conditioned, or modified, to a certain temperature and, depending on the local climate, a certain humidity. The temperature and humidity can be modulated in various ways, but the air delivered to the space needs to be balanced with the air exhausted from it to avoid a buildup of carbon dioxide (CO_2). The fans that move the air, the air volume dampers in the ductwork, and all the grilles and diffusers are adjusted for proper air distribution. Temperature and humidity controls are calibrated and set to normal comfort ranges.

Ideally, after the systems are balanced, an independent contractor "commissions" the building systems. This involves activating all the systems in normal operating mode under normal operating conditions and verifying that all system components are in proper working condition. The systems are then fine-tuned and any substantial remedial work completed before the occupants move in. Even then, some additional remediation may be needed, as CO_2, humidity, and heat levels fluctuate with occupancy.

Ventilation air systems are presently designed for economy as well as efficiency. They recycle a certain amount of indoor air, mix this tempered air with fresh, outdoor air, and redistribute the blended air to the breathing zone. While this saves on heating and cooling, recycled air can become contaminated with pollutants or compromised by the presence of too much CO_2. (While CO_2 is not lethal, an overabundance can cause fatigue, lethargy, inattention, headache, irritability, and drowsiness) When this happens, the mechanical system becomes the distribution pathway for gaseous or particulate indoor air pollutants. Gaseous pollutants, such as the VOCs mentioned above, are chemical-based. Particulate pollutants can be biological, like molds, mildew, and fungi, or inorganic, like silica dust, asbestos, and fiberglass.

Operable Windows—The Downside

There is almost universal insistence on having operable windows in school buildings, but it is impossible for design engineers or HVAC system balancers to accurately predict their use. So the school's occupants themselves are a significant factor in operational problems. The conservative, practical approach plans on all windows and doors being shut. Problems then arise, of course, when windows or doors are opened, upsetting the balance of mechanically induced air ventilation. For example, open windows can reverse the airflow from a lavatory that has been designed with negative air pressure, causing odors to be forced back into a corridor. Open windows can also create localized ventilation loops that disrupt normal air distribution or cause a buildup of CO_2 in spaces occupied by groups of students.

Opening windows can bring about other indoor air quality problems, as well—which is somewhat ironic, since the object of opening windows is to bring fresh air indoors. When fertilizers and spray pesticides are applied outside open windows, these chemicals can easily make their way into a building. Open windows can also allow entrance of insects and other pests, as well as pollen and other plant allergens, all of which can impact the quality of the indoor environment. Dust and debris from adjacent areas can infiltrate, as can odors and fumes from outdoor activities. The problems are as variable as the use of the windows themselves, but, despite the greater mechanical efficiency of sealed buildings, most people still prefer the option of being able to open windows.

Typical ventilation systems for schools do not include filtration systems other than nuisance dust filters that affect only visible particulates. In the absence of such systems, the indoor air is only as clean as the outdoor air. While a variety of air purification systems have been developed, their efficacy and reliability remain largely untested. Systems such as ultraviolet sterilization, bipolar ionization, or photocatalytic cleansing of the ventilation air stream are available, but the up-front cost is usually prohibitive.

Biological Pollutants

While biological pollution is more common in older buildings, molds, mildew, and fungi can grow just as readily in a new building, given the right conditions. Mold spores are ubiquitous and at normal concentrations do not pose problems for most people. But when the right conditions are present, the spores can settle, the mold can multiply and release more spores, and, in just a matter of days, concentrations in the air can become significant enough to require remediation. The requirements for mold and fungus growth are darkness (or, more accurately, the absence of ultraviolet light), moderate temperature, high humidity or moisture, and a food source such as cellulose or some other organic material. These conditions are not uncommon inside wall cavities or in ceiling plenum spaces—hidden areas where mold growth may be difficult to locate until it is so extensive it becomes visible on the exposed surfaces, by which point the problem is very significant.

People's reactions to mold and fungus exposure vary. Some people may merely perceive a nuisance odor, while others react with life-threatening illness; the intensity of reactions and symptoms are unpredictable. Suscepti-bility depends on age, health, genetic predisposition, exposure levels, and on the type of mold or fungus itself. School-age children are, as a group, more vulnerable to exposure than adults, making this a critical issue for middle schools.

Certain types of molds and fungi are particularly toxic and require immedi-ate attention if identified (for detailed information, see New York City Department of Health 2000). Experts in the field of industrial hygiene should be consulted if a mold or fungus problem is suspected. They can identify the species, assess the scope of the contamination and risk, and make recommendations for a course of action. It is important to note that killing the mold or fungus only stops its amplification. Dead spores contain the same toxins as the viable spores. And dead spores are easily aerosolized if disturbed, entering the breathing zone and even the building's ventilation system. Remediation therefore often requires extensive site cleanup, with area containment similar to an asbestos remediation project.

The single most significant factor in the growth of biological pollutants is moisture, which can derive from a number of sources. In summer, warm air can condense on cool surfaces, such as pipes and air conditioning ducts, non-thermal windows and doors, or the non-insulated underside of roof decks in the cool of early morning hours. Moisture can come from leaking plumbing or roofs, from liquid spills, or from rain infiltrating through windows or walls. Significant moisture is tracked into a building on rainy days by people entering the space. Routine cleaning procedures typically use water. In other words, the sources of moisture are many, common, and everyday.

The best way to control biological pollutants is to control moisture. Repair leaks immediately and clean up spills as they happen. Use dry cleaning techniques where possible, and force-dry areas where water is used. Quickly mop up rainwater tracked into the building. Do not let moisture sit anywhere for more than a few hours. If the local climate dictates, install humidity controls to keep the interior relative humidity to 45 percent or less, and insulate pipes and ducts against condensation. If the building is kept dry, molds, mildew, and fungi will not propagate.

Inorganic Particulate Pollutants

Particulate pollutants also derive from building materials. Older buildings—those built up until the early 1970s—probably contain asbestos insulation. Most school districts have cleaned up their buildings in accordance with the federal Asbestos Hazard Emergency Response Act (AHERA) of 1986. Remaining asbestos-containing materials should be catalogued and strictly managed so that they pose no threat to air quality. While asbestos is no longer used in school construction, today's fiberglass, mineral wool, fiber-type thermal and acoustic insulation, and some spray-on fireproofing materials used on structural steel can still contribute to airborne dust problems if not properly specified and installed.

IAQ in the Future Middle School

So far, we've mostly focused on IAQ problems. So how do we go about ensuring good IAQ in the middle school of the future? For new buildings the solution is straightforward. Provide 100-percent fresh air, tempered to comfortable temperature and humidity, at a rate that suits the occupants and their activities, rather than designing to minimum codes or guidelines. Never recycle exhaust air into the breathing zone. Displacement air ventilation systems that provide this volume of fresh air have proved successful—one example is the system used in the Boscawen School in Boscawen, New Hampshire, which was designed by the H. L. Turner Group and which was given an Environmental Merit Award by the U.S. Environmental Protection Agency in 1996 (Sustainable Buildings Industry Council 2001).

If the outdoor air is fouled by smog, dust, or other industrial pollution, the building should include air-cleaning filtration within the ventilation system and the number and control of operable windows should be limited. The ventilation system should, through the use of sensors and controllers, compensate for temporary pressure imbalances caused by operable windows.

For renovated buildings, the systems mentioned above must be adapted to the existing space, and the cost/benefit ratio must be diligently analyzed. Adapting systems to fit existing building parameters is, by its nature, custom work that will increase the design and construction costs of a project. Perhaps the physical constraints of the building or the cost of adapting the systems will be such that the building is no longer even appropriate for school use. Educational planners need to be aware of indoor air quality issues, and IAQ must be considered in the early planning stages of a project to help make this very difficult programmatic decision.

A few final cautions are necessary. The first concerns facility maintenance. Keeping a building clean and dry is the formula for keeping it healthy. But the goal of a clean and dry building must be attained with the thoughtful and judicious use of environmentally sensitive cleaning methods and products. Schools are becoming increasingly specialized, high-performance technical buildings. As such they require a certain level of expertise to maintain them, much the way a high-performance vehicle requires specialized maintenance. These solutions do not come without added cost, but that cost must be balanced against the need for healthy indoor air—a requirement for good health and improved learning.

Second, educators need to be aware that there are many factors—improper lighting, excessive noise or vibration, overcrowding, poor ergonomics—that can produce symptoms similar to those associated with poor indoor air quality. In addition to ensuring the quality of the indoor air, these other stressors must be controlled for overall indoor environmental comfort.

Chapter 12

A Sustainable Approach to Middle School Design

Architecture worldwide changed forever when the Organization of Petroleum Exporting Countries (OPEC) embargoed the United States and other western countries in 1973, causing widespread shortages in fossil fuels. Energy efficiency suddenly became paramount in design, and building codes and standards were revised to reflect the need to conserve energy and reduce reliance on oil. This new energy consciousness heightened interest in developing technologies such as solar and wind power. Unfortunately, when the embargo was lifted and OPEC's oil pipelines once again flowed freely westward, these technologies were marginalized, and never became part of mainstream commercial design. The relatively high up-front cost for these systems and a lack of demonstrable performance reliability proved to be the Achilles' heel of this emerging industry. It faltered and became a special-interest sector relegated to the back-page classifieds of industry periodicals.

The energy crisis of the early 1970s did, however, engender a persistent interest in environmental issues on both an academic and popular level. Today, as a generation of environmentally aware people assumes leadership positions in the professions, the idea of utilizing renewable resources and conserving nonrenewable ones is at last becoming mainstream. We find ourselves at the cutting edge of a 30-year-old idea: sustainable, or "green," design—design, that is, that treads lightly on the environment and works creatively with renewable resources.

Green Design

With this new (or restored) environmental awareness, architects are turning with great fervor to what are called *holistic* building techniques. And because there is general popular agreement that the environment matters, depletable resources are being conserved and renewable resources utilized. Schools are now designed with specific functional areas for recycling programs. Taking recycling one step further, thoughtful consideration of what a building might become after its initial function passes (adaptive reuse) is now part of the initial design process, and some components are designed to be recycled rather than demolished when a building is dismantled. Even building materials are designed and manufactured to be recycled into the same or different products. Carpet used to be torn out, hauled off to a landfill, and replaced. Today, recyclable carpets can be leased: the worn material is removed for recycling whenever new carpet is required. Though not always practiced, conservation of resources has become a mainstream idea.

In fact, capturing nature-provided energy resources is now standard technology for any who want to include such measures in a project. Geothermal heating and cooling—tapping into the constant ground temperature for climate control—is used increasingly in schools. Passive solar collection for hot-water heating is common. Production of electrical power

Julie A. Kim, AIA, contributed to this chapter.

through the use of photovoltaic collection devices (solar energy cells) is becoming a mature industry. Environmentally friendly technologies such as fuel cell electrical generation are gaining favor as their initial costs stabilize. Collecting rainwater for plumbing systems is coming to be considered conventional design, as is collection of wastewater for "gray water" irrigation systems. The use of highly reflective materials and colors to avoid heat buildup on large surfaces such as paved parking areas and large, flat roofs is an easy choice. And even more adventurous roofing strategies—like grass-planted roofs—are finding proponents among public-school designers. These are just a few of the green ideas being included in present-day designs.

A life-cycle cost analysis of various building materials and systems should be part of any design decision-making process and is often mandated by regulatory agencies. These analyses consider not only what it costs to purchase, install, maintain, and eventually replace a material or system but also the costs of the energy required to collect, process, and transport the raw materials used in the manufacture, packaging, and delivery of the system. Along with the construction, installation, and maintenance costs, replacement and ultimate disposition costs of the materials through landfills or recycling now informs the selection of building components.

Likewise, sustainable design requirements are being met by manufacturers competing for "green" budget dollars. In fact, companies with generous R&D budgets are often leading the charge with new products. A good example—already referred to—is the carpet industry. With millions of tons of used carpeting filling up landfills, the carpet industry recognized a problem and moved forward to develop ideas in marketing and manufacturing technologies to reclaim these potential raw-material resources.

Sustainable products are hardly new to the marketplace. Some of the most sustainable materials are those that have been used in schools for the last hundred years, including exterior brick, masonry interior walls, ceramic tile, and terrazzo floors. In older school buildings these materials have long since paid for themselves in savings on maintenance expenses. But the quantity, variety, and availability of sustainable materials is greater now than ever before. In the long run, the use of such materials can be kind to both the environment *and* the operations budget. While it is the purview of the architect to make the best decisions for the specifics of the individual school program and budget, it is incumbent on him or her to make sure that project decision-makers are informed about life-cycle costs and are not bound by a first-cost-only mindset. A byproduct of the typical public-funding process, which establishes separate budgets for building a school and for maintaining and operating it, such thinking stands in the way of either a truly green or truly economically sound project.

The Future Meets the Present

As sustainable design techniques become fundamentals of design philosophy, a new building prototype is emerging. While the building may not *look* so different from the middle school of today, it will operate very differently.

Comfort systems will be much more user-controllable than they generally are today. As reliance on fossil fuels—and, hence, operating costs—declines, the strict controls now placed on building heating and cooling can become more lenient. If an individual room is too cool in the early morning hours, the users can adjust the heat to temporarily compensate. If it is overheating in the afternoon, the cooling can be increased. The central building intelligence system will register these adjustments and incorporate them into the building's day-to-day operating routines. If a classroom develops an overabundance of fumes or odors, sensors will detect the imbalance and purge fans will engage to ventilate the room to proper fresh-air levels.

Advances in lighting technology are already providing balanced illumination and color temperature approximating natural daylight. Other lighting system–related architectural strategies and electronic features—all available now—will come into greater use in tomorrow's middle schools. Light shelves (horizontal devices with a reflective surface) will redirect daylight into building interiors, decreasing the need for artificial light and reducing electric-power consumption. The lighting control system will read the level of daylight entering an interior and correct the balance of natural and artificial illumination for the time of day and the solar orientation of the room. Lighting control systems will communicate with the building management system and adjust the heating, ventilating, and air conditioning (HVAC) systems to economize on heating or cooling, depending on lighting conditions.

It's a point well worth making that green design has two, equally important, aspects: it's good for the environment *and* it's good for the human occupants of a building. That double function can be clearly seen, for example, in the push to maximize natural daylighting of interior spaces. Not only does natural daylighting reduce electricity bills—lessening dependence on the fossil fuels that are often used to generate electricity and, hence, reducing a building's contribution to air pollution generally—It also improves the interior environment for those who study and work there.

The State of Connecticut recently mandated that school districts consider maximizing natural light in new school buildings as well as those undergoing alteration or renovation. Why? because natural daylight is a great mood enhancer, which can lead to greater attentiveness, improved attendance, and higher achievement.

In the middle school of the future, communications systems will be merged. The public address system will no longer be separate from the telephone/

intercom system. Communications devices will be part of an integrated VDV (voice, data, video) network, which itself will be part of a larger intelligent building system that incorporates security, life safety, and building management systems, as well. Imagine the intimacy of a school in which the principal makes routine announcements to all students via video conferencing to each classroom, rather than through wall-mounted speakers that distort sound. Many of these technologies are available today, although the complexity of programming and operating them will require that the staff of the school of the future include trained network systems managers.

Classroom acoustical problems will be resolved through the strategic use of materials that reflect, diffuse, or absorb sound. (This topic is addressed in detail in Chapter 10, "Improving School Acoustics—A Systems Approach.") Indoor air quality will no longer be an issue, as the building will be infused with conditioned fresh air. Displacement ventilation systems might well replace the ducted central air systems, fed from rooftop air handlers, that are currently used. As filtration technology advances, the indoor air will be as clean as—and quite possibly cleaner than—the outdoor air. (For more on this topic, see Chapter 11, "Indoor Air Quality—Problems and Solutions.")

A Sustainable Approach to Siting/Site Design

The individual school's specific requirements and the character of the surrounding environment must drive the site selection process. Urban schools usually have a vertical orientation because of the shortage of suitable real estate in cities. Suburban schools face transportation-related site issues: Where can buses queue? Where can parents, driving their own cars, drop off their kids in the morning and wait to pick them up in the afternoon? Regional schools generally require large athletic fields and facilities. All schools have to deal with deliveries and services.

While site selection is project-specific, there are some sustainable criteria that ought to be considered in any middle school site selection process. For example, sites where mass transportation is both available and likely to be used will reduce the number of trips in private motor vehicles—and thus pollution. Proximity to population centers encourages the use of nonpolluting modes of transportation such as bicycles and walking. Schools should not be located near major industrial facilities, near trucking routes or other heavily traveled highways, or on or near sites that are toxically contaminated or that, because of past use, may present some environmental health hazard. While this last point seems obvious enough, schools have in fact been built on top of landfills, and there is currently a push, through the use of tax incentives, for the development of so-called brownfield sites (reclaimed former industrial or manufacturing sites). While brownfield sites can be successfully cleaned up and may be judged environmentally sound, brownfields might best be developed by private industry and not used for purposes that involve young children—purposes that would make it difficult to justify even a miniscule risk of exposure to toxic contaminants.

(Siting issues are covered in detail in Chapter 8, "Site Design and Landscape Architecture for the Future Middle School.")

Other sustainable design ideas include capitalizing on what might otherwise be considered site problems. In a suburban setting, wetlands and animal habitat issues frequently become problematic. In a sustainably designed school, these will become onsite educational assets—tools for teaching about ecology and conservation. Geological problems with bedrock or poorly draining soils can lead to a sanitary waste disposal problem. A sustainable approach would involve onsite processing, whether by a packaged sewage disposal processing plant or some other alternative processing technique. This, too, might serve as an educational asset, acquainting students with recycling and biomechanical processes.

Future Use of the School Building Itself

Sustainable design includes thinking about the future, both near and far. Near-future concerns address the building construction costs and schedule, and the operating costs in terms of both dollars and the environment. Far-future considerations include the possibility that the building may someday become obsolete as a school because of pedagogical changes, demographic shifts, or other reasons. Could it someday be utilized for municipal offices, housing, business, manufacturing or warehousing—without major reconstruction and needless waste of resources? If these changes can be planned for in the present, the life of a building can be extended by decades.

If major reconstruction would be required to convert the building to some other function, could the materials removed from the building be reused or recycled? All the materials that go into a building need to be considered for their recycling potential. Metals—steel, cast iron, aluminum, and copper— are easily recycled. Many plastics can be recycled to provide raw materials for other products. Non–pressure-treated wood products can be recycled into other wood- or cellulose-based products. Some single-ply-membrane roofing products can be reclaimed. Even if the building itself cannot exist forever, its components may exist as sustainable resources for other buildings or as other products for decades to come.

Chapter 13

Exceptional Kids Need More Feet: Designing Barrier-Free Schools for Special Education Students
by Edwin T. Merritt, Ed.D., James A. Beaudin, AIA, and Jeffrey A. Sells, AIA

At Trumbull High School in the Bridgeport suburb of Trumbull, Connecticut, the Planning and Placement Team applauded junior Shane Spencer's involvement with the audiovisual club and developed an Individual Educational Plan (IEP) for him that called for AV club participation before and after school. Shane's father and mother, who were deeply involved with development of the plan, pointed out that, although the concept was fine, it wouldn't work because Shane, a student with multiple disabilities who is confined to a wheelchair, could not open the school's front door.

After lengthy discussion with the Trumbull Board of Education, it was determined that an electronic door opener costing $2,400 would solve the problem. An agreement, in keeping with the IEP, was reached in which the Board of Ed would install the opener, paying for the device and associated construction costs out of emergency/contingency facility funding.

During the same period, the Trumbull district determined that it needed an alternate education facility for approximately 50 high school students, some identified as special education students and many with emotional and related behavior problems. The district decided that this facility should be configured into existing middle school space. The facility was designed with IEP requirements in mind, and a substantial effort was made to accommodate different students' varying needs. Costs associated with this renovation added up to approximately $200,000.

Another Connecticut high school, this one in the Hartford suburb of Plainville, recently faced an uncomfortable dilemma. In response to a state ruling declaring that playing-field press boxes must be fully accessible, school officials shut down their football field's press box—part of a structure built long before disabled-access legislation was ever introduced—as they searched for an affordable and workable solution. As they investigated the possibility of installing a lift—having already decided that constructing a wheelchair ramp would be infeasible or prohibitively expensive—the old press box went unused.

Educational Entitlements and School Architecture

School districts across the country are facing extraordinary demands on their facilities. The reasons for the seemingly inexorable increases in space needs are many—including, for example, rocketing enrollments, the expansion of community recreational programs, and curriculum development that focuses on providing space for collaboration, hands-on activities, and a problem-solving approach to learning. But one of the prime movers pushing up space requirements is the expansion of educational entitlements due children with disabilities resulting from the Individuals with Disabilities Education Act (IDEA) of 1990. That federal law, combined with the Americans with Disabilities Act (ADA) of 1990 and with state laws and local mandates, has created a situation in which schools' legal and moral obligations to attend to the needs of special education students sometimes conflict with districts' facility and financial resources. Much of the space and money crunch happens at the high school level, but the problems certainly aren't limited to high schools. IDEA extended protections and entitlements to children younger than five years of age, which means that many school districts are wrestling with questions about how to provide barrier-free access to educational opportunity from the earliest preschool years through 12th grade.

School officials are hardly unaware of these developments—or of the space and financial quandaries they so often raise. Yet, to our knowledge, there has been no comprehensive study of the impact that disabilities/special education legislation and case law has had on school districts nationally. Although there have been numerous attempts to study the problem and many special hearings on the topic before national, state, and local legislative bodies, supportive data falls short of being comprehensive. It is just too difficult to uncover all the expenditures or to discern their rationales—or, in fact, to determine with any precision the relationships between particular expenditures and the special education needs that instigated them. For instance, what indicator, other than a transcript of the Board of Ed discussion itself, could possibly lead to uncovering the Trumbull electronic door-opener expenditure? The actual expense was buried in an emergency facility fund. There is a paucity of information about the strategies that districts pursue to make sure that the architectural design of new and renovated schools meets special education and related space needs. If such information were systematically compiled, it might help districts contain costs related to special education, now and in the long run.

In the absence of a national or systematic study, we can offer only anecdotal evidence of the kinds of challenges school districts are facing. But that evidence is, we believe, telling, and it has led us to speculate on the architectural ramifications of special education entitlements. What follows is a discussion of these implications, with an eye toward helping school officials prepare to work with architects to ensure that special education needs are met. Of course, the financial pinch that school districts feel is partly created by the fact that state reimbursements have not caught up with the increased square-footage demands arising from special education entitlements and other factors. Legislative action on this score is, unfortunately, likely to be long in coming. In the meantime, school officials need concrete advice on how to best serve all of a districts' students while keeping special education–related costs as low as possible. As we'll indicate, this is a very tall order indeed.

Specific Space Implications

In the decade since ADA and IDEA were signed into law, Americans (architects included) have learned quite a lot about how to accommodate people with physical disabilities and to ensure their easy access to all sorts of facilities. We have a fair amount of experience and now deal reasonably well with access issues involving elevators, entranceways, (including the provision of ramps and interior automatic doors), lavatories, and so on. We still have a long way to go, however.

As a society, we haven't yet come to grips with some of the subtler aspects of disabilities legislation, which aims at ensuring that disabled people participate equally in *all* the opportunities that we provide to the able-bodied. In schools, this means making sure that, to the greatest degree possible, physically disabled students are able to enjoy access to all parts of the curriculum *as well as* all extracurricular activities. For instance, we can no longer relegate student clubs or groups, like the yearbook editorial team, to constricted, inaccessible, out-of-the-way offices or storage rooms. If a wheelchair-bound student wants to serve as a manager of the football or field hockey team, architecture and landscaping must serve his or her wishes: locker rooms must be fully accessible, as must playing fields and, as we saw above, auxiliary facilities such as press boxes.

So far, this seems simple enough in concept, and the space (and cost) implications might seem relatively clear. In actuality, they can be exceedingly complex. To take just a few examples: When designing new school gymnasiums or rehabbing old ones, architects must take pains to ensure that bleachers are accessible, which might involve the addition of ramps, the implementation of new handhold standards, and the like. Such measures aren't only expensive; they also have an impact on space. (In a renovated gym, the number of seats might be reduced by as much as 20 percent to permit these kinds of changes.) Making a school's pool accessible might involve the installation of an electric lift to lower physically disabled students into the water. Here again, there isn't just a cost impact (the expense of the equipment) but a space impact as well. The poolside areas must be larger or differently configured in order to accommodate the apparatus.

The list of architectural interventions necessary to accommodate physically disabled students has grown quite long—and the impact on space and budget is burgeoning accordingly. In auditorium design, for example, it's no longer satisfactory to designate a certain seating area for wheelchairs; such spaces should be scattered around the house, so that wheelchair-bound students—like all others—have a choice of vantage. Lifts must be provided to enable disabled students to access the pit and the control room.

The design of band and choral-group practice rooms must likewise be reconceived: the old tiered arrangement turns out to be impractical for disabled-access purposes in most school buildings, since wheelchair ramps capable of servicing all the tiers are expensive—*and* require that the room be enormous, since the angle at which such ramps can incline is very slight. (Flat-floored band rooms eliminate the access problem but create difficulties with sightlines and acoustics for which solutions must be found.)

Hallway design must factor in a host of variables relating to access: For instance, wheelchair-accessible water fountains typically protrude fairly far into corridors and may necessitate increasing corridor width. (And, for school buildings, such fountains and their mountings must be extra-strong, since athletically inclined students tend to use them as ad hoc pommel horses!) Corridors must incorporate buzzer-equipped "refuge" spaces to which wheelchair-bound students can retreat when having difficulties or in case of fire. (In multifloor buildings, staircases must also include refuges on each floor landing where people in wheelchairs can wait to be rescued.) To aid visually impaired students, all hallway signage must include Braille versions, and doors to off-limits rooms must have knurled knobs to warn against entering those areas. And lab design, too, must accommodate students with disabilities—including the provision of special-height counters for students using wheelchairs.

It's also important to point out that "barriers" don't just consist of the physical impediments—walls, stairs, doors—restricting disabled students' movement. A "barrier" can involve *what is not there* as much as what is. For example, not only do some assistive devices (e.g., wheelchairs) require space, but many electronic assistive devices require recharging stations; and space for these is not usually anticipated in a school's design. A barrier limiting a physically disabled child's equal access to educational opportunity is thereby being erected "by omission," one might say.

Planning and Placement Team Facilities

Most facility modifications are drawn from decisions taken by the federally mandated Planning and Placement Teams that exist in all public schools across the nation. These teams make decisions based on what they think is realistically possible. If, for example, a child is having a bad allergic reaction in a classroom, the PPT plan might call for installation of an air purifier and/or removal of a suspect rug. The use of whiteboards instead of blackboards has to some extent been driven by dust-related disability complications.

It's obvious that Planning and Placement teams need somewhere to meet. What may not be so obvious is that a well-functioning PPT meeting space has some relatively complex programmatic requirements.

First, the main PPT conference room must be fairly large. It isn't uncommon for a PPT meeting to include the following people: the student, his or her parents, as many as five teachers, a social worker, a guidance counselor, one or more representatives from the school district, one or two attorneys for the Board of Education, one or two attorneys or other advisers representing the student, a stenographer, and possibly a state appointed mediator. That list of participants, as long as it is, is not necessarily complete. This means we are talking about a conference room capable of comfortably accommodating upwards of 20 people. PPT negotiations resemble other legal procedures, in which, for example, parties may at certain points wish to retire from the negotiations in order to consider offers, discuss strategy, and so on. Therefore, it may be advisable for the PPT space to be configured as a suite that includes a main conference room and one or more auxiliary "caucus" rooms where the parties can sequester themselves, if necessary.

PPT spaces also need to be private and, to ensure that recording equipment works properly, insulated against outside noise. They need to be air conditioned as well, since many PPT meetings occur during the summer months, before the beginning of the school year. (A given hearing may last for several days, which makes the need to air condition PPT spaces even more urgent). These combinations of requirements of size, privacy, quiet, and air conditioning mean that it is often wise to make PPT meeting spaces *dedicated* meeting spaces. Needless to say, setting aside an area of a school building specifically for this purpose can have a significant impact on overall square footage.

"Special Education": Expanding the Definition

In some ways, "Special Education," traditionally understood as applying to students with physical disabilities and/or diagnosable learning disabilities, may be too narrow and limiting a term to designate contemporary school districts' efforts to ensure equal educational opportunity for all students. Perhaps we ought instead to speak of "alternate education," a term that would cover not only the legally mandated special education strategies that are designed to assist children with physical and/or learning disabilities but also those strategies that districts are pursuing to ensure that students with family, emotional, or psychological problems also receive the fullest, best educational experience possible. (Many of these students are considered "pre–special education.")

To help students in this latter group, (and to reduce the chance that students with emotional problems will disrupt other students' learning process), many schools today are employing techniques to help students manage their anger, and even to mediate disputes that arise among students at large, with the aim of preventing disagreements from escalating into more serious problems. These strategies, too, have very real effects on space needs and on how space is allocated. For example, whether a school relies on trained student mediators or a salaried anger-management/mediation specialist, rooms must be set aside for this purpose.

As we make progress in learning how to deal with wall, stair, and door barriers, technology is giving us the ability to deal with barriers of a different nature. When students cannot, for some legitimate reason, leave their homes to come to school, schools have traditionally sent tutors to provide at-home instruction. In a technologically enhanced educational environment, however, schools will in all probability be required to telecommunicate lessons in full-motion audio/video format utilizing the Internet or an intranet system. Likewise, computer technology provides in-school solutions for students who have problems hearing, seeing, and/or writing. Students with these kinds of difficulties can be assisted by district-owned laptops with earphones, large-print capabilities, and/or voice-recognition software.

The goal, of course, is inclusiveness: to make sure, whenever and wherever possible, that special-needs students are not segregated but have the opportunity and ability to learn, eat, play, study, and travel to and from campus with so-called "regular" students. The infrastructure necessary to support the new technology includes room for sophisticated wiring and switching gear, repair/maintenance space, production areas, training stations, and simple charging and disbursement stations. And these specialized space needs translate into extraordinary expense.

"Soft" Costs and Inflationary Factors

To appreciate the full impact on design and construction costs of accommodating special-needs students in all areas of academic life, one must also figure in the nearly unavoidable increases in "soft" costs that such efforts entail. For example, school-facility planning costs are proportionally higher than in the past: as case law and state regulatory decisions continue to mount, architects and planners have come to anticipate that a significant amount of redrawing will usually be necessary following state review of plans.

For a variety of reasons ranging from construction industry labor and building-material shortages to the decreasing availability of suitable sites for building new schools (and concomitant increases in the need to perform extensive site remediation before construction begins), inflation rates in school construction have sometimes been perceived as higher than the average across-the-board rates calculated by the Consumer Price Index. (The full set of factors contributing to rises in school construction costs is laid out in Chapter 2, "Cost, Change, and School Construction.") Accommodating students with disabilities exacerbates this inflationary trend because of the rise in the number of code-mandated requirements that must be incorporated into facility design and followed during construction.

Moreover, incorporating features that enhance access for students with disabilities inevitably widens the gap between gross and net square feet. School officials are sometimes puzzled by this, since the gross-to-net ratio can grow even when stringent efforts are made to limit a school facility's size—for instance, by reducing classroom dimensions. But there's really no mystery: many of the disabled-access and related elements mentioned above—wider corridors, hallway refuge spaces, recharging stations, rooms for air-conditioning equipment, and so on—have the effect of increasing gross square footage disproportionately.

Agreement, Knowledge, Patience, and Understanding

In the face of these stepped-up demands on school facilities, what can a school administration do to stem the tide of rising costs related to meeting exceptional student needs? The answer to the question is not abundantly

clear, but some school districts have successfully implemented an administrative approach that emphasizes agreement among officials, sound
knowledge and expert counsel, patience, and a willingness to understand
parents' concerns. Below, we describe this approach—one that, in broad
terms, could be adopted by any school district.

Educators are ethically and professionally charged with the task of doing
what is right to meet students' needs and help them learn. On this basis, one
might suggest that an administrator will always be on solid ground if he or
she advocates paying the bill—no matter how high—for any apparently
valid special needs request.

The problem is that some of the requests come with enormous price tags.
For instance, supporting a residential placement for an emotionally disturbed student might require an annual expenditure on the part of the
district of, say, $75,000. This, of course, would correspondingly reduce the
amount of money available for other important educational projects.
Knowing this, most administrators will try to hold off on making a large
special education expenditure even where such an expenditure will be a
step toward meeting an exceptional student's needs.

But, to contain special education–related expenditures successfully, the
superintendent, the administrator in charge of special education, and the
district's business manager must be in agreement about which requests to
support, which to oppose, and where to draw the line. If a special education
director takes an issue that has not been agreed upon to the Board of
Education, a state mediator, and/or the Exceptional Children's Parents
Organization, the director is likely to win the argument and the town to be
forced to spend the money. The three administrators must therefore learn
how to work together and to present a unified front.

In many cases, even when a school district administration presents a solid
position opposing a parent's request, the parent will call for a hearing with
the state's department of education or will go to court—and stands a good
chance of winning a favorable decision. The Board of Education and
district administration must therefore have the assistance of an adept and
knowledgeable lawyer with experience in the special education field and
knowledge of how the school administration, Board of Education members,
state mediators, and the courts would be likely to react if pressed on a given
issue. In preparing to deal with special education requests, districts have to
be ready to "pay the price" by having a knowledgeable lawyer on staff,
backed by a quality law firm on retainer.

Taking problems into the legal arena is not always prudent or wise, however. Understanding how a particular request accords with legal
requirements and understanding something about the particular parent or
parents making the request—being able to guess with some degree of
certainty the kind of action they might take if the request is denied—are

essential. For one thing, administrators must know when to "fold their cards" and grant a request. In many cases a partial solution to the problem may be acceptable enough that the district can delay having to lay out the comparatively huge amount of money that meeting the full request would require. And sometimes parents' concerns can be assuaged by less costly solutions—assigning a teacher's aid to provide tutoring, for example, or purchasing a laptop with special features designed to ease the student's learning difficulties. Getting all the parties to agree to accept an arbitrator's decision may be helpful in resolving some situations.

In all cases, human relations skills are absolutely necessary when dealing with parents who often feel that they are their children's only advocates. The administration must exhibit patience and understanding. Many an advocate for exceptional children has been stonewalled by school administrators only to rebound and to win the argument with a resolution that is significantly more costly than the initial request. It always pays to bend over backwards to support special education students, their parents, and their advocates in booster groups and parent/teacher associations. Making a real effort to understand the challenges that students with disabilities face goes a long way toward bridging communication gaps.

The record is full of cases where what appeared to be a minority position turned out to have majority support. In the 1999/2000 school year, again in Trumbull, Connecticut, the district administration and eventually the Board of Education agreed to fight for a 19-year-old, mentally retarded high school senior named David. David wanted to swim on the varsity team, but Connecticut Inter-Scholastic Association Conference ruled him ineligible because he was 19. Athletic directors and principals across the state joined hands to fight the Trumbull position, arguing that it would not be wise to let David swim.

David's articulate, dedicated parents were prepared to fight the school district and the state all by themselves. But, sensing the district's compassion, they persuaded the district to battle the state's athletic bureaucracy. The Trumbull lawyer and his supportive law firm took the case on pro bono, and Trumbull won in the local court and on appeal in the United States circuit court. The district was prepared to proceed all the way to the U.S. Supreme Court when the state athletic association realized it was backing a loosing cause and withdrew. Press coverage of the case cast a favorable light on the Trumbull School District and strengthened the administration's hand in dealing with other special education matters.

In general, parents of special-needs students are well aware that school districts have limited funding. They just want to be assured that districts are doing as much as they can to support their children. With patience and knowledge, a middle ground can usually be reached. Administrators who are prepared to suggest a range of alternatives and are willing to negotiate—*and* who are aided by an expert, capable lawyer—will be the most successful at controlling costs while satisfying concerned parents.

In this climate, where demands on school facilities constantly change and inexorably increase, it is incumbent on architects to become as knowledgeable as possible about all the issues affecting school design, to stay abreast of regulatory changes, and to keep school officials informed regarding how state and local mandates and case-law decisions will impact design, construction, and associated costs. Most of all, though, architects must counsel patience—and must do their part to help administrators prepare for the long, and occasionally difficult, road ahead, as our society strives to meet its obligations to special-needs students.

Chapter 14

Harmony in Value Engineering

by Marcia T. Palluzzi, LA

At the onset of any building project, all parties seek to create an environment that inspires. Often the process is tempered by practical, fiscal, and/or political challenges. It is during such controversies that value is established and inspiration becomes visible. Value engineering is the manifestation of the balance between priority and constructability.

Value engineering is most successful when it is fully integrated into the design process. It involves more than just changing or removing building materials or program functions. In fact, it involves seeing the path to the finished project in new ways. It is the component that makes the intangible tangible, often by creating a compromise between an idea and an affordable solution. Our beliefs about money and our understanding of the construction process work hand in hand in the value engineering process.

Our beliefs about money, and especially the voter's beliefs as revealed by the referendum process, can dramatically impact the course of the design process. Perceived need and actual need can be two very different things. It is essential that the building committee and Board of Education, working in conjunction with the architect, craft a financial strategy plan while the schematic building design is under development. Such a plan should include a communications strategy for gaining voter understanding, acceptance, and support of the project. (See chapter 15, "Passing Your School Referendum.") It should also include an analysis of state reimbursement potential, a compilation of possible rebates for energy-efficient systems, and an assessment of the current labor market, availability of building materials, and the timing of similar projects in the region.

Oftentimes, value engineering decisions are made early on, during conception of the project. Expenditures on administrative office space, extensive parking areas, and large athletic complexes are frequently eliminated at the start before other cost options are investigated.

The conception period of a project is, in fact, a critical time in the value engineering process. Feasibility studies, often part of the conception process, provide a valuable analysis of potential paths that a project can take. The decisions to rehabilitate, build additions, or construct a completely new facility all have different cost implications. Consideration of facility needs, enrollment projections, state reimbursement, and energy rebates are some specific factors affecting the design.

Judgments related to initial cost versus long-term durability must be determined in the value engineering process. Balancing these two factors and making related decisions requires clear communication about the cost of materials, maintenance, and life-cycle of the products. For example, it is common to use dry wall instead of masonry on interior walls although the use of masonry is probably more cost-effective over the long run. Floor finishes, particularly in the cafeteria and hallways, will stand up longer and be easier to maintain if they are of high quality. The dollars spent to strip and wax low-grade finishes would in many cases probably more than pay for an upgrade.

Such decisions can also significantly impact the health and welfare of the individuals who will occupy the building. Lighting and acoustical treatments significantly impact vision and hearing. Improperly diffused ceiling lights can obscure lighting on computer screens, causing eyestrain or headaches. Improper computer furniture will affect posture, causing neck aches or backaches or even serious repetitive strain injuries. Acoustical treatments in a band room are critical to preventing damage to musicians' eardrums.

Another approach to reducing costs involves the re-evaluation of needs. Prioritizing the inclusion of certain spaces or reducing the sizes of critical spaces will bring the costs down. Compromising on the spaces or storage areas within the school can, however, have a large impact on the functioning and management of the facility. Cutting back on space is often the first strategy pursued because it is difficult to quantify the value of additional space. At this point in the space-adjustment process it is extremely important to obtain input from the Board of Education and knowledgeable educators to understand any related impact on student learning potential.

Lastly, the building systems should come under scrutiny. Heating and ventilation systems improperly distributed, balanced, and filtered will produce an unhealthy building with dirty ducts and/or hot-cold spots. Leaving air conditioning out of portions of a building will affect year-round building usage. But large, expensive facilities should be able to be used throughout the year. Also relevant in a discussion of mechanical systems is the opportunity to save money on operating the building through energy-efficient equipment. Although such equipment is costly, rebates from utility companies are often available.

So when and where do we value engineer a project? Ideally, it begins to occur during the conception of the project and continues from there. It is clearly a collaborative process, which must balance need, funding, and creativity into a harmonious whole. Conscious effort to be aware of the cost estimating and financial strategic plan for the building will forestall surprises during the bidding process. Rather then pulling easily calculated items out of the equation, value engineering must be based on sound planning and design considerations. Time spent to gather data, communicate findings, and discuss priorities will pay off in the long run. Educated, "quality" decisions—made in a collaborative fashion—have the best chance of being cost-effective and providing the best learning environment for the student of tomorrow.

Chapter 15

Passing Your School Referendum: Community Support Is Based on Credibility

by Patricia Myler, AIA

Gaining the support of the community to fund a school project is a challenging task, particularly in transitional economic times. A referendum campaign, much like a school building itself, has to be carefully designed, because success does not happen by accident. The time and energy invested in planning, organizing, and running a campaign will be rewarded with the support of the community and a positive referendum vote.

It has been our experience that a well-designed and -implemented communications program and campaign plan goes a long way toward achieving that support. The following is an outline of the referendum campaign process as it should generally occur. This process has to be customized, however, to address the distinctive needs of a particular community.

The architect is an important member of the referendum campaign team. The school district needs the expertise and technical guidance of an architectural firm—one specializing in school design and construction—to prepare the necessary design and other documents for presentations and public forums. In addition, an experienced architectural firm can guide the whole team through the referendum process by sharing knowledge gained in similar referendums in other communities.

This guidance is extremely important. The questions raised by the project's opponents, by its supporters, and by those voters who remain undecided must be answered professionally and completely to build the credibility necessary for victory.

Most communities opt for the formation of a Coalition Committee composed of parents and other community members who have a stake in the project. The members of this Coalition Committee—rather than the architect, district officials, or building committee members, who may be perceived to have a bias—should be the key deliverers of the message. Frequent Coalition Committee meetings will be required to coordinate the content of the message and ensure consistency in its delivery.

Ideally, the campaign should be initiated two to three months before the scheduled referendum date. This period is needed to organize the coalition, design the campaign plan, and disseminate the necessary information to the voters. The time of year when the referendum is scheduled is extremely important to its success. The referendum should not coincide with municipal votes, nor should it occur during the summer months, when families with school-age children go on vacation, and low voter turnout—especially among those with the greatest stake in the project's success—can lead to defeat. Also, part-time summer residents may be less likely to support local educational bond issues.

REFERENDUM PROCESS

1998 JANUARY	APRIL	JULY	OCTOBER

community communication

Steps 1, 2, 3
Assess
Define
Communicate

establish the need workshop
educating the voter   *the campaign*

AWARD

November
Referendum

DEMOGRAPHIC   PROGRAMMING   PLANNING   IMPLEMENTATION
ANALYSIS

conceptual design

The Referendum Process

Phase 1: Educate the Voter

The education phase of a referendum process is a necessary first step. This phase brings issues within the school district to the public's attention, thus establishing "the need."

Establishing the Need. It is essential that the needs are established and communicated in order to solicit community support for a potential solution. It is equally important for the school district to understand the perceptions of its "customers" (administrators, teachers, parents, students, community, taxpayers/voters). There must be an up-front commitment to understand these customers' points of view before any attempt is made to engage their support.

Demographic Research. Questionable demographic research can lead to diminished support for public education. The shrinking number of school-age children in the late 1960s and early 1970s led to school closures in many communities. With schools either closed or outdated there is a shortage of classroom and learning space. The public's recollection of this history must be addressed when projects are put forth for renovations, additions, or new schools. The proper demographic research must be executed to establish a credible database for future planning.

Community Relations. The public schools' relationship with the public does not begin with the development of the referendum process. Schools must have a long-range approach to optimize the daily interactions with their customers, and to solidify a supportive and informed contingency. Because of limited community funding, school facilities must also serve the wider community. This shared use can facilitate a cooperative relationship—one that fosters mutual understanding—between the school population and the community. Perceptions of a school or an entire district cannot be reversed within a relatively short referendum campaign. These beliefs about a school system, whether or not accurate or deserved, can account for much of what happens inside the voter booth.

Phase 2: The Campaign—Get the Story Out!
Getting the story out to voters begins with a referendum workshop, or campaign kickoff meeting, in which the campaign process is defined and the design of the campaign plan is initiated.

During this initial meeting, the campaign leadership positions are identified and the associated responsibilities defined. Appointments are made to key campaign leadership positions. Positions may include

- Campaign Chairperson (serves as the chief spokesperson for the campaign and administers the campaign plan)
- Volunteer Coordinators:
  - Research Coordinator (researches targeted pro-education groups, including parents, PTA, and community groups; researches past referendum results; cross-references target groups against voter registration lists)
  - Neighborhood Distribution Coordinator (identifies and implements effective neighborhood drop and public distribution strategies; organizes volunteers and coordinates timing of activities within the campaign plan)
  - Phone Bank Coordinator (arranges for phone bank locations and organizes and coordinates volunteers; coordinates timing of activities within the campaign plan)
  - Business Support Coordinator (solicits support from local businesses and coordinates the placement of posters and flyers with the campaign plan)
- Communications Coordinators:
  - Message Development Coordinator (works with subcommittee to develop and refine key messages to be incorporated into the campaign plan)
  - Community Presentations Coordinator (designs presentations that incorporate the campaign messages and coordinates community presentations with the campaign plan)
  - Letters to Editor Coordinator (develops draft letters incorporating the key messages and organizes and coordinates volunteers for letter writing; coordinates timing of letter placement and press releases with the campaign plan)

It is essential that the lead spokesperson, the campaign chairperson, be perceived as objective and have credibility within the community. In most cases, a school administrator, board of education member, or building committee member, who might be perceived as biased, should not hold this position. Table 15.1 presents a sample campaign plan for a two-month (March/April) campaign for a referendum scheduled for early May.

Task	3/3	3/10	3/17	3/24	3/31	4/07	4/14	4/21	4/28	5/5
Community Presentations										
Develop list										
Neighborhood Drops										
Message 1										
Message 2										
Message 3										
Message 4										
Message 5										
Public Distribution										
Letters to the Editor										
Draft letters										
Message 1										
Message 2										
Message 3										
Message 4										
Message 5										
Press Releases										
School Tour										
Cable TV Show										
Phone Bank										
Call pro-ed voters										
Research										
Identify pro-ed target										
Compare voter list										
ID opposition message										
Develop Campaign Message										
Flyers										
Posters										
Other Campaign Materials*										

Table 15.1. Campaign Plan
* Other campaign materials might include large boards for presentations (including floor plans, elevations), models, PowerPoint presentations, computer-generated video fly-throughs, and so on.

Once the Campaign Plan has been developed, volunteers have signed up, and the schedule has been set, it's time to begin implementing the campaign. Here are some of the steps you'll need to follow:

Implementing the Campaign Plan

Step 1: Identify the Target Groups and Assess Their Electoral Strength

- Research past campaigns and town referendums. Based on past referendum history, establish the number of votes needed to win (50 percent of the number likely to vote plus 1).
- Identify the target groups or voter segments most likely to support the referendum.
- Identify undecided and opponent voters.
- To determine the electoral strength of the target group, transfer lists of voters likely to support the referendum to the voting lists. This crossed-referenced list will serve as the basis for designing the communications program.
- Call identified "yes" voters.
- Maintain up-to-date voting records.

Step 2: Design an Effective Campaign Message

- Find out what the voters think and what they want to know. Based on feedback from public forums, newspaper articles and editorials, surveys, and general discussions, develop a list of the most important questions, issues, and concerns.
- Differentiate the arguments of the opposition. Determine who opposes the project and why they oppose it and what they might support as an alternative. Structure the proposal to neutralize the opponent's arguments and to minimize surprises by predicting the opponents' reactions.
- Keep the message simple and concise. Select three or four key facts that address the voters' major questions. The simple, concise message needs to be repeated consistently in order for voters to absorb the information.

Step 3: Determine the Mix of Tools to Communicate the Campaign Message

The campaign has to determine the best mix of tools for communicating its message. A variety of communication tools are available, including:

- Paid advertising—print and broadcast
- Paid advertising—outdoor media
- Free media
- Direct mail
- Phone banks
- Mailers
- Flyers
- Newsletters
- Press releases
- Press interviews
- Press conferences with TV, radio, newspapers
- Student participation

- Tours through existing, inadequate facilities
- Literature drops
- Neighborhood "walks and talks"
- Letters to the editor
- Public presentations to different groups (including the Board of Education, PTA/PTO, general public, students, media, town council)
- Email bursts
- A referendum website

Available resources will also vary, but they can include volunteers, private funding, and business donations of printing, materials, phone banks, meeting space, and free advertising. The Coalition Committee must evaluate the available resources and develop a strategy to maximize their utilization. Communication tools need to be selected based on the available resources and the optimum forum for reaching your target audience.

Phone banks are a very important communication tool. It is desirable to have a location with multiple phone lines. Here, volunteers can call voters who belong to the targeted segments and deliver a carefully scripted message. This tool can be utilized at the initiation of the campaign as an information-gathering exercise, and again later on to remind the pro-education voters to get out and vote. For a referendum in Watertown, Connecticut, a major corporation donated the use of its facility as a weekly meeting place for the Coalition Committee and as a phone bank location. This support from a local business saved the coalition a large amount of money and provided a central rallying location.

The architect should prepare visual materials including site and floor plans, elevations, renderings, models, and CAD-generated animations. These graphic materials can be used in conjunction with a message developed to "tell the story." Posters and flyers can be developed for posting, mailing, and handing out. Local cable TV stations will provide free airtime to present the plans and animations and to broadcast discussions about the project. The campaign should also make the best use of press releases to local media, organize writing campaigns of letters to the editor, and sponsor public presentations and person-to-person neighborhood "walk and talks." The support of the local press is immensely valuable. Endorsements by local media gain votes.

Campaigns utilizing private funding are likely to be subject to strict regulation, and the Coalition Committee may even have to register as a Political Action Committee (PAC). In most states, a guide to campaign financing is available from the state elections enforcement commission. There are also limitations on the role of public officials and consultants hired with public funds (including the architect) in the referendum process, and these must be fully understood to avoid conflict with these regulations.

Conclusion:

Looking Ahead

About the future one can never say the final word. And so this conclusion isn't a "conclusion" (in the sense of something final) at all. The only sensible way to "conclude" a book about the future is to look ahead, with openness, to the changes the future will bring.

In the years ahead, Americans will continue to focus on the nature and quality of our public education system, debating and experimenting with ways of strengthening the educational experience we give our children and improving the preparation they receive for entering the worlds of college, work, adult relationships, parenting, and citizenship. To accommodate new educational technologies and new approaches to schooling (undoubtedly including some that we cannot now predict), we must design schools to be as flexible as possible. But it's equally clear that our own thinking about what flexibility *is* and how it can best be achieved must also continue to evolve.

To respond effectively to the changes the future may bring, we must ourselves be willing to change our thinking, our strategies, and our priorities. This is a potentially endless task, and one that we—as designers, educators, parents, and citizens—should welcome. In concluding this book, we look forward to publishing further editions, in which the thinking we express here is refined, corrected, augmented, expanded—*changed* in ways that address the ongoing changes in American education, society, and culture.

We believe that our long experience in designing the full range of public education facilities provides us with insights that may be of value to middle school, high school, specialized school, and community college educators and administrators, as well. The other books in the Schools of the Future series are intended to serve these audiences: *The Elementary School of the Future* and *The High School of the Future* are being published simultaneously with this volume; *Magnet and Charter Schools of the Future* and *Community Colleges of the Future* will appear in 2004 and 2005, respectively.

Finally, we mean what we say, throughout this book, when we speak of the value of collaboration and democratic process in school planning, design, and construction. It's our consistent experience as designers that thinking gets better and solutions become more effective as participation in the design process widens and grows. We therefore invite you, our readers, to participate in the making of future editions of this book. If there's anything you wish to respond to—anything we've missed, or overemphasized, or gotten wrong (or gotten right)—we'd very much like to hear from you. Contact us through our website, <www.fletcherthompson.com>.

Sources   Alexander, William M., and Paul S. George. 1981. *The Exemplary Middle School.* New York: Holt, Rinehart & Winston.

Barton, Ronald Rex. 1976. "A Historical Study of the Organization and Development of the Junior High and Middle School Movement, 1920–1975." Ph.D. diss. University of Arkansas.

Cadwell, L. 1997. *Bringing Reggio Emilia Home: An Innovative Approach to Early Childhood Education.* New York: Teachers College Press.

Christopher, Gaylaird, Sonja Yates, Lynne Rauch, Bruce A. Jilk, George H. Copa. N.d. "Transforming the Learning Environment." American Institute of Architects, Committee on Architecture for Education.

Connecticut Department of Education. 1999. "Doing What's Right in the Middle: Promising Practices in Schools with Middle Grades." Available as a PDF, at <www.csde.state.ct.us/public/der/promisingpractices/improvingstudentachievement/>.

Dillon, Sam. 2002. "Heft of Students' Backpacks Turns Into Textbook Battle." *New York Times.* December 24.

Florida, Richard. 2002. *The Rise of the Creative Class: And How It's Transforming Work, Leisure, Community and Everyday Life.* New York: Basic Books.

Frey, Susan. 1999. *The Road to Avalon II: Cultivating Spirituality in the Classroom.* Exp. and rev. ed. Haverford, Pa.: Infinity Publishing.

GAO (United States General Accounting Office). 1995. *School Facilities: Condition of America's Schools, February 1995.* GEO/HEHS-95-61. To access this and other GAO reports online, go to <www.access.gpo.gov/su_docs/aces/aces160.shtml>.

George, Paul S., Chris Stevenson, Julia Thomason, and James Beane. 1992. *The Middle School—And Beyond.* Alexandria, Va.: Association of Supervision and Curriculum Development.

George, Paul S., and John H. Lounsbury. 2000. *Making Big Schools Feel Small: Multiage Grouping, Looping, and Schools-Within-a-School.* Westerville, Ohio: National Middle School Association.

Gross, Jane. 2003. "What's Big, Yellow and Humiliating? Full Lot at Greenwich High Means New Reality: The Bus." *New York Times.* January 27.

Jackson, Anthony W., and Gayle A. Davis. 2000. *Turning Points 2000: Educating Adolescents in the 21st Century.* New York: Teachers College Press.

Lewis, L., et al. 1999. "Condition of America's Public Schools." *Education Statistics Quarterly,* fall.

National Middle School Association. 2001. *This We Believe . . . and Now We Must Act.* Thomas O. Erb, ed. Westerville, Ohio: National Middle School Association.

New York City Department of Health. 2000? "Guidelines on Assessment and Remediation of Fungi in Indoor Environments." New York: New York City Department of Health Bureau of Environmental and Occupational Disease Epidemiology. Published on the Web, at <www.ci.nyc.ny.us/html/doh/html/epi/moldrpt1.html>.

Pinker, Steven. 2003. "How to Get Inside a Student's Head." *New York Times*. January 31.

Progressive Architecture. 1971. "The New Old School." Unsigned article. February. Pp. 92–93.

Seep, Benjamin, et al. 2000. *Classroom Acoustics: A Resource for Creating Learning Environments with Desirable Listening Conditions.* Melville, NY: Acoustical Society of America, Technical Committee on Architectural Acoustics.

Sterling, Bruce. 2002. *Tomorrow Now: Envisioning the Next Fifty Years*. New York: Random House.

Sullivan, Kevin. 1996. "Middle School Program and Participatory Planning Drive School Design." *Middle School Journal*. March. Pp. 3–7.

Sustainable Buildings Industry Council. 2001. *High Performance School Buildings: Resourcer and Strategy Guide*. Washington, DC.

Winter, Greg. 2003. "Gates Foundation Providing $31 Million for Small Schools." *New York Times*. February 26.

Zernike, Kate. 2001. "The Feng Shui of Schools." *New York Times* (Education suppl.). August 5.

On Ocoee Middle School:

"Audio Systems Improve Comprehension." 2001. *School Planning & Management*. October.

"First Look: Designing a New Era in Education." 2000. *Florida Caribbean Architect*. Spring.

Kilsheimer, Joel. 2002. "From the Ground Up." *Scholastic Administrator*. Winter. Pp. 30–32.

"New Generation of Schools." 2002. *Building Operating Management.* March.

"Ocoee Middle School." 2001. *American School & University.* November.

Rittner-Heir, Robbin M. 2001. "Sounds Like a Winner." *School Planning & Management.* January.

Rittner-Heir, Robbin M. 2001. "The Revolution in I.D. Cards." *School Planning & Management.* February. Pp. 53–56.

"SIF: The Schools Interoperability Framework Initiative Is Helping to Build Smarter Schools." 2002. *School Foodservice & Nutrition.* January.

"SIF Report." 2001. *Curriculum Administrator.* March.

"Voices over the Din." 2001. *New York Times.* November 11.

Contributors

Edwin T. Merritt, Ed.D., is Director of Educational Planning & Research for Fletcher-Thompson, Inc. Over his 29-year career as a school superintendent (in three different districts), Ted Merritt was involved in more than 25 new construction, renovation, and major maintenance projects. A futurist and an expert on educational technology, he currently serves as a consultant on technology planning for the Connecticut State Department of Education. Mr. Merritt has received many awards, including the Connecticut State Superintendents' Golden Shield Award for Exemplary Service (1999), the General Connecticut Coast YMCA "Strong Kids Builder" Award (1999), the Bridgeport Regional Leader of the Year Award (1998), and the Rotary Club's Paul Harris Fellowship (1998), and he has been a National and State Parent/ Teachers' Association Honoree (1993, 1999). He has written for *American School & University* and *School Business Affairs,* among other publications.

James A. Beaudin, AIA, is the Principal of Fletcher-Thompson, Inc.'s Education Practice Group. Over his career, Mr. Beaudin has been involved in the design of almost 100 schools in 45 communities—for a total of more than 10 million square feet of public and private school construction. Since 1990, the firm, under his direction, has created more than 7.5 million square feet of educational space, with a combined construction value in excess of $500 million and comprising projects for every educational level, from pre-kindergarten through high school. Besides new construction, projects directed by Mr. Beaudin have included renovations, code-compliance improvements, system-wide studies, and educational programming and specification development. Under his leadership, Fletcher-Thompson's Educational Studio has received numerous awards and other recognition. Articles authored or co-authored by Mr. Beaudin have appeared in *American School & University, Facilities Design & Management, School Business Affairs,* and *School Planning & Management* magazines.

Patricia A. Myler, AIA, is Director of Pre-K through Grade 12 Facilities and an Associate at Fletcher-Thompson, Inc. Since joining the firm in 1995, she has served as a studio leader and project manager and is currently Director of the firm's Hartford, Connecticut, office, focusing on educational projects that have ranged from feasibility studies for elementary, middle, high, and magnet schools; to additions and renovations; to new primary, magnet, middle, and high schools. She has also provided pre-referendum consulting services to several Connecticut school districts. She is the co-author of a recent *School Business Affairs* article, "Going Up?," on the feasibility of vertical expansions of existing school facilities.

Daniel Davis, AIA, a Senior Design Architect with Fletcher-Thompson, Inc., has more than 20 years of experience designing a broad range of project types, including educational, institutional, commercial, corporate and industrial facilities. He is a professor in the University of Hartford's Department of Architecture, where he teaches architectural history and design. His architectural writings have appeared in a variety of publications, ranging from local newspapers to national professional journals. His projects have been published in leading architectural magazines and have won prestigious design awards.

Richard S. Oja, AIA, is a Senior Project Manager at Fletcher-Thompson, Inc. For more than 12 years, he has managed public school projects, from project inception through programming, design, bidding, construction, and post-occupancy evaluation. He has worked on a full range of educational facilities, from small elementary schools to major suburban and urban high schools. He has focused on schools' indoor environmental quality issues, giving presentations and publishing articles, including a recent piece in *Facilities Design & Management,* on the topic.

Barry M. Blades, ASLA, is a landscape architect and principal of Blades & Goven, landscape architects, located in Shelton, Connecticut. With over 20 years of experience, he has served as designer, project manager and/or principal-in-charge on numerous elementary, middle and high school projects located throughout Connecticut and New York. His current projects include Rochambeau Middle School in Southbury, Conn., Memorial Middle School in Middlebury, Conn., and 6 to 6 Magnet School in Bridge-port, Conn. Mr. Blades also has extensive experience in the acquisition of environmental permits from regulatory agencies and in assisting educa-tional clients with feasibility studies and evaluations for potential school projects. Blades & Goven, LLC, offers consulting landscape architectural, site planning, and environmental design services to clients in the public and private sectors.

Katherine C. Clark, Ed.D., principal of Ocoee Middle School, has for 27 years served as a teacher or administrator in the Orange County [Florida] Public Schools, the nation's 14th-largest school district. Dr. Clark has been interviewed for numerous national publications, including *Florida and Caribbean Architectural Journal, School Planning & Management, District Administration, Scholastic Administrator, The American Food Service Journal,* and *SIF Report.* She has received several awards, includ-ing an award for being one of the "Top 25 Educational Technology Advocates in the Country."

Timothy P. Cohen has more than 13 years of experience in the architectural field. Before joining Fletcher Thompson he served as a designer at a Hartford, Connecticut–based architectural firm, where his primary responsi-bilities included master planning, programming, and design. As a Project Designer for Fletcher Thompson, Mr. Cohen is responsible for project design quality and for ensuring that owners' expectations and project budgets are appropriately reflected in the design solutions.

Joseph G. Costa, AIA, an Associate and Project Manager with Fletcher-Thompson, Inc., has more than 18 years of professional experience. His project management duties, on a diverse range of project types, have included full project responsibility from conceptualization to implementation, manpower allocation and budgeting, cost analyses, scheduling, contract negotiation, consultant administration and coordination, construction documentation, and construction administration.

Julie A. Kim, AIA, a Project Manager with Fletcher-Thompson, Inc., has 20 years of professional experience in commercial, institutional, and educational design. Recent work includes the Wexler-Grant Community School in New Haven, Connecticut, and pre-referendum studies for school projects in the towns of Guilford, Connecticut, and Rye, New York. Ms. Kim was project manager for the Seymour Middle School in Seymour, Connecticut.

John C. Oliveto, P.E., Principal of Construction Support Services at Fletcher Thompson, is responsible for administering the firm's construction administration assignments and serves as project field representative on selected projects. He is also responsible for design phase reviews aimed at improving the quality and efficiency of construction documents. He has performed construction support services for a number of Connecticut educational projects, including additions and renovations to the Eleanor B. Kennelly School in Hartford and renovations to the 6 to 6 Early Childhood Magnet School in Bridgeport. In addition, he heads up production of architectural specifications for the firm's three architectural studios.

Marcia T. Palluzzi, LA, is registered landscape architect. While she was at Fletcher-Thompson, Inc., her work focused on the pre-planning process, programming, land-use studies, and regulatory approvals for educational and other projects.

Robert J. Poletto, P.E., served as Fletcher Thompson's Chief Mechanical Engineer.

Jeffrey A. Sells, AIA, is the Design Leader of Fletcher-Thompson, Inc.'s Education Practice Group, responsible for the design approach on all of the firm's educational projects. He has designed new elementary and high school buildings as well as additions and renovations of elementary, middle, high, and magnet schools in districts throughout Connecticut. He has also designed college and university facilities, including the Thomas Dodd Archives and Research Center at the University of Connecticut. His work has been featured in professional publications and has won numerous awards and special recognition. His written work has appeared in *Engineering News-Record, School Business Affairs, American School and University,* and *The CABE Journal,* and he has been a collaborator on, or primary contributor to, articles for *Contract* and *Building Design & Construction* magazines and the *Connecticut Post.*

Photo Credits

Introduction, page xi: Fanning/Howey Associates, Inc. rendering

Chapter 1, page 3: (clockwise), David Sundberg/Esto; Fletcher-Thompson, Inc. Staff; Courtesy Mount Olive Middle School; Emery Photography, Inc.; Robert Benson Photography; James D'Addio
page 4: David Sundberg/Esto
page 5: David Sundberg/Esto
page 6: James D'Addio Photographer
page 7: James D'Addio Photographer
page 8: James D'Addio Photographer
page 9: Robert Benson Photography
page 10: Robert Benson Photography
page 11: Robert Benson Photography
page 12: Robert Benson Photography
page 13: Robert Benson Photography
page 14: middle and bottom, Robert Benson Photography; top, David Sundberg/Esto
page 15: Courtesy Mount Olive Middle School
page 16: Courtesy Mount Olive Middle School
page 17: top and middle, Emery Photography, Inc.; bottom, Fanning/ Howey Associates, Inc.
page 18: top, Fanning/Howey Associates, Inc.; bottom, Emery Photography, Inc.
page 19: Emery Photography, Inc.
page 20: top, Ocoee Middle School; bottom, Emery Photography, Inc.

Chapter 2, page 21: Fletcher-Thompson, Inc.

Chapter 3, page 33: Fletcher-Thompson, Inc. rendering

Chapter 4, page 45: Woodruff/Brown Photography

Chapter 5, page 57: Bernstein Associates

Chapter 6, pages 67-76: Fletcher-Thompson, Inc.

Chapter 7, page 77: Robert Benson Photography

Chapter 8, page 117: Blades & Goven, LLC
page 118: Blades & Goven, LLC

Chapter 9, page 125: Emery Photography, Inc.

Chapter 10, page 131: Emery Photography, Inc.

Chapter 11, page 141: Fletcher-Thompson, Inc.

Chapter 12, page 147: Bernstein Associates

Chapter 13, page 153: Robert Benson Photography

Chapter 14, page 163: James D'Addio Photographer